THE
FIRST
CLASH

THE
FIRST
CLASH

The Miraculous Greek Victory at Marathon
and Its Impact on Western Civilization

JIM LACEY

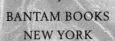

BANTAM BOOKS
NEW YORK

Published in the United States by Bantam Books,
an imprint of The Random House Publishing Group,
a division of Random House, Inc., New York.

BANTAM BOOKS and the rooster colophon are registered
trademarks of Random House, Inc.

Grateful acknowledgment is made to Pantheon Books,
a division of Random House, Inc., for permission to reprint excerpts from
The Landmark Herodotus: The Histories by Robert B. Strassler, translated by
Andrea L. Purvis, copyright © 2007 by Robert B. Strassler. Reprinted
by permission of Pantheon Books, a division of Random House, Inc.

LIBRARY OF CONGRESS CATALOGING-IN-PUBLICATION DATA
Lacey, Jim
The first clash: the miraculous Greek victory at Marathon and its impact
on Western civilization / Jim Lacey.
p. cm.
Includes bibliographical references and index.
ISBN 978-0-553-80734-9
eBook ISBN 978-0-553-90812-1
1. Marathon, Battle of, Greece, 409 B.C.—Influence.   2. Greece—
Civilization—To 146 B.C.   3. Iran—History—To 640 A.D.   I. Title.
DF225.4.L33   2011   938'.03—dc22   2010046214

Printed in the United States of America on acid-free paper

www.bantamdell.com

2 4 6 8 9 7 5 3 1

First Edition

Book design by Virginia Norey

Dedicated to
Ali and James

The mountains look on Marathon—
And Marathon looks on the sea;
And musing there an hour alone,
I dream'd that Greece might yet be free
For, standing on the Persians' grave,
I could not deem myself a slave.

—LORD BYRON,
"THE ISLES OF GREECE"

Contents

CONTENTS

THE AEGEAN

Adriatic Sea

ILLYRIA

MACEDONIA

Pella

Myrkinos

THASSOS

Aegea

EPIRUS

THESSALY

EUBOEA

Chalcis
Eretria

Delphi

BOEOTIA

Thebes

Plataea

Marath

✖

Megara

Athens

Kary

ATTICA

Corinth

AEGINA

Argos

ARCADIA

Tegea

MESSENIA

Sparta

Messene

LACONIA

Mediterranean Sea

0 Miles   50   100   150

0 Kilometers   100   150

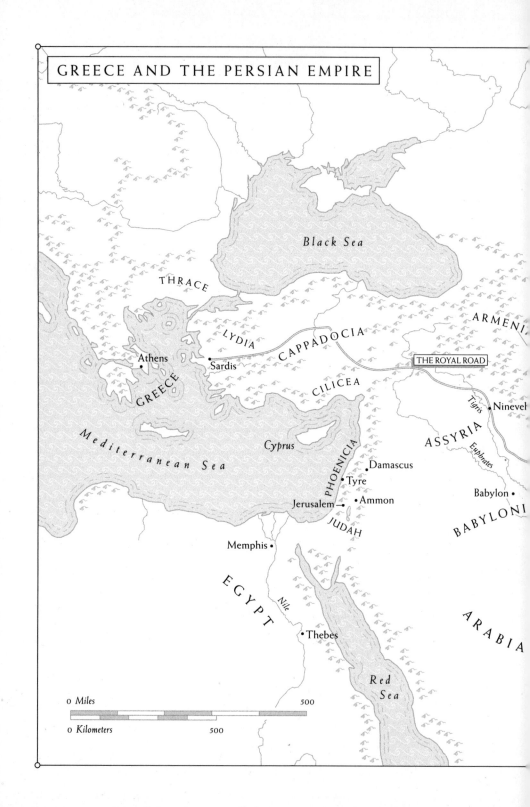

GREECE AND THE PERSIAN EMPIRE

Black Sea

THRACE

LYDIA

CAPPADOCIA

ARMENI

THE ROYAL ROAD

Athens

Sardis

GREECE

CILICEA

Tigris

Ninevel

ASSYRIA

Mediterranean Sea

Cyprus

PHOENICIA

Damascus

Euphrates

Babylon

Tyre

Jerusalem

Ammon

BABYLONI

JUDAH

Memphis

EGYPT

Nile

ARABIA

Thebes

Red Sea

0 *Miles*   500

0 *Kilometers*   500

N

Caspian Sea

SOGDIANA

Bactra

BACTRIA

Ecbatana

MEDIA

Susa

PERSIA

Persepolis

Indus

INDIA

Arabian Sea

© 2010 Jeffrey L. Ward

Dramatis Personae

Amasis—Egyptian pharaoh who took the throne by force and held it for forty-four years. He spent the last several years of his life preparing to meet an expected Persian offensive into Egypt. He died just before the decisive Battle of Pelusium, which saw the Egyptian army defeated by Cambyses II.

Aristagoras—Tyrant of Miletus. He is credited with starting the Ionian revolt. After the revolt began, he traveled to Greece to gain Spartan support. Failing in that endeavor, he managed to enlist the limited support of Athens. The small force Athens sent to Ionia managed to burn the Persian city of Sardis before returning home. Persian enmity over Sardis's burning was the direct cause of the 490 BC Persian invasion and the Battle of Marathon.

Aristides—One of ten Athenian generals at Marathon and the leader of the Antiochis tribe. Several years after the Battle of Marathon, he lost a political struggle with Themistocles and was banished from Athens. He was recalled to help Athens fend off Xerxes in the 480 BC invasion and commanded the Athenian army at the decisive Battle of Plataea.

Artaphrenes—Persian satrap of Lydia and Ionia during the Ionian revolt.

Astyages—King of the Medes, overthrown by Cyrus and his Persian allies. Afterward, Cyrus claimed his throne and used the combined Persian and Median armies to build the greatest empire the ancient world had yet seen.

Callimachus—Athenian polemarch (commander) at the Battle of Marathon. He was killed at the climax of the fighting.

Cambyses II—Cyrus's son and successor. After winning the Battle of Pelusium in 525 BC, he went on to conquer Egypt. He died, under disputed circumstances, in 522 BC, while returning to the heart of the empire to crush a revolt.

Cimon—Son of Miltiades and a hero of the Second Persian War against Xerxes. He was politically powerful at the time Herodotus was reciting his history in Athens.

Cleisthenes—Son of Megacles, a brilliant politician and the sworn enemy of Hippias. He was the driving force behind the establishment and defense of Athenian democracy.

Cleomenes—Spartan king in the twenty years leading up to Marathon. This remarkable Spartan played kingmaker in Athens, annihilated an Argive army, and humbled Aegina. In no small measure, Cleomenes' actions in the few years before the Persian invasion made the Greek victory at Marathon possible.

Croesus—King of Lydia (560–546 BC) until he was defeated by Cyrus outside of his capital city of Sardis. His defeat saw the Lydian Empire overthrown and merged into the growing Persian Empire.

Cylon—Athenian Olympic hero who, with the support of the city of Megara, made an early bid to become tyrant of Athens. The bid failed, and although he escaped, most of his followers were slaughtered after they surrendered. The killers were led by a member of the Alcmaeonidae clan. The "blood guilt" associated with this act persisted for over a century and was always a major influence on Athenian politics.

Cyrus—Starting as the petty king of a small Persian kingdom, Ansan, he led a successful revolt against the Medes. Before his death, he had conquered the Lydian and Babylonian empires and incorporated them into the Persian Empire. Cyrus was the greatest empire builder the ancient world saw until Alexander the Great over two centuries later. He ruled from 559 BC to 530 BC.

Darius—A Persian noble who along with seven other young nobles made a bid for the Persian throne after the death of Cambyses II. After a year of civil war, Darius eventually secured his hold on power. He proved himself a first-rate administrator and was responsible for building the infrastructure and institutions of the empire that allowed it to last for two hundred years. It was by Darius's command that the Persian army was sent to destroy Athens in 490 BC.

Datis—Persian commander at the Battle of Marathon.

Demaratus—Spartan co-king with Cleomenes. After a strained relationship, Cleomenes engineered his removal. He later escaped to the Persian court and was an adviser to Xerxes during the Persian invasion in 480 BC.

Gobryas—Babylonian general who went over to Cyrus with a substantial portion of the Babylonian army in 541 BC. He joined Cyrus in his conquest of Babylonia and was responsible for capturing the city of Babylon and holding it until Cyrus arrived.

Harpagos—Median general who betrayed his king, Astyages, and brought a large segment of the Median army over to Cyrus's side. Harpagos's support of Cyrus was the decisive moment in Cyrus's rise to ultimate power. He later became Cyrus's most trusted general and was responsible for reducing the Greek cities of Ionia to submission to Persian rule.

Hippias—Son of Pisistratus. He assumed the role of tyrant after his father's death. Although competent, he was not as adept as Pisistratus at balancing the many threats Athens faced. He was deposed by Cleisthenes and went to reside within the Persian Empire. He was with the Persian army at Marathon, hoping for reinstatement as Athens's tyrant in the event of a Persian victory.

Histiaios—Tyrant of a Greek city within the Persian Empire. He was with the Persians during their invasion of Thrace and is credited with protecting the bridge over the Danube, allowing Darius's army to escape destruction in Scythia. He was a key Greek leader in the later stages of the Ionian revolt.

Isagoras—He opposed Cleisthenes and seized power with the support of the Spartan king Cleomenes. When the Athenian assembly resisted his bid for power, the Spartans withdrew their support and he was banished from Athens.

Mardonius—Persian general instrumental in crushing the Ionian revolt. He was put aside by Darius after a failed expedition into northern Greece but was with Xerxes as his top military commander in the invasion of 480 BC.

Megabazos—Persian general under Darius. After the failed attempt to conquer Scythia, he was left behind to complete the conquest of Thrace. It was his suspicion of Histiaios's loyalty that led to that tyrant being ordered to Susa, where he could be watched more carefully.

Megacles—Early ally of Pisistratus and later a sworn enemy. He is not to be confused with an earlier Megacles who killed Cylon (an Olympic hero who made an early bid to be tyrant of Athens) after promising him safe conduct.

Miltiades the Elder—The first tyrant of the Chersonese, sent there by Pisistratus to help protect Athens's access to grain. He was a close ally of Croesus and the uncle of one of the heroes of Marathon, the second Miltiades.

Miltiades—Stepnephew of Miltiades the Elder. He also became the tyrant of the Chersonese but returned to Athens after the Ionian revolt and was one of the leaders of the Athenian army at Marathon.

Nabonidus—King of Babylon from 556 BC to 539 BC. He was defeated in battle by Cyrus, who promptly added Babylon to his growing empire. Nobonidus had previously lost the support of Babylon's powerful priestly caste and most of his people by refusing to properly honor the traditional Babylonian gods.

Phanes—Greek mercenary general in the service of the Egyptians. He switched sides before the Persian attack on Egypt in 523 BC. He was instrumental in the successful Persian invasion and became one of Cambyses II's most trusted generals.

Pisistratus—First tyrant of Athens. He oversaw Athens's rise to commercial and political power.

Smerdis—Son of Cyrus and Cambyses's brother. He was most likely murdered on Cambyses's orders, either just before the Persian invasion of Egypt or soon thereafter. While Cambyses and the Persian army were in Egypt, a false Smerdis rose up within the empire and claimed the throne. This led to a civil war, which after many bloody battles saw Darius victorious and the new ruler of the Persian Empire.

Solon—Athens's great lawgiver. He provided Athens with the basic structure of its governance and legal system. He was also instrumental in rallying Athens to continue its war with Megara until the island of Salamis was conquered. Although there were setbacks, this event marks the start of Athens's remarkable rise.

Themistocles—One of ten Athenian generals at Marathon. He commanded the Leontis tribe during the battle. In 480 BC, he was the most powerful politician in Greece and the hero of the crucial Battle of Salamis.

Xerxes—Darius's successor as king of Persia. He led a failed second invasion of Greece ten years after the Battle of Marathon (480 BC).

Introduction

S ince its inception over two and a half millennia ago, Western civilization has faced many threats, but none as dangerous as when Persia's
mighty army attempted to smash it in its infancy. It has lately become
fashionable in the West to understate the threat Persia posed. After all, in
the popular imagination the ancient East, particularly the Persian Empire,
is viewed as a rather effeminate lot devoid of martial abilities.[1] Nothing,
however, could be further from the truth. In reality, the great empires of
the East were built and maintained by war. Each, in turn, stood supreme
for only as long as its army proved the most capable, fierce, and ruthless in
the region. When a foe arose capable of overthrowing the military power
of the ruling peoples, the vanquished went into rapid decline and a new
people and empire ascended. In the sixth century BC, this process gave
birth to the Persian Empire under their great conqueror Cyrus. Over a period of several decades starting in 559 BC, Cyrus's Persian army swept all
before it, creating an empire stretching from northern India to Egypt. For
the next two hundred years, Persian arms reigned supreme over an area as
vast as the Roman Empire at its height and would topple, finally, only
under the successive hammer blows inflicted by Alexander the Great.

During those two hundred years, Persia suffered only two major military setbacks. The first occurred against the Scythian nomads occupying
the vast steppes of southern Asia. Persian forces marched against enemies
who possessed no cities or fixed wealth requiring defense and who had a
vast hinterland in which to retreat. Into this barren land, made even more
desolate by foes who burned everything behind them, the Persian army
marched endless miles in pursuit of an elusive enemy who refused battle.

Frustrated and exhausted, the Persians could save themselves from ruin only by retreating back into the empire, with ferocious Scythian horsemen tearing at them all along their line home.

The second military setback occurred when the Persian army marched against the Greeks, a very different kind of enemy from the Scythians. Persian kings thought the fractious city-states of Greece were an easy target, for the Greeks had little choice but to defend the cities on which their entire identity depended and therefore could not flee before Persian arms. Moreover, as far as the Persians could see, these cities spent most of their energies on continuous rounds of internecine warfare. There appeared little chance the Greeks could put aside their hatred and distrust of one another long enough to unify against a common foe. At the start of the fifth century BC, however, even a unified Greece probably would not have appeared as much of an obstacle to the "Great King" of Persia. As for the individual city-states, they must have appeared to the Persians as mere specks to be swept aside on the tide of conquest. In this analysis, Persia's kings made two mistakes. The first was that in spite of a general dread of Persian military power, many Greek cities, led by Athens and Sparta, were ready to unify against an invader. The more fundamental error, however, was underestimating the fighting power even one city-state could bring to any battlefield where its soldiers could engage with an enemy in close combat.

Twice the Persian armies came to conquer Greece. The first of these invasions ended when the Athenians wrecked a Persian army at Marathon. Because of its huge size, the second invasion in 480 BC—immortalized by the sacrifice of the three hundred Spartans at Thermopylae—is the best known. Rarely is it noted that the Greeks found the will to resist this second invasion only because of Athens's heroic stand at Marathon a decade before. For then, Athenian hoplites had stood almost alone on the Plain of Marathon, facing an overwhelming Persian army only two dozen miles from their home city.[2] Feeling themselves unable to wait for the assistance of a Spartan force already on the march and despairing of help from any other city, Athenian commanders ordered their hoplites to attack. Less than two hours later, the Persian force was wrecked and its disorganized survivors were retreating out to sea.

In the two and a half millennia since the Battle of Marathon, a myth has arisen that the Athenian army was a conglomeration of rustics with little experience in war. Only the threat of an imminent Persian invasion had made it a matter of some urgency to put as many of these farmers and tradesmen as possible into hoplite armor. If this were true, then Athens's victory at Marathon was indeed a miracle. In fact, that they would even hazard a battle to begin with was in itself a miracle or a case of mass insanity. As this book will make clear, although they would have preferred the backup of the Spartans, the Athenian army was far from being an amateur force. In fact, it was an experienced and battle-hardened army that shortly before Marathon had stood face-to-face against a Spartan army and had made the Spartans themselves blink.

Still, Athens's victory over the tremendous power of Persia both startled and amazed the other Greek cities. It is a safe assumption that the Persian Empire was equally surprised. For the Greeks, the example of Marathon stiffened spines and gave them the confidence to face the even more powerful Persian invasion of 480 BC. For the captive states within the Persian Empire, it gave hope that they might one day throw off the Persian yoke. Here was positive proof that Persian arms were not invincible. In fact, soon after Marathon, Egypt rose in a revolt that was suppressed only after a massive Persian military effort. Egypt's revolt and growing unrest within the empire drove home the point that the Great King of Persia could not let the decisive judgment of Marathon stand. Although Persia prevailed, the Egyptian sacrifice gave the Greeks time to prepare for the second invasion all knew was coming.

Had Athens's hoplites failed at Marathon, however, a second invasion would never have been necessary. The Persians would have destroyed Athens, and a reinforced Persian army would likely have conquered or forced the submission of the remainder of Greece during the next campaigning season. With Athens lost and the remainder of Greece absorbed into a great Eastern Empire, Western civilization would have been smothered in its cradle. No wonder, then, that when Sir Edward Creasy wrote *The Fifteen Decisive Battles of the World* in 1854 he began with the story of Marathon.[3] In the more than 150 years since Creasy wrote his work, the world has been racked by two great world wars and almost innumerable other conflicts, yet his judgment still holds. As far as the future of Western civilization is concerned, no battle was as important, or as decisive, as that fought at Marathon twenty-five hundred years ago.

For historians, the Greco-Persian conflicts and above all the Battle of Marathon hold a unique importance, as they represent the first major clash between a nascent Western civilization and the already old civilizations of the East. The cultural fault line between East and West deter-mined by the Greco-Persian wars has remained a focal point for civiliza-tional conflict over the subsequent twenty-five hundred years.

As important as Marathon was to the survival of the political and cul-tural aspects of Western civilization, for the student of military history Marathon has special appeal, as it is the first military engagement of an-tiquity for which we have a detailed contemporaneous record of the battle, its antecedents, and its aftermath. While our primary source, Herodotus, is called the "Father of Lies" almost as often as he is called the "Father of History," the assembled evidence, taken as a whole, shows that his account of the battle is remarkably accurate.[4] Unfortunately, Herodotus himself admitted that he was interested only in relating the "great" deeds of the Greeks (rather than all of the details), and his account consists of a few short paragraphs that present just the highlights of the battle.[5] Worse, he apparently never served in the battle line as a hoplite, and therefore his descriptions of battles and military affairs are always sus-pect. This, in turn, has led to a small cottage industry among ancient his-torians, as each vies to present the most original interpretation of what Herodotus states.

Unfortunately, too many of the great classicists tried to interpret He-rodotus as history when they would have been on firmer ground if they had examined his writings as works of biased journalism. Too many have forgotten that Herodotus earned his living by reading his material in front of Athenian audiences, who paid him for the privilege. As his prosperity rested on the happiness of the Athenians listening to him, Herodotus rarely relates facts that would have angered his audience. Moreover, like any good journalist, Herodotus treated his sources well. Those who talked to him came across favorably, while those who shunned him often saw their ancestor's place in history trashed. Herodotus was not above fabri-cating conversations to bring his stories to life and make them appear more factual. Furthermore, while those scholars who have made careers of studying Herodotus were great classicists, few of them were ever soldiers or had any particular interest in or knowledge of military history.[6] Over the years, this has caused them to write a number of questionable argu-ments about the nature and character of warfare and battles, particularly the Battle of Marathon.

Still, all historians are only as good as their sources, and for historians of the Greco-Persian wars, Herodotus remains the most important ancient source. As such, volumes have been written on his reliability, starting with Plutarch's attack in *On the Malice of Herodotus* and continuing to the present day.[7] The key problem historians face when trying to judge Herodotus's reliability is dealing with the dearth of other material from the period with which to compare his work. Undoubtedly, there are times when Herodotus says things so outlandish that it is impossible to take him seriously. However, as it concerns the main phases of the Greco-Persian wars and in particular the run-up to the Battle of Marathon, what the great historian has to say appears plausible. In fact, where there is other extant evidence from the period, Herodotus comes off very favorably. His history of events in Persia sits comfortably alongside the information provided in the Persian Behistun inscription and the Babylonian Chronicles.[8] Moreover, each new archaeological find tends to confirm the essence of what Herodotus reports.

In short, although a historian needs to be careful when dealing with Herodotus, as he must with any single source, it is never wise to stray too far from what the "Father of History" has to say on any particular event. Of course, many historians have ignored this caution. In their search for an alternative to Herodotus, many have seized upon an alternative narrative produced approximately a hundred years after the Battle of Marathon by Ctesias, a Greek in Persian service. Many of the well-known classical historians of the nineteenth century put great store in Ctesias's version of events. Unfortunately for these historians, the later decipherment of contemporaneous Persian sources proved that Ctesias was at a minimum an unreliable narrator. Despite his proven unreliability, many historians still uncritically use him as a source. As A. R. Burn states, "The name of Ctesias still lurks with distressing frequency in the footnotes of modern works on the Persian Wars."[9] To this, I also must plead guilty. I too have used Ctesias's work in this book, but have done so sparingly and always with a great deal of circumspection.

There are of course a number of other minor sources that present some added information about the Battle of Marathon, but they must all be used with caution. There is, for instance, Cornelius Nepos, a first-century Roman chronicler who may have had access to a more ancient work by Ephorus.[10] Several generations of authors have used his testimony as it was retold in a Byzantine *Suda*, a thousand years after his death, as proof that the Persian horses were landed at Marathon but were away grazing on the day of the battle. However, one must be careful about giving too much weight to a story written five hundred years after the battle and retold in a source further removed from the original author than we are from the height of the Byzantine Empire.

The same must be said of Plutarch, who presents us with biographies of two Athenian generals at Marathon—Aristides and Themistocles. He was also writing several centuries after the events of Marathon and, along with another historian of the period, Diodorus Siculus, shows signs of contamination by the writings of Ctesias. Still, where Herodotus is silent, historians can glean useful knowledge from these sources, as they often still had available to them the writings of contemporary historians that have long been lost to us.

While the work of the great classicists provides an excellent foundation, only a deep knowledge of military history, the nature of war, and the realities of close bloody conflict can allow one to create an accurate reconstruction of a battle whose true dimensions have long eluded historians. It is also crucial to understand the development of the Persian and Greek military systems, along with those elements of state power that bear on the ability of both parties to wage war. Only by placing Marathon within this larger historical and institutional context is it possible to understand the outcome of the battle.

For almost two centuries, historians have marveled over how a supposed bunch of hurriedly collected rustics beat a professional battle-hardened Persian army. For most of them, the lopsided result—sixty-four hundred Persians dead for fewer than two hundred Athenians—is one of the many unfathomable mysteries of history. However, given the facts, what is truly remarkable is not that the Greeks won, but rather that any Persians left the Plain of Marathon alive.

This leads us to consider one of the greatest debates still raging among military historians: Is there a definable way of Western warfare that is superior to that of any other culture? Victor Hanson, who started this debate, marks the Battle of Marathon as the first indication of a discernible difference between Western and Eastern methods of war. Because Professor Hanson (on this topic, at least) has abandoned the intellectual battlefield, historians have begun increasingly to doubt the existence of the "Western way of war" and its alleged superiority to other methods of warfare. In no uncertain terms, this book declares them wrong and picks up the cudgels Professor Hanson has let fall. Although I have taken issue with some of what Hanson has written, on this central issue he is correct.

Writing this book has been a venture of discovery. It is my sincere wish that the synthesis of scholarship and experience offered here sparks a fresh debate on not only the Battle of Marathon, but also the entire field of ancient military history. The final word on the Greco-Persian wars has not yet been written. In all likelihood, it will never be written. Unless the future brings us a major find that forces a reexamination of our current evidence, historians must make use of the limited sources that exist today. I contend that the problem a student of the Battle of Marathon confronts is that this evidence has been so misused or misinterpreted by several generations of historians that the true events of the battle have been lost. What follows is my interpretation of the evidence. I expect that it will spark a large amount of serious debate, and I look forward to engaging in it.

THE MOMENT OF BATTLE

At the dawn of the fifth century BC, Persia stood triumphant. For over five decades, her warriors had crushed all who opposed them. In that time, no city had ever withstood a Persian siege, and all the armies of the known world's most powerful civilizations had met their ruin trying to halt Persia's inexorable march of conquest. On their near invincible warriors, Persian kings built the world's first global empire, stretching from the Mediterranean Sea to India, destroying, in the process, a dozen smaller empires and absorbing the people of a hundred races.

In 490 BC, the mighty Persian king Darius looked west, toward two insignificant Greek city-states that had insulted his empire. Tiny Sparta had sent emissaries to the Persian capital warning the "Great King" to cease his attacks on the Greek cities in Asia; more insulting, Athens had summoned the audacity to send troops onto Persian soil and to burn a Persian city, Sardis, before scurrying home to safety. Tiring of the insults, King Darius sent emissaries to Athens and Sparta demanding the gifts of submission—earth and water. In answer, the Spartans threw the king's messengers into a well and told them to help themselves to all the earth and water they desired, while the Athenians simply put the messengers to the sword.

Enraged, Darius ordered his army to destroy Athens and to enslave the survivors. However, trouble within the empire forced Darius to delay retribution. Eight years after Athens had reduced Sardis to ashes, the dreaded Persian army finally arrived in Greece and mustered its strength on the Plain of Marathon, a scant two dozen miles from Athens. For nine days, ten thousand Athenian hoplites watched the Persian army prepare for battle and wondered how they would be able to resist an army of professional warriors three times their number. Some prayed for the gods to intervene, while others hoped the Persians would delay just a day or two longer. For every Athenian present at Marathon knew that the Spartan army, boasting the best warriors in the world, was marching hard to their aid.

On September 12, 490 BC, the waiting ended. The Persians were moving, and Athens, in mortal danger, could wait no longer. Spartans or no Spartans, Athenian commanders prepared to attack. Before dawn, ten thousand hoplites formed up in columns and waited for the trumpets to signal the order to advance. Eight men deep on the flanks and four deep in the center, the phalanx of bristling spear points and blazing shields began its slow, inexorable march toward the enemy. At first, the Persians could not believe their eyes and wondered how such a meager force could ever hope to break their lines. Some thought it was just a demonstration and would be followed by a hasty retreat. Others simply thought the Greeks mad.

The Athenian hoplites began to pick up the pace, first to a fast walk and then to a trot. The hoplites crushed together, shoulder to shoulder and shield to shield, as each tried to cover as much of his exposed right side behind his neighbor's shield as possible. Dread and fear melted away now that the army was advancing. Men who had soiled themselves in the line drew strength from the surging men surrounding them. At six hundred yards' distance, the mass of men began to scream their fierce and nerve-shattering battle cry: *Alleeee!*

Hastily, the Persian commanders aligned their troops. Men holding wicker shields went to the front as thousands of archers arrayed themselves behind them. The Persian army showed no panic. They were professional soldiers, victors of a hundred bloody battles. In another moment, the archers would release tens of thousands of deadly bolts into the sky. The spearmen would wait for the arrows to decimate their foe and then advance to slaughter the shattered remnant.

But the Persians had never before faced an army like this one. Athenian hoplites learned the art of war against other hoplites, and their kind of war was not decided by a hail of arrows. It was settled by a collision of wooden shields and deadly iron-tipped spears, wielded by heavily armored men. It was a horrible and terrifying confrontation of pushing, screaming, half-crazed men who gouged, stabbed, and kicked at their opponents until one side could bear the agony no longer and broke. The victors would then launch a murderous pursuit of their defeated foes as the bloodlust propelled them forward.

This was the kind of war charging down on the Persians, and it arrived at almost incomprehensible speed, for at two hundred yards' distance the Athenian trot became a sprint. Finally, the Persian archers let fly, but to no effect. Never having seen such a rapid advance, they mistimed their shots and most of the arrows flew harmlessly over the charging hoplites. Hastily, the archers reloaded and the shield bearers uneasily began inching backward as ten thousand metal-encased killers were almost upon them.

In a shuddering instant, hoplites smashed into the lightly protected Persians and convulsed their defensive line. Then the killing began.

PART I

AN EMPIRE
MADE IN WAR

Chapter 1

AN EMPIRE RISES

In 547 BC, Croesus, the king of Lydia, had reason to feel satisfied. To his west, where the Greek cities of Ionia dotted the Aegean coastline, a long, costly war had finally ended. These often troublesome Greeks were presently awed by Lydian power and were now paying him annual tribute. To the north, from which the terrifying Scythian horsemen in previous generations had swept down in devastating raids, it had been quiet since his father, Alyattes II, broke the back of Cimmerian power decades before.[1] To the south, Babylonia remained a strong and dependable ally, a state of affairs that was unlikely to change as long as mighty Babylon felt threatened by the power of the Medes, who occupied the lands east of both Lydia and Babylon.

Since the crushing of the Cimmerians and the demise of the dreaded Assyrian Empire in 613 BC, the Medes had been Lydia's most serious threat. For five bloody years, during the reign of Alyattes II, Lydia fought an exhausting war to halt Median expansion. Herodotus reports that the war ended only when in the midst of a great battle both sides withdrew in terror as a solar eclipse darkened the field.[2] Whatever the influence of the eclipse, the truth is that the war so exhausted both sides, they willingly allowed Babylon to arbitrate an end to the fighting.

The "Peace of the Eclipse" lasted a generation. In that time, Lydia, the first state to create a standardized coinage, grew rich. So rich, in fact, that even today Croesus's name is synonymous with vast wealth and riches. However, the Medes, while not as rich as Lydia, had also grown powerful and ever more threatening. So it was with a certain amount of contentment that Croesus had watched the Medes spend the recent years engaged in a bloody civil war with their cousins the Persians. But by 547, that war had ended and a new Persian-Median king, Cyrus, was solidifying his hold on power. For Croesus this was a troubling development, as the combined power of the Medes and Persians was a dire threat and the youthful Cyrus appeared restless. To forestall a Persian invasion of Lydia, Croesus determined to wage a preemptive war before Cyrus could complete his consolidation of power. But first he had to determine if the gods would bless his enterprise.

According to Herodotus, prior to starting his war with the Persians, Croesus sent envoys to determine the accuracy of each of the major oracles used by the Greeks to foretell the future. After putting each to the test, Croesus decided that the oracle of Delphi was the most accurate. He sent envoys bearing rich gifts to inquire as to the outcome of a war between the Lydians and the Persians. He was much cheered by the Delphic oracle's promise that if the Lydian army marched against the Persians, a great empire would be destroyed. Unfortunately for Croesus, it did not occur to him to ask another important question: Which great empire would be destroyed? He interpreted the oracle's words as it best suited his desires and forwarded immense gifts to Delphi, and to several other temples, to secure the full support of the gods.

When the threat Cyrus presented first arose, Croesus also began a period of active diplomacy in an attempt to assemble allies for the coming fight. This resulted in promises of support from Babylonia, Egypt, and even Sparta. If only he had waited for these forces to gather at his capital, the Persian state might well have died in infancy. But believing immediate action was necessary and buoyed by Delphi's promise of success, Croesus determined to strike out with only his own forces on hand. Beyond the promises of Delphi, Croesus's confidence rested on the fact that Lydia possessed what was probably the most formidable army in the Near East. It consisted of heavy armored infantry (much of it from the Greek cities along the Aegean) and a formidable host of local levies. However, the mainstay of the Lydian army was its elite heavy cavalry, universally feared for its expert use of lances from horseback.

With the gods propitiated by numerous gifts of gold, the Lydian army launched itself against King Cyrus. In 547 BC, the Lydians marched into Cappadocia, which had been under Median lordship since Assyria's collapse. After crossing the Halys River, which had been set as the Median-Lydian boundary by the Peace of the Eclipse, Croesus captured the supposedly strongly fortified city of Pteria and devastated the surrounding country, while waiting to see how Cyrus would react to the provocation. He did not have long to wait. Cyrus, apparently forewarned of the attack, was ready to move immediately after receiving information as to the direction of the Lydian offensive. Moving rapidly from his new capital at Ecbatana, Cyrus gathered further recruits along his line of march, and in what must have been a matter of a couple of weeks, the Persians pitched their camp within striking distance of the Lydian army. Herodotus indicates that the battle that took place was fierce and that many fell on both sides. However, when the fighting ended, at the onset of darkness, there was still no victor. Croesus, who must have been shocked by the speed and strength of Cyrus's response, blamed his lack of success on the Persians' greater numbers and determined to fall back on his capital, Sardis, and await the arrival of his allies.

If his army was still in good condition and he had the city of Pteria as a base, and presumably had access to Sinope on the Black Sea, then there was no reason Croesus could not have wintered his army in Cappadocia and awaited his allies. Therefore it is likely that his army, though not vanquished, received a severe battering. Furthermore, his previous policy of ruining the surrounding country had probably left the countryside denuded of supplies. Croesus was now paying for his policy of systematic devastation, which had greatly shortened the time he could linger in Cappadocia; even under the best of circumstances, an army could remain stationary only a short time before it consumed all of the area's available resources. After failing to win a decisive victory against the Persians, he did not have the choice of staying. Circumstances compelled him to retreat or starve. Still worse lay ahead of him, for Croesus had neglected to stock his capital at Sardis with sufficient provisions to sustain his army through the winter. So upon his arrival at the capital, he was forced to disband all of his army, except for his elite cavalry, and ordered it to reassemble in the spring. At the same time, he sent envoys to Egypt, Babylonia, and Sparta and requested them to bring their armies to Sardis in three months, whereupon their combined might would see Cyrus off.

Cyrus was now left in an unenviable position. The same reason that had compelled Croesus to abandon Cappadocia was now acting on him: A devastated country would not supply his army through the winter. In such circumstances, all precedent called for Cyrus to fall back to Ecbatana, where he could refurbish his army for the next season's campaign. Realizing that his enemies would gather in vast numbers against him in the spring, Cyrus knew that the prudent course only delayed his doom. Therefore he launched his army into an unheard-of winner-take-all winter campaign and followed Croesus's retreating army into Lydia.

Surprised at his foe's audacity, Croesus weighed his options. Most of his army had left for their homes, and it would be months before any of his allies would appear to assist him. Still, the walls of Sardis were considered impregnable, and most leaders would have considered holing up inside of them until the winter frost decimated the Persian army or until his allies would eventually come to the rescue. Instead, Croesus opted to give battle with the much-reduced forces available to him. Historians have often commented on the folly of his choice, but under the circumstances it was probably the best available. While it is true the Sardis region had not been devastated like Cappadocia, it still could not have had much food left on hand. It had been the mustering point for the Lydian invasion, and as such the Lydian army would have consumed much of the reserve food stores before marching into Cappadocia. Furthermore, the army would have packed much of what was left on wagons and mules to supplement whatever it collected on the march. By early winter, the reserve food stores must have been very low, if they existed at all. Given these circumstances, the idea of a siege of many months must have filled Croesus's head with visions of famine. As Croesus had not taken the precaution of restocking his magazines within the city, what food stores did exist were probably still stored in the countryside, left for Cyrus to use. As long as Cyrus was not averse to seeing the rural population starve (and it is a safe guess that he would find this acceptable), then his food situation was probably markedly better than what Croesus faced in the city, where he had to feed both his own population and his army. Moreover, as is frequently the case, military commanders tend to magnify their own difficulties while discounting those faced by their opponents. In the final analysis, Croesus probably saw no option except to risk all on a final decisive battle. If he lost, he could still in the last resort retreat behind the protection of Sardis's walls.

Despite dismissing the bulk of his army, Croesus still possessed the Lydian cavalry, a formidable force, while the plains in front of Sardis afforded perfect terrain for their operations. For Cyrus's part, he had to consider carefully how to engage such a dangerous foe. Taking the advice of Harpagos, his most trusted general, Cyrus had the baggage camels unloaded and placed at the front of his lines to act as cavalry. As the Lydians did not use camels in their operations, Cyrus hoped that the sight and foul odors of these strange beasts would panic the Lydian horses.

This is precisely what happened. Unable to control their horses, the Lydian cavalrymen dismounted and prepared to stand and fight as infantry against the Persian assault. It was a doomed struggle. Stripped of their mobility and lacking heavy armor, the Lydians were easy prey for the Persians' massed archers, who always made up the bulk of the Persian infantry forces. Once the archers had done their work, Cyrus unleashed his own cavalry into the disordered Lydian masses. Although there was some fierce fighting at points, the Lydians were soon routed and the survivors streamed back into the city.

While Herodotus says that the Persians settled down for a siege, he also states that Cyrus offered a large reward to any of his soldiers who fought their way to the top of Sardis's walls. This probably reflects the fact that food was short, winter was fast approaching, and Cyrus would find himself in a bad situation if he was still conducting a siege when the armies of Babylonia and Egypt arrived. With those factors in mind, he launched a major assault on the walls, but it failed. As he lacked a siege train, Cyrus determined to starve the city into submission in the hope that it would soon give up.

Herodotus tells a remarkable story of a Persian soldier watching a Lydian climb down from the Acropolis along crags in the cliffside to retrieve a helmet that had fallen from the walls. The soldier then returned by the same route, all the time watched by the alert Persian sentry. This section of the walls was poorly guarded because the cliff was so steep that the Lydians considered it unscalable. However, now a Lydian guard had shown the way, and the next day a specially selected force of Persians ascended the heights by the same route. The attacking Persians surprised the Lydians. By daybreak, the Acropolis was in Persian hands and the city gates opened. Persians swarmed into the "impregnable" fortress, and Cyrus gave the city over to sack.[3]

Is Herodotus's version of the story true? At almost the precise point that such an attempt would have occurred, archaeologists have discovered the remains of a soldier in his mid-twenties who appears to have been thrown from the walls of Sardis's Acropolis. Forensic archaeologists found that the man was in remarkably good health until he suffered a stab wound through his seventh rib. Interestingly, the soldier's arm was broken in two spots consistent with what one would expect from a surprised man desperately warding off sword blows. Finally, in his hand was a stone—perhaps he was a slinger—meant to be used in a final act of desperation. Just a few feet from the soldier's body was found the only helmet retrieved in the Sardis excavations, which was dated to the period when Cyrus attacked. Is this the soldier who climbed down the cliff and inadvertently showed the Persians a route to take the fortifications? Is this the very helmet that soldier tried to retrieve? The truth will never be known, but it is tantalizing evidence that tempts historians to use it to fill the gap in our knowledge. It should be noted that the rest of the archaeological record unearthed during these excavations is entirely consistent with Herodotus's account.

Diverse traditions present varying fates for Croesus, ranging from one suggestion that he had himself immolated as the Persian army swept into Sardis to another where he was spared by Cyrus and elevated to a place of trust and honor. This latter version is what Herodotus offers, but Babylonian records contradict the historian's. While most Greek traditions have the god Apollo saving Croesus at the last minute, it should be noted that the Greeks had to create this conclusion no matter what the true facts were. For them, Croesus had to survive, as their religion would not let them accept or conceive that Apollo would allow him to die. After all, Croesus had presented Apollo, through his oracle at Delphi, rich gifts in return for a victory. It would have been beyond the pale for the god to both deny him the victory and allow him to die. At the moment, the best that history can offer is that Croesus's fate is unknown, with a prejudice toward his being allowed to live, as Cyrus appears to have made this a standard policy through most of his conquests.[4] What is positively known is that an upstart Persian king had vanquished the once powerful Lydian Empire and made its capital, Sardis, a mere provincial city in the growing Persian Empire. A generation later, a small Athenian force would burn Sardis to the ground before scurrying back to Greece and safety. In doing so, Athens would gain the undying hatred of Persia and history was set on the course that eventually led to Marathon.

But who was this Cyrus who suddenly springs into the pages of history? What is known about the man whose conquests would grant him the appellation "the Great" and make him the founder of the world's greatest empire until the advent of Rome? Cyrus's story begins soon after the Peace of the Eclipse years before, when the Medes had turned their attention to securing the loyalty (or failing that, the subjugation) of the numerous seminomadic tribes within their domain.

By 585 BC, when Astyages took the throne, they had formed a true polyglot empire of Iranian-speaking tribes, including the Persians. With a secure border on his Lydian frontier and the Babylonians cringing behind what they called the Median Wall, Astyages was able to concentrate his energies on securing his eastern border and further consolidating his kingdom.[5] As many of the region's tribes gave up their nomadic ways in favor of permanent settlements, they adopted new government structures. Many, including the Ansan tribe of Persian heritage, saw their tribal chiefs elevated to petty kings. Although these kings continued paying tribute to the Medes, like powerful medieval barons they ruled their own territories with little interference from the Median king. When Astyages eventually realized the danger that these independent power bases represented to his own hold on power, it was too late, as one of these petty kings, Cyrus, was already preparing for war.

It was not until toward the end of his long reign that Astyages confronted this revolt, the first real military threat to his rule. Cyrus, then a minor noble within the empire, had succeeded to the title of king of Ansan and had consolidated his power over the numerous disaffected Persian tribes in his region. If this were all Astyages had to worry about, it would have been a small matter. For at this point, even the combined might of all the Persian tribes was no match for the professional, battle-hardened Medes. However, as Astyages' rule progressed, he had become progressively more paranoid and suspicious of those around him. In the process, he turned much of the Median nobility against him. As he relied on these men to command his army, he was in the unenviable position of having to embark on a civil war without any assurance that his own army would remain loyal to him.

To understand the politics of the time, we have to turn to legend and see what truths we can gather. According to Herodotus, early in his reign Astyages had a dream that his daughter, Mandane, would somehow be his undoing. To forestall this, Astyages decided that when she came of age she should not marry a powerful Median nobleman, who would then be positioned to overthrow him. Rather, he gave her to a minor Persian noble, Cambyses, renowned for his peaceful disposition and therefore unlikely to ever be accepted by the Medes as their ruler. In a later dream, however, Astyages learned that it was not Mandane's husband he had to fear. The true danger was to come from the offspring of this marriage. So when Mandane did become pregnant, he summoned her to the Persian court and stood by as the foretold son was born. Astyages, afraid the child would one day supplant him, ordered that the infant be abandoned on the side of a mountain and exposed to the elements until he had died.

The infant's murder was entrusted to Harpagos, a relative of Astyages and also his most trusted general and adviser. Harpagos understood that this assignment placed him in terrible danger. Failure to obey Astyages' orders would mean his death. However, Astyages was old now and had no male heir. If he died, it was not unlikely that Mandane and her husband would take control of the empire, and they would surely want revenge on the man who had killed their firstborn son. Trying to make the best of his dreadful predicament, Harpagos gave the child over to Astyages' herdsman to kill. Fortunately for the infant, the herdsman's wife had just given birth to a stillborn baby, and she convinced her husband to expose her already dead child to the elements and keep the king's grandson, Cyrus, as their own.

When Cyrus was ten years old, Astyages discovered the ruse but was convinced by his seers and dream interpreters that the danger of Cyrus replacing him had passed. He decided to allow the child to return to his parents in Persia—but not before he had punished Harpagos for his failure to kill the infant. Pretending he was happy about his grandson's deliverance, he told Harpagos to go home and send his young son over to play with Cyrus. When the boy arrived, Astyages seized him, slew him, and cut him limb from limb. Some of these limbs he had broiled for a banquet that night, whereupon he served Harpagos the flesh of his own son for dinner. Upon learning what his meal consisted of, Harpagos contained his fury and told Astyages that the meal was pleasing, as was everything the king presented to him.

As was noted, the story is legend, and the often unreliable Ctesias gives a very different version of events.[6] Even Herodotus mentions that there were several other stories about Cyrus's youth but fails to tell us what they were. So we are left to gather some truth from legend. Babylonian sources confirm that Cyrus was the son of Cambyses and that he was the king of Ansan. What we learn from Herodotus's story is that Cyrus was also at least half Mede and a direct descendant of the Median king. At a time when there was considerable intermarriage among the nobility of many of the region's tribes, this suffices to explain why the Medes so readily accepted Cyrus's future overlordship. Moreover, whatever may be the ultimate truth of this gruesome tale, one can surmise that the king did not stifle any impulse to visit degradations upon his nobility. If he did inflict this or some other unbearable insult on Harpagos (and that general's later actions surely indicate he did), his closest friend and adviser, it can be safely assumed that the rest of the Median nobility feared for their own safety at the hands of such a capricious ruler.

Herodotus further indicates that Harpagos bided his time until Cyrus was of age and had risen to the Ansan throne before reaching out to him with inducements to revolt. This would establish Harpagos in the position of kingmaker, which may be giving him too much credit. What is known is that by 559 BC, Cyrus was king of Ansan and busily forming a coalition of other local Persian tribes determined to resist Astyages' rule. By 555 BC, this coalition was in open revolt, and Astyages, finally deigning to take notice of the upstart king of Ansan, ordered Cyrus to present himself at his palace at Ecbatana. Cyrus replied that he would arrive sooner than Astyages would like, and with an army at his back.[7]

Alarmed, Astyages raised an army and sent it south to confront Cyrus. According to Herodotus, the gods had unbalanced Astyages' mind and caused him to give Harpagos command of this army. Even if one does not believe Herodotus's story about the king feeding Harpagos his own son, it appears certain that Harpagos was nursing some other severe grievance against Astyages. Discounting the direct influence of the gods on his mind, Astyages' decision to entrust Harpagos with command of the army surely rates as an ill-considered personnel decision. When Harpagos's Median army finally met the Persians, most of it wasted no time in joining their commander and going over to Cyrus's side.

After he learned of his army's treasonous collapse, Astyages immediately ordered the execution (by impalement) of the dream readers who had told him it was safe to let Cyrus live. He then called forth the general levy and personally led out the host of the Medes to face Cyrus. Again, there was no battle, as the remaining Median nobility followed Harpagos's lead and went over to the Persians. Astyages was turned over to Cyrus in chains. Cyrus, probably realizing that if the Median nobility wanted their king dead, they would have done it themselves, held Astyages prisoner, and in 553 BC, Astyages passes from the pages of history.

Because Herodotus's narrative when placed in chronological order goes directly from the fall of Astyages to the Persian war with Lydia, most histories have done the same, neglecting the fact that there was a period of approximately six years separating these events. Although the historical record for this time is a blank, one can probably assume that no matter how much the Median nobility had come to hate Astyages, many were not overjoyed at having to bow to a Persian upstart. Furthermore, Cyrus began his revolt with the support of only a portion of the Persian tribes. He required time to persuade or force the other tribes to join his confederation. Finally, the northern and eastern borders of the Median Empire were always restless, and it would have been odd indeed if the steppe nomads had not taken advantage of the turmoil within Media to move south with the hope of picking up some easy loot. For all these reasons, Cyrus was forced to spend the early years of his reign consolidating his hold on power.

This consolidation was as much a matter of politics as it was warfare, and here Cyrus showed a particular genius. Not only did he refrain from killing his vanquished grandfather, Astyages, but he also retained much of the Median nobility in their places of honor and power in both the government and the army. In fact, the rise of Cyrus was not so much a conquest of the Median Empire as it was a change in management, a task greatly eased by the fact that Medes and Persians were close ethnic cousins. In fact, to the Greeks they were so indistinguishable that they used the term *Mede* to describe both Medes and Persians. Both races already shared a common law and a distant linked heritage. Each also brought something important to the ethnic union. The Medes possessed an organized imperial state, experience in statecraft, and a military organization steeped in the efficient Assyrian methods of war, battle, and siege operations.

The Persians brought a vigorous leader and a population eager for the good things available in the settled areas of Mesopotamia—things that they could obtain only by war and conquest. These conquests began with Cyrus's defeat of Croesus and the destruction of Lydian power, but many more were to follow.

Chapter 2

LOOKING TO THE WEST

Lydia's collapse brought the growing Persian Empire into contact with the Greek city-states of Ionia for the first time. Prior to his invasion of Lydia, Cyrus had sent messengers to each of these cities, asking them to support his cause by revolting against Lydian rule. But only the city of Miletus had seen which way the winds were blowing and revolted accordingly. The rest of Ionia had grown rich off the trading opportunities that flowed from being part of the Lydian Empire and from the leadership of the commercially enlightened Croesus. Reluctant to put their trading profits at risk, and sure that the powerful Lydian army would repulse the invaders, most of Ionia focused on business and did its best to ignore the war.

Now that the Lydian Empire was in ruins, its former possessions passed into Cyrus's hands. Frightened that Cyrus would interpret their neutrality as opposition, the Ionians hastened to send messengers to Sardis to plead for Cyrus to accept their subjugation on the same terms that Croesus had allowed them. Cyrus, still angry at their refusal to help him when he needed it most, refused their entreaties. Furthermore, although it is not mentioned in the contemporary records, one can assume that Cyrus's encounter with the Greek heavy infantry in the Battle of Pteria must have left an impression on him. He may have considered it unwise to leave such a potentially powerful military force in his rear when he turned his army against Babylon. Informed that they would suffer Cyrus's wrath, the Ionian cities began to fortify themselves and to prepare for war. As part of their preparations, they sent an envoy to plead for Spartan help. The Spartans, who were always reluctant to send their soldiers very far from home, refused to send an army to the Ionians' aid but did send an emissary to meet with Cyrus.

When the Spartan envoy was ushered in for an audience with Cyrus in Sardis, he reportedly told the Persian king that he should desist from attacking any of the Greek cities in Ionia. If Cyrus ignored their warning, he would incur Sparta's displeasure. Incredulous, Cyrus turned to the Greeks in his service and asked, "Who were the Spartans, and how many of them were there?" Upon being given the answer, Cyrus dismissively told the Spartan envoy, "I have never yet feared any men who had a place in the center of the city set aside for meeting together, swearing false oaths, and cheating one another." Continuing, Cyrus said that if he lived long enough, he would give Sparta more to concern itself with than the affairs of Ionia.[1] This is the first example in history of the East–West cultural divide that in many ways still exists today, for Cyrus was demonstrating his contempt for the emerging democratic and market-oriented values of Western society. Although Cyrus may have been speaking out of ignorance, his response and the fact that there were Greek advisers at his court provide sufficient evidence that Cyrus was already interested in learning as much as possible about the Greeks. Moreover, his comments reveal that what he had learned about Greek politics and society so far had failed to impress him. In fact, he apparently held Athenian and Spartan methods in contempt. And so it was that the first attempt of European Greeks to involve themselves with affairs in Asia failed to make much of an impression.

Whatever Cyrus's intentions for the Ionian cities, he did not immediately move against them. In fact, he did the exact opposite. After spending a few months in Sardis, presumably consolidating his hold on the non-Ionian portions of the former Lydian Empire, Cyrus took the bulk of his army and returned to his capital, Ecbatana. Herodotus reports that he returned to the east in order to prepare for wars of conquest against Babylon, the Bactrians, the Saka, and the Egyptians. Nevertheless, it is just as likely that there were unresolved issues back in recently conquered Media that required his attention.

Because Herodotus's narrative takes Cyrus directly from his return to Ecbatana to his assault on Babylon, many histories of the period do the same thing. Unfortunately, existing sources are silent on Cyrus's activities during the seven years between these events, leaving historians to make their own deductions. The Great King's intent after defeating Croesus was to march directly on the Ionian cities, both to subdue them and to punish them for their insolence. That he instead marched east with the bulk of his army and left Lydia only partially consolidated, with a number of Greek cities still in open revolt, likely means that news of unrest in the east had reached him. Moreover, the fact that he did not personally command the force sent to crush a rebellion that broke out in Sardis after his departure is a further indication that a serious threat in the east demanded his full attention.

Whether it was halting another invasion of the steppe tribes or the need to further consolidate his rule of the newly acquired Median kingdom has to be left to speculation. What is known is that a large amount of territory in the east that was never controlled by the Medes was under Persian rule by the time Cyrus's successor, Darius, assumed the throne, approximately a decade after Cyrus's death.[2] As it is unlikely that Darius or his predecessor, Cyrus's son and immediate successor, Cambyses II, had time to undertake operations in the east, it must have been Cyrus who won these new conquests.[3]

While Cyrus dealt with the east, his general, Mazares, after crushing a revolt in Sardis, marched south to conquer the Ionian cities. He first laid waste to the region around the Maender River and after capturing Priene had the inhabitants carried off as slaves.

Soon after this campaign, Mazares died and Harpagos assumed command of the Persian army. Harpagos, the former commander of Astyages' Median army, was a professional soldier well versed in siege warfare, with which the Greeks had little familiarity. As the Ionian Greeks proved unable to coordinate their activities and were reluctant to meet the Persians in open battle, they made the mistake of electing to hide behind their walls, secure in the knowledge that their fleets could keep them supplied with necessities. As city walls had always proven impregnable to Greek hoplites, who never trained or equipped themselves for siege warfare, and as the Persians did not yet possess a navy, this must have seemed a sound strategy. However, against a general, and an army, that had learned the mechanics of siege warfare from the masters of the trade, the Assyrians, it was a disastrous course.

As Herodotus relates:

> Now that Cyrus had appointed him general, Harpagos went to Ionia, where he captured the cities there by investing them with earthworks. For whenever he had forced the people of a city to shut themselves up within their walls, he would then pile mounds of earth up against the walls as he laid siege to the city.[4]

The first city Harpagos besieged was Phocaea, the populace of which reacted to their inevitable defeat by loading the entire population onto ships and sailing away. Unfortunately, the rest of their tale was not a happy one. The refugees were expelled from Chios, the first island where they attempted to settle. They then determined to sail to Corsica and establish a new city there. However, before departing the eastern Mediterranean, they sailed back to Phocaea and massacred the Persian garrison that Harpagos had left in the vacated city. To escape Persian retribution, they then sailed to the western Mediterranean, where they managed to antagonize Carthage, the growing power of the region. Carthage wasted no time in declaring war and soon defeated the Phocaeans in a naval battle off Corsica. Afterward, the Phocaean survivors were taken ashore and stoned to death by the Carthaginians.

The population of Teos also picked up stakes and sailed away, but the remainder of the Ionian cities either surrendered or were quickly subdued by Harpagos. According to Herodotus:

> All of the Ionians who stayed behind faced the challenge of resisting Harpagos. These men fought courageously for their country. But they suffered defeat and conquest and then stayed in their cities, submitting to Persian rule.[5]

Given his Greek audience, Herodotus could not say plainly that the Ionians cravenly surrendered on the approach of the Persian army. But given the pace of the Persian conquest—Ionia apparently fell in one campaigning season—it does not appear that the Persians conducted any great number of prolonged sieges. Herodotus states that Harpagos now marched south, into Caria and Lycia, with Ionian soldiers as part of his army. It would thus appear that whatever hostilities had occurred between Ionia and Persia had not led to prolonged animosity.

The Carians did no better than the Ionians, and with thinly veiled disgust, Herodotus relates:

> Now, the Carians did not distinguish themselves in opposing Harpagos; indeed they submitted to him without performing any glorious deeds, and the same can be said, too, of all the Hellenes who lived in that region of Asia.[6]

It was left to the Lycians to give the Persians a taste of what a war between civilizations might be like. The Phocaeans, by sailing back to their home city to murder the Persian garrison, gave the Persians a preview of how bitter Greek resistance to their rule might become, but it was the Lycians' commitment to victory or death that should have awakened the Persians to the fact that there were some peoples who would never submit to their rule. As Harpagos and his polyglot army marched into Lycia, he was attacked on the Plain of Xanthos. After a long, hard fight, the Lycians were defeated and retreated behind their city walls. Herodotus relates:

> Once trapped in their city, they gathered together their women, children, possessions, and servants on the acropolis and set fire to it, burning up everything. Then, having sworn powerful oaths, the men went forth again to do battle against Harpagos. They all died fighting.

The city of Caunus followed the Lycian example, leaving Harpagos with nothing but a wasteland to occupy in southern Asia (modern southwestern Turkey).

Greek had met Persian in the field, and the Persians had conquered. From this encounter, the Persians learned a number of lessons. First, it was apparently impossible for the Greeks to overcome their petty rivalries and coordinate their resistance. From this, the Persians came to believe that the best policy against the Greeks was to divide and conquer. Furthermore, a policy that combined threats of overwhelming military force with bribes was often sufficient to get most Greek cities to do their bidding. Finally, while the heavily armored Greek infantryman (hoplite) was individually a formidable soldier, the Ionian Greeks did not train for concerted action on the battlefield. Unfortunately for the prospects of further Persian conquests, this last lesson did not apply to the Greek mainland, where hoplites trained exclusively for concerted battlefield action.

During almost two generations of Lydian sovereignty, the martial ardor and capabilities of the Ionian cities had atrophied. For the warlike Persians, the rapid and complete collapse of Ionian resistance demonstrated that the Greeks were a feeble race when it came to war. It was left to a later generation of battle-hardened Spartan and Athenian hoplites to prove otherwise.

Chapter 3

EMPIRE AT LAST

With Lydia overthrown, the Ionians subdued, and his eastern borders temporarily secure, Cyrus turned his full attention toward mighty Babylon.[1] This was the great prize, the strongest and wealthiest city in Mesopotamia, the glory of which even in Cyrus's time reached back deep into the mists of distant ages. After the fall of the Assyrian Empire, Babylon's rulers, Nebuchadnezzar and his successors, had launched their armies in an almost unending series of wars designed to re-create the Babylonian Empire on a scale greater than that of Hammurabi. It was during these wars that Jerusalem was conquered and a significant portion of the Jewish population was shipped east in what has become known to us as the "Babylonian Captivity."

This transshipment of large portions of a conquered people was a favorite tactic of the Assyrians, who used it not only as an instrument of terror, but also to break the national will of newly conquered peoples. Babylon apparently adopted the policy from their previous overlords for the same reason. Unfortunately for their rulers it was to have tragic consequences, as these transported populations constituted an angry fifth column, which Cyrus was to use to his advantage.

Even as Babylon's kings sent their armies to conquer lands lost during Assyria's ascendancy, they remained wary of the restless power of the Medes. To counter that threat, they spared no expense in building the Median Wall. This ancient Maginot Line stretched across the entire expanse between the Euphrates and Tigris rivers and secured the empire's northern frontier. Unfortunately, the wall likely fed an artificial feeling of security that allowed Babylon's king, Nabonidus, to neglect the rising danger of the combined Median-Persian force, led by an avaricious military genius.

While Cyrus was securing his eastern frontier, Nabonidus spent much of his reign away from Babylon, in Tayma. The excuse has been offered that this oasis was a key nexus of the major Arabian trade routes and as such was the locus of Babylonian economic power. However, this is still the kind of responsibility best handled by a trusted garrison commander coupled with a few customs agents. In reality, Nabonidus was busy reconstructing on a magnificent scale the Temple of Harran, where his mother was a priestess. This temple was dedicated to the moon god, Sin, and it is clear that Nabonidus placed this god far above the traditional Babylonian gods, particularly Marduk. By placing Sin, formerly a relatively minor deity, at the head of the Babylonian pantheon of gods, Nabonidus was running a great political risk, as he was deeply angering Babylon's powerful priestly caste. These priests regarded the king's continuing absences from Marduk's great new year festival (Akitu) as a direct insult to themselves and to their god. As they believed the king's participation in this festival was the surest guarantee of good harvests and continued prosperity, his absence made a deep impression on the Babylonian people. When these resentments were coupled with the rising dissatisfaction among the merchant classes, weary of tax exactions used to pay for unceasing conflicts and the cost of the Harranian temple, Babylon began to seethe with discontent.

Cyrus was aware of these difficulties and used them to his advantage. Although the evidence is fragmentary, it appears that he began active operations along the Babylonian frontier as early as 541 BC. These attacks may have represented probing for weak points or raids designed to test the effectiveness and loyalty of the Babylonian army. However, it is more likely that they formed part of a coordinated propaganda campaign, which Cyrus began a full year before he was actually prepared to wage all-out war. Each attack provided further proof to the inhabitants of the frontier provinces that Nabonidus was either powerless to protect them or uninterested in doing so. Simultaneously, Cyrus's agents began reaching out to the discontented groups within Babylon. The Book of Isaiah captures the effectiveness of these activities:

> Thus saith the Lord unto Cyrus, my anointed, whose right hand
> I have grasped, that the nations shall obey him, and I will break
> the Strength of Kings: I will open gates before thee, and cities

shall not be shut. I will go before thee and level mountains; I will shatter gates of bronze, and smash bars of iron, and will give the hidden treasures of darkness. . . . [2]

In fact, the Old Testament mentions Cyrus twenty-three times, always with lavish praise. Undoubtedly, Cyrus's propaganda was equally success-ful with other transplanted populations and discontented groups. What we do know is that the commander of Babylon's northern army and Gutium province, Gobryas (also referred to in many histories as Ugbaru), saw which way the tide was running and transferred his loyalty to Cyrus.

By 539 BC all was ready, and Cyrus launched his armies south. At the city of Opis, the Persians, joined by Gobryas and his troops, met the Babyloni-ans and defeated them. Almost immediately, the people of the region rose in revolt against Babylon. But they rose a bit too early and were apparently slaughtered in great numbers by Nabonidus's retreating forces.[3] Cyrus crossed the Euphrates at Opis, south of the massive Median Wall, which was taken in flank and rear and rendered useless.[4] Just as Cyrus made good use of Harpagos after he deserted Astyages, he also put Gobryas to good use. Having split his army in two, Cyrus took command of one portion himself and marched along the rear of the Median Wall, apparently in pur-suit of Nabonidus and the remnants of the Babylonian army. After a two-week pursuit, Cyrus appeared before the walls of Sippar, on the east bank of the Euphrates, and the city threw open its gates. Nabonidus, who much to his surprise had found himself barred from entering Sippar, was still unable to meet the Persians in battle on the open plain, so he fled to Babylon.

Gobryas, in command of the other portion of the Persian army, had marched directly on Babylon. Upon arriving well ahead of Nabonidus, he also found the city gates open and marched into a welcoming Babylon without a fight.[5] When Nabonidus arrived from Sippar, the city had al-ready fallen, and he was taken captive. The chronicles are silent as to his fate.[6]

Cyrus's careful preparations had paid off: The whole of Babylon's em-pire had fallen to him after just one battle. Everywhere he was greeted as a liberator, and he apparently worked assiduously to keep his pre-war promises and to maintain his popularity. The Nabonidus Chronicle relates that Gobryas kept his forces in hand and placed a special guard around the

Babylonian temples to prevent looting.[7] Two weeks after Gobryas captured the city, Cyrus arrived (October 29). According to the Babylonian
Chronicles, his path was lined with green twigs and a "state of peace was
imposed upon the city." The chronicle continues: "Cyrus sent greeting to
all Babylon. Gobryas, his governor, installed subgovernors throughout
Babylon." Once again, Cyrus wisely placed a trusted Babylonian face on
his rule, at least through the critical transition period. Unfortunately, Gobryas died soon after, but by that time the important work was done and
Cyrus's place on the Babylonian throne was secure. As the Nabonidus verse
relates: "To the inhabitants of Babylon a joyful heart is now given. They
are like prisoners when the prisons are opened. Liberty is restored to those
who were surrounded by oppression. All rejoice to look upon him as king!"[8]

Cyrus immediately reversed Nabonidus's placement of the moon god,
Sin, ahead of the foremost Babylonian god, Marduk. He also ended the
former ruler's other unpopular religious policies, which were responsible
for much of the city's discontent. More famously, he released the Jews
from their Babylonian Captivity and ordered his governors in Syria to supply funds to help them rebuild their temple in Jerusalem. Although there
is no evidence to the fact, this was probably a policy he extended to other
transplanted populations as well. Cyrus tarried in Babylon for several
months to consolidate his rule before returning to his capital at Ecbatana.
Before leaving, he had inscribed on a stone cylinder:

> I am Cyrus, King of the world, the Great King, the legitimate
> king, King of Babylon, King of Sumer and Akkad, King of the
> four corners of the earth . . . of a family which has always exer-
> cised kingship; whose rule the gods love. . . . All the kings of the
> whole world, from the upper to the lower sea, those who sit in
> throne rooms, those who live in other . . . all the kings of the west
> dwelling in tents brought their heavy tribute and kissed my feet.
> And Cyrus restored sanctuaries and houses and gave peace to
> Babylon.[9]

For the next eight years, until 530 BC, there is no further mention of
Cyrus in the historical record. There is, however, a story in Arrian's *Anabasis* (written over six hundred years later) claiming Cyrus lost the bulk
of an army while trying to conquer the Indus valley.[10] If Cyrus did invade
India, he would have first had to control Gandhara (modern Kabul), and
since the Behistun inscription lists this region as one of the satrapies

Darius inherited from earlier kings, there is at least this confirmation that Cyrus campaigned in the area. However, it is just as likely that the Great King spent the bulk of this period consolidating the massive empire he now ruled. The Behistun inscription, which Darius ordered written after he ascended to the throne almost a decade later, takes it for granted that twenty great satrapies had already been designated prior to the start of Darius's rule. Each of these areas was ruled by a satrap (*khshathrapavan*, translated literally as "protector of the kingdom") and linked into a complex administrative system that must have taken considerable time and energy to implement.

*The Cyrus Cylinder, produced after Cyrus conquered Babylon, tells of
how the former king, Nabonidus, was unfit to rule, and details how
Cyrus was pleasing to the Babylonians' chief god, Marduk.
In short, it is an excellent piece of propaganda defending
Cyrus's conquest.*   The British Museum

When Cyrus again appears in the historical record, we find him on the empire's northeastern frontier with his army, either attacking or defending against the Massagetes—probably a Scythian tribe. In typical fashion, Herodotus tells a colorful but probably fanciful story of this encounter.[11] What is certain is that Cyrus was defeated and killed in battle. According to Herodotus, the Massagetae queen (Tomyris) had a wineskin filled with blood and thrust Cyrus's severed head into it so as to "slake his thirst for blood."[12]

In any event, the Persians retrieved Cyrus's body and took the great conqueror's remains to Pasargadae, where they buried him with his arms and jewelry in a gold sarcophagus. He left to his son Cambyses the largest empire the world had ever known—an empire that was to last until Alexander the Great two hundred years later.

The Tomb of Cyrus the Great at Pasargadae, Iran. It honors Cyrus, the greatest conqueror in the ancient world until the time of Alexander the Great, and the founder of the Persian Empire.   The Art Archive/Alfredo Dagli Orti

Chapter 4

THE RISE OF DARIUS

The oldest son of Cyrus, Cambyses, remains one of the great enigmas of history. If one believes Herodotus's account, Cambyses was both cruel and mad. The great historian presents a lengthy list of the king's transgressions, including the sacrilegious murder of Egypt's sacred Apis bull, the kicking to death of his pregnant wife, and the scourging and murder of Egyptian priests. The truth is probably somewhat more complex. For instance, Egyptologists have proven that the sacred Apis bull did die soon after Cambyses conquered Egypt, but they have also uncovered a stone tablet showing the bull's respectful burial.

Herodotus's account often represents the evidence and opinions offered by persons with a vested interest in presenting Cambyses in the worst possible light. Therefore there is good reason to discount many of the negative stories about Cambyses. Moreover, as Cambyses' successor, Darius, who had usurped the throne, had no interest in glorifying his predecessor, making the official records of his reign untrustworthy on this matter. For instance, much of what Herodotus tells us comes from Egyptian priests, whom he met almost half a century after Cambyses' death. Herodotus would have had no way of knowing that these stories were the result of malice engendered by official propaganda and that they had nothing to do with actual cruelty or sacrilege on Cambyses' part. It is likely that the priests disapproved of Cambyses because he reduced the payments promised them by the pharaoh Amasis, who bought their loyalty with great gifts to the temples. A papyrus at the French Bibliothèque National provides evidence that Cambyses was reducing the official gen-

erosity to which the priests had become accustomed. It details Cambyses'
orders to reduce the taxes (in kind) going to the temples:

> Of the cattle that once were given by the people to the temples
> of the gods, let them give only half of it. Regarding the poultry,
> do not give it to them any more. The priests are perfectly capa-
> ble of rearing their own geese.

The loss of half their revenues and the indignity of having to raise their
own poultry is a more likely source of animosity than anything presented
by Herodotus.[1] As for the Behistun inscription, it must be remembered
that Cambyses' successor, Darius, was in all likelihood a usurper with a
vested interest in maligning the reputation of his immediate predecessor.[2]

Whatever the final truth about Cambyses' character, his accomplishments and failures are easier to ascertain. Although the events of the first
several years of his reign are not recorded, he probably spent most of that
time campaigning on the empire's northeastern frontier. At the very least,
it can be assumed that there was unfinished business with the Massagetes,
who had killed Cyrus and still required pacification. There was also a significant amount of work required to consolidate all of Cyrus's new addi-
tions to the empire, such as present-day Afghanistan. Moreover, after
Cyrus's death there may have been an extended period of internal insta-
bility that consumed much of Cambyses' attention. Xenophon, in his fic-
tional work the *Cyropaedia*, may have preserved an accurate historical
tradition when he states that after Cyrus's death, "immediately his sons
quarreled and cities and nations revolted and everything took a turn for
the worse." The Behistun inscription provides supporting evidence that
Cambyses may have faced a challenge to his power. On that inscription,
Darius records that Cambyses had his brother, Smerdis, secretly murdered
before embarking on his Egyptian campaign.[3] Finally, with the east settled,
challengers dead, and the empire stable again, Cambyses turned his attention to a project Cyrus had entertained before his death—the invasion of
Egypt.[4]

Egypt was ruled by the pharaoh Amasis, who, after seizing the throne
by force, ruled for forty-four years. He was an old soldier himself and must
have made a realistic appraisal of the situation. As long as the Persians
lacked a fleet, Amasis likely felt secure with the unforgiving Sinai desert
between Egypt and the Persian army. However, after Babylon's fall, the

greatest seafarers of the ancient world, the Phoenicians, transferred their allegiance to Cyrus and placed their fleets under Persian suzerainty. Cambyses could now launch an amphibious attack from Phoenicia, or if he marched overland, he would have a fleet in constant contact from which to draw supplies. To counter this, Amasis strengthened the Egyptian fleet and secured a number of alliances with the islands of the eastern Mediterranean. In return for Egyptian gold, these island kingdoms were to send their fleets to Egypt to counter the Persian threat.

Unfortunately for Amasis, as soon as the Persian forces moved, these arrangements collapsed. Fearing Persia's growing power, Egypt's allies looked first to their own interests. Rather than assist Egypt, they sent their fleets to assist Cambyses. In this regard, the example of Samos is informative. In 525 BC, the island was ruled by Polycrates, who had seized power with his two brothers. After murdering one brother and exiling the other, he had become sole ruler. Taking advantage of Ionia's slow recovery after the Persian conquests, Samos became the Aegean's foremost trading power. As the island grew rich, Polycrates fortified his capital city and its harbor. He also invested in a fleet of over one hundred vessels, which he used both for state-sponsored piracy and to enforce Samos's trading dominance. According to Herodotus, Polycrates had, in exchange for gifts, forged an alliance with Amasis. However, when the Persians began to march, Polycrates offered a substantial portion of his fleet to Cambyses. When the attack on Egypt began, he outfitted forty ships for war and then, trying to kill two birds with one stone, manned them with those Samians he considered most likely to cause his regime future problems. To Cambyses he sent a secret message that the Samian crews should not return from the campaign, though one must assume he would welcome the return of the ships.

The Samians departed, thought better of it, and sailed back to attack Samos. Defeated by Polycrates, the Samian exiles made their way to Sparta and pleaded for assistance to help them overthrow Polycrates. The Spartans had strong ties to many of the Samians in the defeated party, but as always they were reluctant to send any substantial force far from Sparta. However, Sparta's Peloponnesian ally Corinth, probably as a result of trading rivalries, was keen to participate in an assault on Samos and convinced the Spartans to cooperate.

The expedition was a fiasco. After forty days, the Spartans gave up the siege and sailed away. Herodotus brands as scandalous lies rumors that Polycrates bribed the Spartan commander to depart. However, he was getting his information from the direct descendants of these Spartans. As for Polycrates, his arrogance and power eventually proved an irritation to Persia. Later, the Persian satrap of Sardis, Oroites, tricked him into visiting the mainland, where he was captured and put to death in a manner Herodotus considered "too disgusting to relate." In death, he was left for viewing impaled on a stake.

As Samos dealt with its internal problems and fending off the Spartans, Cambyses' preparations went forward. In this, he was ably assisted by a deserter from Amasis's cause, the commander of the pharaoh's Greek mercenaries, Phanes. After some undisclosed disagreement with Amasis, the Greek soldier escaped, but in his haste he was forced to leave his two sons behind. Phanes brought with him invaluable information about the condition of Amasis's forces and plans for the defense of Egypt. He also strongly advocated that Cambyses ally himself with the Nabataeans, as they were familiar with the desert and would ease the army's passage through the Sinai.

Cambyses proved just as ready to heed Phanes' advice as his father had been to take that of Harpagos against Lydia and of Gobryas against Babylon. By arrangement, a massive Nabataean camel train loaded with water met the Persians en route and escorted them across the desert. After a two-week passage, the Persian army approached the gateway to Egypt, Pelusium, at the mouth of the Nile. There, they learned that Amasis had died and his son Psammenitos (Psamatik II) commanded the Greek mercenaries guarding the city. When the mercenaries saw that Phanes was leading the Persian army, and thus had betrayed them, they paraded his sons to where he could witness their execution. They then cut the sons' throats, caught their blood in a large bowl, and mixed it with water and wine. Each of the mercenaries then sipped from the bowl to taste the blood of Phanes' sons. By this profane act, the mercenaries declared that the coming battle would be to the death, with no quarter asked or expected.

Nothing is known of the ensuing battle except what Herodotus reports:

> The fighting became quite fierce, so that a large number of men
> fell on both sides, but finally the Egyptians were routed.[5]

Herodotus also reports that he could still see the bleached bones of the combatants littering the desert floor when he passed through the area forty years later. The routed Egyptian mercenaries did not halt their retreat until they reached Memphis, where they sealed themselves up in the city. Cambyses, hoping to avoid a siege, sent a Mytilenian ship with a Persian herald with surrender terms to Memphis. But the enraged mercenaries "destroyed the ship and tore the crew limb from limb."[6] After a short siege the city surrendered, and Cambyses ordered two thousand Egyptian notables (ten for each man aboard the Mytilenian ship) put to death, including the son of the new pharaoh. Cambyses permitted Psammenitos to live, at least until the Persians discovered him plotting a revolt, after which he was immediately executed.

Cambyses spent the next three years consolidating Persian rule in Egypt, during which time he conducted two further military expeditions. In the first, Herodotus tells of a fifty-thousand-man army sent to the Siwa Oasis either to seize it for future operations or to destroy it. Reportedly, the entire army was lost in a sudden sandstorm. As there are no other sources to confirm this event, historians have long doubted it occurred. But recently, geologists searching for oil found the remains of what appears to be a Persian military force near Siwa. There is speculation that these remains are at least a portion of Cambyses' lost army.[7]

The second expedition was an invasion of Ethiopia, supposedly led by Cambyses himself. Herodotus reports that this expedition too met with disaster, as the Persians had made no preparations prior to setting out and starvation soon decimated the army. Given the meticulous preparations Cambyses had made for the invasion of Egypt, it seems odd that he would conduct a second major invasion without any preparation. The fact that Nubia (northern Ethiopia) became part of the Persian Empire during this period makes Herodotus's report of defeat followed by a humiliating retreat seem improbable.

Moreover, the power of the Persian army does not seem to have suffered during this period. In fact, Cambyses' veterans became the indispensable core of the army his successor, Darius, would use to crush a series of revolts to his rule the following year. If it had been decimated in ill-considered campaigns on the Egyptian frontier, the Persian Empire would not have lasted another two years, never mind two hundred. The most likely interpretation of the evidence is that Cambyses sent out a strong reconnaissance, far short of fifty thousand men, to Siwa and this force was probably lost. As for Ethiopia, Cambyses did make a strong incursion into that country and made some gains. After heavy fighting and likely some supply problems, he settled for Nubia and brought his army back to Memphis. It is also quite possible that Cambyses retreated from Ethiopia because he was receiving the first news of revolts, or at least serious unrest, in the heart of the empire that demanded his immediate attention.

Whatever happened, Cambyses and his veteran army were soon on the march back to Persia. Along the way, he was informed that a revolt had indeed taken place and a Median usurper claiming to be his brother, Smerdis, had seized the throne. Herodotus states that soon after hearing the news, Cambyses was accidentally cut by his own sword while mounting his horse. The wound festered, and he died a short while later, but not before imploring his nobles not to let a Mede gain supremacy of the empire.

The revolt of the false Smerdis was the greatest crisis the Persian Empire faced until Alexander's invasion two hundred years later. It was also one of the great unresolved scandals of the ancient world. The evidence for the course of events comes from two main sources—the Behistun inscription and Herodotus—both in general agreement. It is also clear that Herodotus drew his description of events from the official story that Darius put forth after he secured the throne for himself. That Darius, the author of the Behistun inscription, was keen for the entire empire to know his version of events is clear from papyrus fragments of the inscription that archaeologists have discovered in various ruins throughout the empire. Both sources agree that Smerdis was an impostor and that Cambyses had sent an assassin to kill his brother, the real Smerdis, prior to this revolt. Where they disagree is whether Cambyses ordered this execution before leaving for Egypt (Darius's version) or after he was already in Egypt (Herodotus's version).

Among historians, there remains a school of thought that claims that Cambyses never killed his brother and that it was the actual Smerdis who seized the throne during Cambyses' absence. In this telling of events, Darius, who apparently took command of the army after Cambyses' death, created the fiction of a false Smerdis to better justify his own usurpation of royal power. This version of events, where Cambyses did not commit fratricide, has a lot to commend it, particularly as it explains why so many were ready to believe the pretender was the actual Smerdis. It also explains how the murder of the real Smerdis could have been hidden from the Persian people and the nobles.

In this version of events, rather than being murdered, as would be the expected fate of any possible challenger to the throne, Smerdis was left behind as regent. However, this new tale has its own problems. Unfortunately for those holding this position, there is no ancient evidence extant that even alludes to this being the case. It is also likely that if any persons actually believed it was the real Smerdis whom Darius deposed, their version of events would have to have come to Herodotus's ears. And since this would have proven Darius's duplicity and illegitimacy, it would have been just the kind of story his audience would have welcomed. Therefore, with no evidence to the contrary available, it would be unwise not to accept the essence of what the existing sources present us.

The pretend Smerdis, probably with the help of his brother, a Magian priest whom Cambyses had left in charge of his household, seized the throne in March 522 BC. Garnering support by declaring a peace policy to a war-weary population brought the brothers some initial support. Further popularity was bought by declaring a three-year moratorium on what must have been ruinous war taxes for the bulk of the population. In April, Babylon accepted him as its ruler, and by early July, most of the empire had accepted him as the legitimate ruler of the empire.[8] However, there are indications that almost from the start there was a growing resentment of his rule among the powerful Persian nobles and even some Median nobles and Magi priests.[9] The reason for this discontent is not clear. Nevertheless, some assumptions can be made. First, the nobility could not have been happy to see its power being usurped by the priests. Furthermore, it could not have taken long for Smerdis to discover that governing was impossible without a constant stream of tax revenues. Unable to retract his three-year tax holiday for the masses, Smerdis would have had only one other source of sizable revenue: forced exactions from the accumulated wealth of the nobles and temples, a sure means of alienating his most powerful subjects.

As the high and mighty of the empire began turning away from Smerdis and his brother, the new leadership of Cambyses' army bided their time. With Cambyses dead, seven Persian nobles had come together to take command of the army and plot the overthrow of the pretender. According to Herodotus, the Persian nobles were Otanes, Gobryas, Intaphrenes, Hydarnes, Megabyzus, Aspathines, and a late joiner, Darius.[10] All were young men who possessed substantial constituencies within the empire. In Darius's case, for instance, both his father and grandfather were still alive, and probably both were serving as satraps with powerful local forces under their command. When Darius eventually assumed the throne, it was to these young nobles and co-conspirators he most often turned for help in running the empire, and with one exception, they all maintained substantial power throughout his reign.[11] At the conclusion of his Behistun inscription, Darius went so far as to commend each of his successors' honor and assist the families of these men in perpetuity.

Unsure of their position or how much support they had at home, the seven nobles did nothing for the moment. When the pretender's heralds eventually arrived to order the army to abandon its leaders and swear allegiance to Smerdis, they were met with silence. The army, which was probably mostly Persians at this point, rejected the pretender and remained loyal to Darius and his noble friends. This was not surprising, as armies at this time were prone to identify themselves with their commanders and not with any central state. This was particularly true if those commanders were promising them great rewards, as the seven nobles most assuredly were. It is also worth noting that these soldiers were probably aware that after declaring a three-year tax holiday, Smerdis would have little with which to reward them.

The Nabonidus Chronicle documents the reign of Babylon's last king, Nabonidus, as well as the rise and conquests of Cyrus. It is crucial to historians of the period, as it presents a chronology for the last half of the sixth century.   The British Museum

As the seven conspirators bided their time, discontent within the Persian and Median nobility continued to build. Soon, Smerdis's growing insecurity caused him to retreat to the Median fortress of Sikayauvatish, which isolated him from the general population, who still supported him.[12] At about this time, a Persian noble named Prexaspes announced that he had killed the real Smerdis on Cambyses' orders. Prexaspes, father of one of the seven nobles, Otanes, then rather conveniently committed suicide. Rumors were already circulating among the masses that Smerdis was an impostor, and Prexaspes' revelation undoubtedly fanned the flames. As Smerdis was in self-imposed exile, he could not influence the people, and popular support dwindled rapidly. To a peasant in the sixth century BC, the king was not only a secular ruler, but a direct conduit to the gods and often considered a god himself. Only a king favored by the gods could through his direct intercession on his people's behalf ensure a good harvest. In fact, one of the primary reasons the people of Babylon turned away from their king, Nabonidus, in his war with Cyrus was that he had failed to attend the great religious festivals and therefore was not there to ask the gods for bountiful harvests. As far as the people were concerned, if Smerdis was a pretender, then the gods would refuse to favor him and their harvests would fail.

Although some of the seven conspirators feared the empire's unsettled condition, they chose to act and entered the great fortress of Sikayauvatish without hindrance from the guards. However, in the main courtyard they were met by a troop of eunuchs who demanded the seven state their purpose for being there. Committed now, the seven young nobles gave a shout, drew their weapons, and slashed the eunuchs to death. Continuing their charge, they passed through the king's harem and into his private quarters. Inside they found Smerdis and his brother, who desperately attempted to defend themselves. Smerdis drew a bow, but the nobles were too close for it to be of much use, so he retreated into a dark bedroom. His brother, attacking with a spear, wounded Aspathines in the thigh and Intaphrenes in the eye before being cut down.

Darius and Gobryas followed Smerdis into the bedroom, where Gobryas wrestled the pretender to the ground. Darius stood off to one side, uninvolved, until Gobryas called for his help. Saying that he was afraid to strike as he might injure his friend, Darius continued to hesitate. Gobryas then shouted for Darius to strike even if it meant his sword would kill them both. In the darkness, Darius thrust, killing Smerdis and fortunately missing Gobryas.

What to make of this act? One cannot properly count it as a revolt, as the seven conspirators were not acting against what people were then fairly certain wasn't a rightful king. However, as Cambyses had not left a male heir, the seven were not exactly acting on behalf of a rightful authority. In reality, Smerdis was the revolutionary, trying to wrest ultimate power away from the Persian newcomers and place a Median king back on the throne. In this light, Darius and his co-conspirators were leading a counterrevolution designed to ensure that the Persians remained on the top rungs of the leadership ladder.

Through common agreement, the seven nobles placed Darius on the throne. Although he came late to the conspiracy, he had become its driving force and natural leader. It was also important that he was a member of the Achaemenid royal family, as was Cyrus. Darius, however, was from the older Ariaramnes branch of the family, while Cyrus's branch was considered upstarts by the rest of the Persian nobility. The fact that the throne did not go to Darius's father or grandfather, who were still alive and closer relations to Cyrus than Darius, demonstrates the military character of this coup and suggests the forcefulness of Darius's character.

The pretender was dead, and a new generation had risen to rule the Persian Empire. Unfortunately, the genie of insurrection was not yet ready to be placed back into the bottle.

Chapter 5

TRIAL BY FIRE

Darius was king, but his empire was crumbling. Having become accustomed to de facto independence during the period of revolution and counterrevolution, many of the empire's provinces and client states revolted against what they perceived as a greatly weakened central power. In this, the moment of his greatest crisis, Darius demonstrated a cool, calculating, and ruthless determination to overcome—whatever the odds. Fortunately, he was not alone, for despite Darius's undoubted personal abilities, he still would have failed were it not for the loyal support of his friends and the army.

In the east, Darius's father, Hystaspes, held Parthia; to the southeast, two other loyal satraps held the provinces of Arachosia and Bactria.[1] All three men were loyal to Darius and also capable commanders and administrators. Although they were often hard-pressed over the next year, they won battles, held their ground, and allowed Darius to concentrate his energies on the more dangerous revolts in the heart of the empire. To deal with these, Darius had the veteran troops of the Egyptian campaign at his disposal. So despite Darius's claims in the Behistun inscription that his army was always small, he neglects to mention that it was far and away the best trained and most experienced combat force in the empire. Moreover, it displayed a remarkable degree of loyalty and stood unwaveringly behind Darius throughout the crisis. But Darius had one other advantage of inestimable value. Despite an overwhelming need to act in concert, none of his enemies ever acted in combination. This failure of the individual provincial revolts to coordinate their military activities allowed Darius to turn on and crush each in succession.[2] Still, it was a period of intense combat and danger, the extent of which Darius spelled out at the conclusion of the Behistun inscription:

> *After I became king, I fought nineteen battles in a single year and*
> *by the grace of Ahuramazda nine kings and I made them captive.*

The first revolts were launched only four days after Darius slew the false Smerdis. Babylon and the province of Susiana were the first to make a break for freedom, the latter declaring itself an independent kingdom under a new king. Despite being able to spare only a small force to crush the Susianans, it proved sufficient to cow the rebels. Tightly bound, the new Susianan king was brought before Darius and promptly executed.

Suppressing Babylon, however, was a more serious affair, and after preparing for two months, Darius himself led the bulk of his army out of Media to deal with it.[3] The Babylonians placed their loyalty and faith behind a local noble, Nidintu-Bel, who, claiming to be a son of the deposed Nabonidus, took the great royal name of Nebuchadnezzar. Aware that Darius was on the march, Nidintu-Bel led his hastily assembled army north to contest passage of the Tigris River. As typically happens when hastily raised levies meet battle-hardened professionals, Nidintu-Bel's army was, in Darius's words, "smote utterly." Nidintu-Bel did manage to reconstitute his forces at Zazana on the Euphrates, but again the Babylonians were overmatched by Darius's veterans. This time, though, the Babylonian army was pushed back against the river and annihilated. Nidintu-Bel, with the luck of a true survivor, managed to escape the battlefield and fled to Babylon. Darius's rapid pursuit of his fleeing foe, however, left the Babylonians little time to prepare for a siege even if they were so inclined. But Darius was impatient and did not desire even a short siege. Without pausing after his arrival, he ordered the city taken by immediate storm. After having two field armies massacred, the population was dispirited and incapable of repelling a determined assault. With Nidintu-Bel's capture and execution, Babylon once again recognized Darius as its king.[4]

While Darius rested his army at Babylon, he learned that Media, believing he would be tied down in a prolonged siege, had risen in rebellion. Even more troubling was news that many of the empire's eastern provinces were also in open revolt.

Understanding that controlling Media was the key to ultimate success, Darius could spare few of his forces for action in the east. Fortunately, several satraps in critical provinces remained loyal. Unaided by Darius, they were able to repel and in some cases destroy the rebel armies in their regions. Only to the Persian homeland itself did Darius dispatch any of his veterans. Here another rebel, declaring himself to be yet another true Smerdis, seized the Persian crown. Darius, despite the threat posed by a resurgent Media, could not remain idle while a pretender sat on the Persian throne. So, taking advantage of the new Smerdis's decision to send a large portion of his forces to attack another eastern province, Darius sent a portion of his own small army into Persia.[5] There it defeated a rebel force at Rakha and rejoined Darius in time for his campaign in Media. The new Smerdis was eventually cornered by a loyal satrap and executed along with his supporters.

With his loyal satraps more than holding their own, Darius focused his attention on the Median rebels, who were joined by rebellions in nearby Armenia and Parthia. When the revolts and civil wars began, Darius had tarried in Media for two months to ensure the region remained stable and loyal, even as the Babylonian revolt raged. Despite this precaution, Media rebelled almost as soon as Darius's army entered Babylonian territory. The Medes were led by one of their own nobles, Fravartish, who claimed descent from the royal family of Cyaxares, the father of Astyages and the king who freed Media from the Assyrians. As such, he appealed to the Medes as their rightful ruler, as opposed to the usurper Darius.[6] While Darius settled affairs in Babylon, Fravartish seized Ecbatana, and the Medes began flocking to his standard. For Darius, this was the most dangerous revolt he faced, as his veteran army possessed a substantial Median contingent. Although Darius could count on the loyalty of his Median soldiers when facing any other enemy, they would be suspect in any fight against fellow Medes.

Although caught by surprise, Darius did not hesitate. Even as he continued the pacification of Babylon, he sent a portion of his army, presumably the Persians, to halt the southward march of the newly assembled Median army. This force, under a Persian officer, Hydarnes, fought the Medes to a standstill at the Battle of Marush in January 521 BC but was unable to advance farther. The Median army, though inexperienced, probably had an increasing advantage, as Fravartish's forces continued to be supplied with new levies. Nevertheless, Fravartish appeared content to hold his position and guard the border. The fact that Darius's father, Hystaspes, still had an undefeated army in Parthia (the Median rear) must have entered into Fravartish's calculations. If the Median army advanced too far south, Hystaspes could march into the Median heartland unopposed or even into the rear of the Median army, trapping it between himself and Darius's army. Still, standing idle in the face of a commander as skilled and aggressive as Darius was a risky strategy.

In Babylon, Darius furiously raised new forces and was able to detach a significant number of his veterans to deal with Armenia. Assuming that he had sent his Persian troops to face Fravartish's Medes, the force he sent against Armenia was probably made up mostly of his own Median troops. He was counting on their personal loyalty to him, but he did take the precaution of ensuring that loyalty with payments of Babylonian gold and promises of large hauls of booty in Armenia.[7]

Putting down the Armenian revolt proved a difficult and protracted affair. Over several months, Darius was forced to dispatch two armies for the purpose. The first marched along the Tigris River into the heart of Armenia. Although this army won a major battle against a hastily raised Armenian force, it was unable to march farther, as Fravartish's Medes were on its right flank and could cut it off in the event it went too deep into Armenia.[8] When Darius eventually began his advance against the Medes, the Armenian invasion also recommenced. This time, it consisted of two separate armies marching parallel to each other along the Tigris and Euphrates rivers. In a lightning advance, the two armies fought four major battles and crushed the main Armenian field forces. Despite these losses, a determined Armenia remained in rebellion until Darius himself entered the region some months later, but from this point forward the province presented no military threat.

Probably in April 521 BC, Darius marched out of Babylon to the aid of Hydarnes, who was still warily watching the growing Median army he had earlier fought to a standstill at the Battle of Marush. Before starting his march, Darius sent out orders to each of his loyal satraps to renew their own offensives against the rebels and to coordinate their activities with his. Remarkably, Darius managed to direct the simultaneous efforts of several widely dispersed field armies toward a common purpose, an achievement almost unparalleled in ancient military affairs. Achieving such coordination remains difficult even in the modern era; doing so without the aid of modern communications marks Darius as one of history's foremost military practitioners and qualifies him to be included among the ranks of the "great captains."

The decisive all-fronts offensive began in May 521 BC. On the eighth day of that month, Darius's army met the Median host at Kundar. As Darius's account states, "Then we joined battle. Ahuramazda brought me help; by the grace of Ahuramazda did my army utterly overthrow that rebel host."[9] Darius commemorated this great victory by later having the Behistun inscription carved into the craggy rocks that overlooked the battlefield. Defeated, the Median commander, Fravartish, retreated toward Ragae, hotly pursued by Darius's cavalry.[10] After he was run to ground, Darius demonstrated that some of Assyria's tradition of brutality still remained popular among its formerly subject peoples. For as Darius proudly boasted:

> I cut off his nose, his ears, and his tongue, and I put out one eye, and he was kept in chains at my palace entrance, and all the people beheld him. Then did I impale him in Ecbatana; and the men who were his foremost followers, those at Ecbatana within the fortress, I flayed and hung out their hides, stuffed with straw.

With Fravartish defeated, Darius sent assistance to his father in Parthia, while he advanced with the bulk of his army into Armenia. At his approach, the dispirited Armenians, who had already suffered severely at the hands of Darius's generals, put aside their weapons and returned to the Persian fold. Darius, believing that there was only some mopping up left to do, began his march back to the heart of the empire. He reached Arbela in late July 521 BC. Here he rested his army, as messengers arrived to announce that everywhere his loyal satraps were victorious over the remaining rebel forces.[11] Inexplicably, Babylon, unable to accept that Darius was everywhere victorious, revolted one more time. This time the people followed an Armenian named Arakha, who also styled himself as a new Nebuchadnezzar. As there was still much work to be done after the grim fighting throughout the northern provinces of his empire, Darius could not immediately march on Babylon. Instead he sent Intaphrenes, one of his co-conspirators in seizing the throne, against Babylon. Intaphrenes led a Persian army south and captured the city without much fighting on November 27, 521 BC. As usual, Darius ordered Arakha and all of his chief followers mutilated and impaled.

The main fighting was now over. It had been a brutal year, but at its end Darius reigned supreme. As he inscribed for future generations, he had fought nineteen battles and overthrown nine kings.[12] But still the fighting was not over. The Scythians, who were always looking for weakness within the empire to launch further devastating raids, had intervened on the side of Darius's enemies during the main fighting and were now restless. Like Cyrus before him, Darius could not leave the northern portions of his empire, already weakened by over a year of vicious fighting, at the mercy of these pitiless hordes. He therefore led his veterans north into modern Turkistan. In a novel maneuver, Darius boarded a large portion of his army on ships gathered along the Caspian Sea and launched an amphibious assault in the rear of the Scythians. Taken by surprise, the bulk of the Scythian army was either destroyed or captured. For the first time in generations the northern frontier of the empire was secure, while the Persians added the province of Saka to the empire. With this addition, the Saka cavalry, the finest light and heavy cavalry in the world, was now at Darius's disposal. This cavalry was later to play a major but mostly unrecognized role at the Battle of Marathon.

There was just one more matter to settle before Darius felt himself secure on the throne. The satrap controlling Lydia and Ionia, Oroites, remained neutral during Darius's time of troubles. In fact, he took advantage of the turmoil to add to the territory under his control and had executed several high-ranking Persians, even murdering one of Darius's personal messengers. While he was fighting the rebels, Darius could do nothing to avenge such slights. Furthermore, even after he was victorious on all fronts, Darius remained reluctant to march directly on Oroites, who Herodotus states "possessed great political and military strength, including 1,000 elite Persian troops."

It was on these Persian troops that Darius placed his hopes for a quick resolution. According to Herodotus, Darius sent a royal messenger to Oroites' court to deliver a series of proclamations. The Great King ordered his messenger to watch the reaction of the guards to each proclamation and determine whether their loyalty was to Oroites or Darius. When the messenger noted that the Persian soldiers were reacting to each royal pronouncement with respect verging on awe, he dared to have read aloud one of two final messages: "Persians, King Darius forbids you to serve as guards to Oroites." Upon hearing this, the guards immediately stood easy and let down their spears. Emboldened by the guards' reaction, the messenger handed over one last proclamation for reading: "King Darius instructs the Persians in Sardis to kill Oroites." After this dispatch was read aloud, the guards drew their daggers and slew Oroites.[13]

By 518 BC, almost three decades before the Battle of Marathon, Darius was the undisputed master of the Persian Empire. But it still remained an empire in name only, consisting mostly of a hodgepodge of nations held together by fear of Persian arms. Cyrus had begun the job of emplacing an administrative infrastructure, but it remained incomplete at his death. Moreover, his son Cambyses paid little attention to administrative matters, as he was more interested in expanding the empire and proving he was as worthy a warrior and conqueror as his father. It therefore fell to Darius to complete the consolidation and organization of the empire. He did this so thoroughly that his Achaemenid family line stayed on the throne for almost two hundred years of internal peace.[14]

Chapter 6

THE MIGHT OF PERSIA

Almost two years of civil war had shown Darius how easily his empire could disintegrate. To forestall a recurrence, he turned his attention to creating the governmental and financial structure required to meld his fragile empire into a single, indivisible unit. It was in this regard that he displayed a particular brilliance. For if Darius was a first-class general, then he was also that rare breed of warrior who possessed a genius for administration.[1]

Foremost among Darius's priorities was the shoring up of his dynastic rights to the throne. Although he was an Achaemenid, he came from a branch of the family that was not particularly close to that of Cyrus. Furthermore, if strict laws of primogeniture were adhered to, Darius's father and not Darius himself had the stronger claim to the throne. For the time being, however, the army's unquestioned loyalty was sufficient for Darius to hold power. But that might not be the case if a dynastic struggle erupted at a later date. So to solidify his rule, Darius turned to the first ladies of the empire. As the Persian religion, Zoroastrianism, encouraged polygamy and even marrying sisters, Darius was free to marry all of them.[2] Sometime in the first year of his reign, he also married Cyrus's two daughters, Atossa and Artystone.[3] Atossa bore him four sons:

- Xerxes in 520 BC, who became the next Achaemenid king.
- Masistes, who was one of the senior commanders in Xerxes' doomed campaign to conquer Greece a decade after the Battle of Marathon, and satrap of the key province of Bactria.
- Achaemenes, who became the satrap of Egypt and commanded

the navy during Xerxes' campaign against Greece in 480 BC. He was killed in 459 BC by Egyptian rebels.

- Hystaspes, commander of the elite Bactria and Saka troops during Xerxes' invasion of Greece.

Darius also married Parmys, the daughter of the true Smerdis (son of Cyrus and brother of Cambyses), along with the daughter of Otanes. This last marriage was necessary to keep Otanes' family close to the regime, as he was one of the seven who had overthrown the false Smerdis and had initially been favored by some of the others to become king. He had moved aside voluntarily so that Darius could assume the crown, and in reward Darius declared that he and his house would be subject to no man. This meant that Otanes' family obeyed the king's will only as they saw fit, a condition that still persisted when Herodotus wrote his history. It was therefore important to lock in the noble Otanes' family as closely as possible to the Achaemenids and thereby ensure its loyalty and continuing support.[4] With the legitimacy of his house ensured through dynastic marriages, Darius next turned his attention to consolidating the empire.

After years of neglect and war, there was much to be done. The administrative system that linked the satrapies (provinces) to the central government was destroyed. Communications routes, on which the economy rested, were in shambles and unsafe for traders to travel. Moreover, the empire's finances were wrecked, and there was no cash in the treasury to pay for the maintenance of the realm. Worse, although Darius had defeated his internal enemies, by doing so he had wrecked the provincial forces that had formed the backbone of the rebel armies. This left his relatively small field army as the only defenders of an empire whose expanse had no previous equal. The pressing need was to rebuild frontier fortresses and provincial forces so that they could resist the scourge of raiders from outside the empire's borders. Accomplishing such a task demanded that Darius find large of amounts of ready cash.

Darius did not have the luxury of dealing with each of these problems in turn, as they were all urgent and required his immediate attention. So he turned from war and became one of the great administrators of the ancient world.[5] When he was done, Darius had built such solid supports under the empire that it lasted for two hundred years without any substantial changes to its structure. While some historians have complained that this structure became ossified over time and was unable to adapt to changing circumstances, it still compares well with those of any of the other great empires known to history. For instance, the Persians did not rely on terror, as had the Assyrians, to hold subject peoples in line, nor did the empire tear itself apart in civil wars at the death of its leader, as did that of Alexander the Great. The administrative structure established by Darius was by no means perfect, but when compared with the institutions of other ancient empires, the results are consistently favorable.

In undertaking this task, Darius acted counter to his upbringing as a warrior and forced his Persian and Median subjects to do the same. As Herodotus relates, this was not a popular direction:

> The Persians say that Darius was a retailer, Cambyses a master of slaves, and Cyrus a father. Darius tended to conduct all of his affairs as a shopkeeper, Cambyses was harsh and scornful, but Cyrus was gentle and saw to it that all things good would be theirs.[6]

Although Darius built a great palace complex at Persepolis within the traditional borders of Persia, the location was not suitable as the administrative center of the empire. Darius therefore confirmed Cambyses' selection of Susa as the empire's capital. During the summer months, the royal court (and presumably most of the empire's administrative infrastructure) moved two hundred miles north to the cooler Median capital of Ecbatana, which had also been the administrative center of Cyrus's empire.

Susa was as close to a perfectly placed city for administrative purposes as could be imagined. It sat almost equidistant from the farthest edges of the empire from east to west and was also centrally placed on the north–south axis. Moreover, it rested upon the key ancient trade routes, was situated on a fertile plain between two protecting rivers, and most important was on the edge of traditional Persian lands, the source of the empire's strength and elite military manpower.

Darius began by reorganizing his provinces into twenty satrapies and immediately assessed a tax on each.[7] According to Herodotus, Darius received 14,560 talents in taxes from the empire on an annual basis, although this was not likely to be his only source of revenue (for instance, neither tribute from nearby nations nor imperial customs duties were included). To put this in perspective, during Darius's reign a single talent could pay the wages for a trireme's two-hundred-man crew for two months or the wages of three laborers for twenty years.[8] As trained soldiers tended to receive a higher rate of pay than day laborers, a talent would pay the salary for a single soldier for twenty years.[9] In other words, if the empire had no other expenses to pay, which was far from the case, it could pay a full-time professional force of over a quarter of a million men out of annual revenues. Two generations after Persia's defeat at Marathon, Athens began the Peloponnesian War with 6,500 silver talents in its treasury, and annual revenues were about 1,000 talents (400 internal and 600 from tribute from other members of the empire).[10] So even at the height of Athens's power, annual revenues were approximately a fifteenth of Persia's. It needs to be remembered that Athens did not have an empire at the time of the Battle of Marathon, nor had it yet exploited the richest veins of the Laurion silver mines. An estimate of annual Athenian revenues in the years preceding Marathon should therefore be placed at under 250 talents, with only a percentage of that available for war. This was approximately a *fiftieth* of Persia's revenues.

Within Persia, this massive transfer of wealth to the center did not represent the full tax burden on the peoples of the empire. As none of these tax receipts were typically transferred back to the provinces, the local satraps collected additional revenues to pay for their own upkeep, infrastructure projects, and defense. This last obligation likely amounted to a sizable sum, as many of the satrapies had hostile neighbors on their borders and were expected to see to their own defense against all but the strongest attacks. However, the tax burden did not end there. In addition to the satraps, there were a large number of subsatraps, regional governors, and other administrators who collected taxes to pay for their own maintenance, which was often extravagant. For instance, the subsatrap for Judah during this time fed 150 of his officers from his own table every day.[11] But even this was not the end. All levels of the Persian government also collected taxes in kind, and tens of thousands of sheep, mules, and horses and tons of foodstuffs, incense, ebony, and ivory were taken by the tax collectors every year.

All of this constituted an enormous burden on the empire's economy. It would not have been so bad if the government had spent the money or found some other way to keep these funds in circulation. However, it would be two thousand years before Britain discovered that it was better economically to keep its specie in circulation to grow the economy and still have it available through taxes and loans in an emergency. Prior to this, every good ruler tried to store as much bullion as possible in his treasury as insurance in the event of war or bad times. The Persians proved to be masters of the art of hoarding. This would be plainly demonstrated after Alexander brought the empire crashing down: Reportedly, after the Macedonians captured the Persian royal treasuries, Alexander seized almost 200,000 talents in gold and silver. This must have seemed a fantastic sum for an adventurer who had begun his march of conquest with only 60 talents in his own treasury and owing 500 talents to creditors. It should be noted that this massive sum of Persian treasure was what remained after Darius III had already drawn down vast sums to pay for the war against Alexander and after he made off with 8,000 talents when he fled in the face of Alexander's approach.

At the beginning of Darius's reign, the tax burden was onerous and must have built up a degree of resentment, particularly as the pretend Smerdis had promised a three-year tax holiday. However, the historical record does not indicate any trouble or rebellion over the issue. To some degree, this was because after nearly two years of war, most recognized that Darius possessed a formidable military instrument and the will to employ it ruthlessly. A more important factor, though, was that at least at the start of his reign, Darius did not hoard his tax revenues. He clearly understood that the empire was broken and that it would take lavish spending to fix it. In the beginning, this massive spending on reconstruction rehabilitated an economy broken by war.

Darius's first order of business was to start work on the great royal roads, which stitched his empire together. In scope, these roads were probably equal to the Roman road network at the height of that empire and were designed to serve the same purposes. Cyrus had begun the initial work on this immense construction project. To ease the workload, he directed that the roads follow already existing ancient caravan routes. However, Cyrus only began the project, and there remained much to do following his death. Cambyses made no progress in this area, and it was left to Darius to carry the work forward with a purpose.

Herodotus provides an excellent description of just a section of the Persian road network, from Sardis to Susa, which gives us some idea of the scope of the endeavor and its critical role in holding the empire together. According to Herodotus, it took ninety days for a man to cover the total distance of this section of the road on foot (at seventeen miles per day). At the end of each day's journey, a traveler would find a government station with accommodations that the ancient historian rated as excellent. Along the way there were a series of guardhouses and toll posts, and at strategic locations (such as the crossing of the Halys River) there were strong fortresses garrisoned by Persian troops. In other historical sources there are references to additional arms of the road linking Susa with Bactria, India, and the Median capital (Ecbatana).[12]

For Darius, the royal road served two fundamental purposes. First and foremost, like the Roman road system, the extensive network greatly eased the job of moving the Persian army to any threatened frontier or to any satrapy that dared raise the banner of revolt. Its other purpose was to increase the span of royal control by reducing the communication time between various points of the empire. Herodotus even describes the equivalent of a Persian Pony Express, where way stations with fresh mounts were spaced a day's ride apart, and messengers handed off their dispatches to the next rider at the end of each day. As Herodotus states, "Neither snow nor rain nor heat nor dark of night keeps them from completing their appointed course as swiftly as possible."[13] Through this post system, Darius was able to send messages from his capital to the governor of any satrapy in a week or less, a phenomenal speed for the time. As others throughout the empire began to use the roads to send messages, Darius instituted a reporting system along the network. Royal inspectors monitored road traffic and read every note being sent within the empire. Regular reports were then sent to Darius detailing the correspondence of every important person in the empire (unimportant people were predictably not allowed to use the post service).

Herodotus further relates a probably apocryphal story of how far some individuals would go to sneak a message past the inspectors. Histiaios, who will play a considerable role later in this book, shaved the head of a loyal slave and tattooed the order to start the Ionian revolt on the bald pate. Once the hair grew back enough to cover the instructions, the messenger was sent on his way.

Darius also lavished money on building a new ornamental capital at Persepolis, as well as on building and beautifying monumental structures throughout that city. He also underwrote monumental buildings in many of the empire's other great cities and throughout the satrapies, including construction projects such as an early Suez Canal.[14] In an early proof of Keynesian economic theory, this government spending propelled the empire's moribund economy into overdrive. Economic growth was further boosted by a renewed and flourishing trading regime, as merchants took advantage of the general peace, the construction of secure new roads, and investments in port facilities to move their wares where they could be sold at the greatest profit. In no small measure, Darius bought the stability of his empire through massive expenditures of government funds. By keeping most of the empire's specie in circulation and continually adding more from the royal mints, he made it possible for every region of the empire to enjoy a spell of unparalleled prosperity.

But Darius was the head of a warlike people who were proud of the fact that they had built and held an empire by force of arms. Darius was all too aware that his right to rule was linked directly to his determination and ability to lead the Persians to even greater glory. He could not long continue as a "shopkeeper" if he was to remain in power. Moreover, his experiences in the civil war were a strong reminder of the fact that the Persian army required active employment outside the empire's frontiers or it would soon create intolerable mischief within. Darius was a warrior, and the call of the saddle and active campaigning was always tugging on him. Therefore as soon as Darius deemed his reorganization had gone far enough to ensure a modicum of stability, he ordered the mobilization of his army at Susa and prepared to march. The regions north of the Hellespont were to be added to the empire.

In doing so, Darius set in motion a series of events whose ramifications went far beyond the battlefield. Foremost among these was that he led the first expedition by an Eastern ruler into what is commonly delineated as "the West."

Darius's turn toward war had one immediate negative consequence: The virtuous economic policies of the first years of his reign came to an abrupt end. Renewed war called for new taxes, but now, instead of spending the revenues on infrastructure investments, they were to be wasted in war or hoarded in vast treasuries. This rapid removal of currency from circulation first slowed economic growth and then threw it into reverse. Particularly hard hit were the trading centers along the Ionian coast, which could no longer obtain sufficient currency to continue their economic expansion. Moreover, the impressment of the Ionian trading fleet to provide logistical support for the war opened the door for competitors to seize lucrative trading opportunities. Here was the root cause of the coming Ionian revolt, which soon plunged the empire into its greatest crisis since the end of the civil war, and for the first time pitted the Persian Empire directly against the armed might of the Greek mainland.

PART II

THE RISE OF GREECE

Chapter 7

THE RISE OF ATHENS

For most of its early history, Attica was the rural backwater of Greece. Its only achievement worthy of note prior to the classical age was to unify itself into a single political structure with Athens at its center. Given the nature of Attica's poor soil, which was barely sufficient for most of its farmers to produce a subsistence crop, one could be forgiven for thinking its prospects bleak at the dawn of the seventh century BC. That it did eventually become a Mediterranean superpower was a result of two major developments that revolutionized Athenian life and the effects of which continue to permeate Western civilization today. The first of these was to put at risk the certain but limited prospects of an agriculture-based economy for a perilous but potentially far more profitable one based on trade. This transition made Athens the richest city-state in Greece and gave it the economic might first to resist Persia and later to build an empire of its own. The second and no less significant act was Athens's break from the traditions of Greek politics through its rejection of aristocracy and tyranny in favor of democracy.

Neither of these outcomes was ever certain. For democracy, in particular, the foundation was always shaky, and several times it appeared as though the challenges to creating a democratic society would prove insurmountable. Only after decades of discord was Athens at last able to temper the baser instincts of its noble families and to form a government that gave a voice in the city's affairs to the mass of male citizens.

With respect to the Battle of Marathon, both of these developments were of great significance. From Herodotus we know that Athens put at least nine thousand of its own hoplites into the battle, and I argue it probably had several thousand more hoplites in the immediate vicinity of Marathon. Considering that even a single trained, fully armed, and armored hoplite was an expensive proposition, the cost of fielding over ten thousand hoplites was far beyond anything Athens could have afforded if it had stuck to its agricultural roots. Only by vastly increasing its wealth through trade was it able to afford the mobilization and equipping of an army capable of matching the might of Persia.[1] As for the effects of democracy, even the Greeks of the period felt it gave them a moral supremacy on the battlefield, and as Napoleon said, "even in war moral power is to physical as three parts out of four." As Herodotus noted about Athens's first decisive military victory as a democratic city:

> And it is plain enough, not from this instance only, but from many everywhere, that freedom is an excellent thing since even the Athenians, who, while they continued under the rule of tyrants, were not a whit more valiant than any of their neighbors, no sooner shook off the yoke than they became decidedly the first of all. These things show that, while undergoing oppression, they let themselves be beaten, since then they worked for a master; but so soon as they got their freedom, each man was eager to do the best he could for himself.[2]

Despite Herodotus's claims about the effects democracy had on Athens's military capability, this superiority was not, at the time, apparent to the people of Attica.[3] Athens had only recently become a trading nation, and although by the time of Marathon it was far wealthier than a generation before, it was still a distant way from the riches that would later propel it to greatness. No one in Greece, probably including the Athenians, thought Athens possessed the wealth necessary to stand up to the might of Persia. After all, the Greek city-states of Ionia had all been rich trading centers, and each had been battered into submission by Persia in the years just preceding the Battle of Marathon. As for the benefits of democracy, many Ionic cities that had also started down that road had seen their free hoplites cut down before the unbeatable hordes of the Persian despot. Truth be told, free-trading democratic states had not fared well in their conflicts with the centralized, despotic Persian superstate. On the Plain of Marathon, Athens would make democracy's last stand.

That this lot fell to Athens could not have been predicted from the city's early history. For even in Athens, democratic institutions did not easily take root. Instead, they were the result of a bloody massacre that was followed by decades of civil strife, as Athens's great noble clans vied for ultimate power. This small nobility soon transformed itself into an established aristocracy who jointly controlled the region.

In 632 BC, an Athenian noble and Olympic hero, Cylon, supported by his father-in-law Theagenes (tyrant of Megara), seized Athens's Acropolis and declared a tyranny.[4] Unfortunately for his prospects, Cylon had failed to prepare the ground for revolution, and the common people, staying loyal to the local aristocracy, failed to rise up and join him. Moreover, the fact that the Athenians could see foreign soldiers from hated Megara on the Acropolis sapped any sympathy the mob may have had for Cylon's cause.

The government, under the direction of leading members of the Alcmaeonidae clan—one of Athens's noble families—reacted vigorously and besieged Cylon and his followers. Cylon, with his brother, managed to escape to Megara, but his followers remained trapped on the Acropolis and agreed to surrender only on the condition their lives would be spared. However, when they descended from the Acropolis, the rival Alcmaeonidae, led by Megacles, were waiting. The Alcmaeonidae slaughtered without mercy all of Cylon's defenseless supporters. It can probably be assumed that the Alcmaeonidae had an ongoing feud with Cylon's clan that in their eyes justified their brutality. However, for the superstitious Attic peasants, this mass murder of unarmed men made the Alcmaeonidae "odious to men" and tainted the clan with perpetual blood guilt. Although the Alcmaeonidae were powerful enough to stave off retribution for their act for thirty years, they were eventually tried by an assembly of three hundred nobles. As a result, the Alcmaeonidae were condemned and cast into perpetual exile. Moreover, every Alcmaeonidae who died between the murderous act and the passing of this sentence was exhumed and his bones cast beyond the boundaries of Attica. From this point on, the family was judged accursed, and for the next hundred years or more, their political enemies would wield this stain with tremendous effectiveness.

In the immediate wake of the massacre of Cylon's followers, Athens found itself at war with Megara, while the continual feuding among its own noble families threatened to destroy Athenian society. In an attempt to restore civil order, Athens in 621 BC gave one of its citizens, Draco, the power to draft a code of laws to be accepted by all. Although history has been left barely a trace of the original code, its penalties were judged so severe by later generations that a new word was created for punishments that appear to far exceed the crime: draconian. However, Draco's law code was not without useful effect. Foremost among its achievements was that it ended or at least greatly curtailed the blood feuds that kept Athens in a state of perpetual multiparty civil war. In the future, these interclan rivalries would be fought out in the political arena. This political competition could and often did turn violent, but the outbreaks became episodic rather than endemic.

For a time after the installation of Draco's code, Athens entered into a period of prosperity. Peace was eventually made with Megara, and for the first time Athens began to expand its interests and influence in the greater world. This was felt primarily in its expeditions to the Black Sea region, where there was always a surplus of purchasable grain to feed Attica's growing population. This trade and the natural expansion of its interests led Athens into its first distant war, with the city-state of Lesbos over control of the Dardanelles. However, the strains of this war coupled with the growing avarice of the noble families placed a fiscal strain on Athens that its primitive economic institutions could not yet stand.

As the fiscal requirements for war grew, the nobles took advantage of their political power to disenfranchise most of the population of Attica through the use of stringent debt laws. Unfortunately for the oppressed peasant class, Draco's constitutional formula left them few avenues to redress their grievances. As the poor and middle class had no legal power to question the actions of the noble families, the air became rife with talk of revolution. As Aristotle noted, "The cruelest and bitterest grievance of the many against the existing order was their slavery. But they were also discontented with all else. For at this time the mass of the people had a share in almost nothing."[5] What the moment demanded was a man who could lead and take bold measures to ensure just laws that could end a social crisis that was verging on all-out civil war.[6] As often happens in history, a man great enough to meet the crisis of his time arose: Solon, whose name is still synonymous with lawgiver.

Solon was born in Athens in 638 BC and was a distinguished member of the Athenian nobility. He began his rise to power as a result of his advocacy of renewed war with Megara. Sometime before 595 BC, Megara regained control of the island of Salamis, which Athens had won in its earlier war with Megara. From Salamis, the Megarians were in a position to throttle the expansion of Athenian trade and forever keep it locked among the second-rate cities of Greece. It was not, however, from a lack of Athenian exertion that Megara still held Salamis. In fact, Athens had strained mightily to retake the island. However, by 595 BC it had bled itself white in the process, and the war-weary city had made it a crime punishable by death for anyone to publicly advocate a continuation of the war.

Supposedly, Solon noted that many of Athens's young men wished to continue the war but remained silent for fear of punishment. Solon decided to make use of this current of discontent to push for a renewal of the Megarian war. Not trusting that power and influence were enough to protect him, Solon took the extra precaution of having family members put it about that he had gone mad. He then entered the Agora (marketplace) and read a stirring poem of his own composition, concluding with:[7]

> Forward to Salamis! Let us fight for the lovely island and wipe
> out our shame and disgrace.[8]

The poem had such an effect that Solon was forgiven his crime, the law against advocating war was repealed, and the war with Megara was renewed with "greater vigor than ever before."[9] The military effort was led by a young noble and friend of Solon, Pisistratus, who hailed from the hill country outside the Plain of Athens. Under his command the Athenian army marched directly for Megara, which appeared to be suffering from its own internal dissension. After a hard fight, the Athenians captured Megara's port, Nisaea, and cut off that city from the outside world. With this prize in hand, Pisistratus agreed to let Sparta arbitrate the dispute. Sparta, much to Athens's satisfaction, decided that Salamis would go to Athens and that Nisaea would be returned to Megara. This time the annexation of Salamis was permanent, and Pisistratus became the hero of the hour.[10]

With the conclusion of the Megarian war, Solon was riding a tide of popularity and was elected archon in 594 BC and given unlimited authority to act as he saw fit for the benefit of the state. Solon used his powers to remake Athenian society and institutions. Among his first acts was the creation of nine archons to administer Athens on a daily basis. These archons were appointed by the Areopagus (a collection of former archons) on the basis of their noble birth and wealth. Solon also created an assembly of Athenian citizens, the Ecclesia, which had a voice in the biggest decisions of the day but excluded the poorest and most numerous classes of

Athenian society, the *thetes*. Solon also undertook to establish a new economic order in Attica. In this, he was more successful than in his constitutional reforms. Much of the debt that was forcing the peasant class into bondage was relieved, new coinage was issued, and Athens began its first major moves away from an agriculture-dominated economy to one based on trade and commercial affairs.

When he was done, Solon left Athens, and according to Herodotus, he bound the city to maintain all of his reforms for ten years. They in fact lasted only about four years before the old societal rifts began to reassert themselves.[11] When Solon eventually returned to Athens, he found the city as fractious as ever. He spent his final years trying to settle disputes and relieve civil dissension but met with little success. However, although Solon's attempts at reform failed spectacularly in the short term, they did establish the system out of which eventually grew the institutions of democracy. It was left to Pisistratus, the military hero of the Megarian war, to impose order.*

We pick up the story of Athens in 562 BC. In the East, Croesus was about to mount the throne of Lydia, and Cyrus was still three years away from being made king of a small Persian tribe. Taking advantage of the civil disorder in the city, Pisistratus resolved to become tyrant of Athens. To do this, he required a strong base of political support, which was not readily available. Prior to his rise, and in the wake of Draco's and Solon's reforms, Athenian politics was dominated by two parties: the Party of the Coast and the Party of the Plains. As Pisistratus was unable to dominate either of these two parties, he created a third party, the Party of the Hills. For anyone not steeped in Athenian constitutional history, following developments in Athens from this point leads to a hopeless morass. The following table describes the three parties, their relationships to the great clans, and their aims.

---

* Solon, although he was formerly Pisistratus's mentor, turned against him when he seized power in Athens. He was one of the very few to speak openly against Pisistratus in the Agora. When asked why he took such risks, he stated that his old age protected him from fear. For his part, Pisistratus continued to honor the aging Solon until his natural death.

Party	Primarily Represented	Key Members and Associated Noble Family
The Plains (Pedieis)	The wealthy inhabitants of the plains near Athens (a large number of Athens's noble families—the Eupatridae—belonged to this group).	**The Philaidae (sometimes called the Kimonid or Cimonid)** *Key Members* Isagoras (a member of the party, but his family is uncertain)—Opposed Cleisthenes; seized power with the support of the Spartan king Cleomenes but was later banished. Miltiades the Elder—First tyrant of the Chersonese, sent there by Pisistratus to help protect Athens's access to grain. Miltiades—Stepnephew of Miltiades the Elder. He also became tyrant of the Chersonese but returned to Athens after the Ionian revolt and led the Athenian army at Marathon. Cimon—Son of Miltiades and a hero of the Second Persian War against Xerxes. He was very powerful at the time Herodotus was reciting his history in Athens.
The Coast (Paralioi)	The mercantile interests of the coast and within the city of Athens itself.	**The Alcmaeonidae** *Key Members* Megacles—Early ally of Pisistratus and later a sworn enemy. He is not to be confused with an earlier Megacles who killed Cylon (an Olympic hero who made an early bid to be tyrant of Athens) after promising him safe conduct. He thereby tainted his entire clan with a perpetual blood guilt.

Party	Primarily Represented	Key Members and Associated Noble Family
The Hills (Hyperakrioi)	The poor people who farmed or otherwise used the poor soil of the hills for pasture. This party also represented many of the poor and disenfranchised in Athens.	Cleisthenes—Megacles' son, a brilliant politician and the sworn enemy of Hippias. He would be the driving force behind establishing a true democracy in Athens. **The Pisistratidae** *Key Members* Pisistratus—First tyrant of Athens. He began and oversaw Athens's rise to power. Hippias—Son of Pisistratus. He was deposed by Cleisthenes (who had Spartan help) and went to reside within the Persian Empire. He was with the Persian army at Marathon, hoping for reinstatement as Athens's tyrant in the event of a Persian victory.

Pisistratus built his party from the poor and disenfranchised of Athenian society. They were to prove remarkably loyal, and his political base stood with him both in success and even during his times of failure and exile.[12] With the full support of his Party of the Hills, which made up for a lack of money with numbers, Pisistratus made his bid for ultimate power. After staging an attempt on his life, he appeared in the Agora, beaten and wounded, claiming that he had been set upon by his enemies and just barely escaped being murdered. After he told the assembly, which was packed with the city's poor and the men of the hills, that he was targeted because he spoke up for their rights, they voted him a personal bodyguard of fifty armed men. Possessing the only permanently organized armed body in the state, in 560 BC Pisistratus seized the Acropolis and with it the Athenian treasury.[13] As the majority of the people supported him, the Parties of the Coast and Plains, already at each other's throats, could not find common cause to resist the power grab.

Pisistratus was now master of the state. It took five years before the other two parties were able to settle their differences sufficiently to use their combined resources to force him from power and into exile. However, the anti-Pisistratus coalition quickly collapsed again. Megacles, leader of the Party of the Coast, quarreled with his Plains allies and possibly even with his own party. As a counterweight, he reached out to Pisistratus and offered to assist his return to power if Pisistratus agreed to marry his daughter and unite the two families. Pisistratus agreed to the terms and began preparations for a suitable entry into Athens. Herodotus relates a legend that his supporters found a woman of unsurpassed beauty and dressed her up as the goddess Athena. Supposedly, the common folk were deceived when a herald went ahead of a gilded chariot bearing Pisistratus and the young lady, announcing that the goddess Athena herself was returning the tyrant to power.

Pisistratus went through with the wedding, but it was a sham. Megacles may have had a notion that any male offspring of this marriage would succeed Pisistratus to power. If he did, he was soon to be disappointed, as Pisistratus already had two sons from a previous marriage, Hippias and Hipparchos, and he had no intention of damaging their interests in favor of a grandson of Megacles. Furthermore, it is quite possible that he did not want to damage the future of the Pisistratidae clan's standing in Athenian society by the blood guilt that still clung to the Alcmaeonidae clan, of which Megacles was a member.

When Megacles learned that Pisistratus had no intention of giving him a grandson, he again made common cause with the Party of the Plains, and Pisistratus again went into exile. This time it was to last ten years. At this point, Pisistratus understood that if he was to regain power in Athens and hold it, he would require money and troops. For the next decade, Pisistratus dedicated his every effort to a relentless pursuit of both. At first, he found refuge and support in Macedonia, and from there he was able to extend his influence to the area around Mount Pangaeus in Thrace (now northern Greece), which possessed rich silver deposits. A superb politician, Pisistratus also began gathering allies throughout the Greek world, who sent him enough money to purchase influence in Attica and begin equipping a sizable mercenary force.[14] When his preparations were near completion, Argos sent him one thousand hoplites, and the tyrant of Naxos personally joined him with troops and money. In 546 BC, Pisistratus considered himself ready.[15]

From a base near the city of Eretria, Pisistratus crossed over the narrow strait to the Plain of Marathon. Here, his preparations and the continued cultivation of the loyalty of the hill people and Athens's poor paid their expected dividends. They flocked to his banner, while the Athenian government found it was having trouble fielding an adequate force to resist the tyrant's return. After a short delay, Pisistratus began his advance on Athens, twenty-six miles distant. At Pallene, barring his way, were the leaders of the Parties of the Coast and Plains, along with whatever forces they could assemble. Their army was apparently caught at leisure and failed to form before Pisistratus's attack fell upon them. The Battle of Pallene was over in minutes as the routed defenders of Athens streamed back toward the city. Showing the cunning he was famous for, Pisistratus sent messengers after the fleeing Athenians, telling them that if they returned peaceably to their homes, they would be left secure and unmolested. Most Athenians, whose hearts were never in the fight, took him up on the offer. The road to Athens was clear, his enemies were in flight, and from those important families too slow to get away Pisistratus took hostages that he stored with his ally Naxos.

After two failures, Pisistratus's tyranny finally took root, and he ruled for the next seventeen years. During that time, he took Athens from being a troubled, second-rate city and set it on the path to greatness. Despite his hold on absolute power, Pisistratus held the reins of power lightly, keeping all of Athens's old institutions in place. To any observer the government of Athens was little changed, but now it was guided by the will of one man. The nearest parallel we have for this in the ancient world is Augustus's rise to supreme power in Rome. He too kept the mechanisms of government virtually unchanged, including the dignity of the Roman Senate, but Augustus himself became the guiding force of all that was done.

As a first step, Pisistratus made sure that those who supported him during his long exile were properly rewarded. The great estates of the nobles were broken up and disbursed among the mass of common laborers. In this one act, Pisistratus created a yeoman class that would one day be available as hoplites in the Athenian battle line. It also stripped the nobles of the economic basis of their power, effectively crushing the power of the Party of the Plains for almost a generation. These new landowners were required to pay a tenth of their produce in taxes, which must have seemed a light burden to men who had previously had nothing.

This revenue source probably became the backbone of the government's finance, but it was far from its only revenue source. Pisistratus kept his hold on the silver mines he controlled in Thrace, and to this he added the silver from the Attic mines at Laurion, which started to be worked much more extensively from this point forward.[16] This combined silver hoard was minted into a new Attic currency with a bust of Athena on one side and an owl on the other. The weight of these coins and their purity soon ensured they were in high demand. Moreover, their entry into the economic system in large quantities greatly improved Athenian trade and added to the prosperity of many who had previously supported the Party of the Coast, effectively bringing them into alliance with Pisistratus.

This was not all Pisistratus did to advance the Athenian economy. In a policy reminiscent of the first year of Darius's reign, but maintained for a much longer period of time, Pisistratus spent liberally. He financed farmers and entered into an extensive building program, which had the added benefit of mopping up the remaining excess labor in Athens. Moreover, he began the process of transitioning Attica's farmers from grain production to the growing of olives. The effects of these changes cannot be underestimated, as they had profound consequences for Athenian society and diplomacy and later in the decision to fight at Marathon.

Olives were a cash crop and brought substantially more revenues to farmers than grain. As Athens produced much more olive oil than could profitably be used in Attica, it was forced to begin trading with other cities. This trade, along with the introduction of new silver coinage, soon made Athens the greatest and richest trading city in Greece. However, the transition to olives as Athens's cash crop was not without its downside. Foremost was that Athens was unable to grow the grain necessary to feed its growing population. Although there were several regions that produced excess grain, the farms around the Black Sea produced the greatest surplus. It was not long, therefore, before Attic traders were making regular trips to the Black Sea, a region that soon became critical to Athens's survival. Because of this the Hellespont, the gateway to the Black Sea, became an area of strong Athenian strategic interest, and from this point forward we see increasing Athenian influence in the area, including a number of Athenians who became tyrants of cities in the area. Miltiades, an eventual hero of Marathon, was one of these.[17] Another drawback of this agricultural transformation was that olive trees are easily destroyed. This must have been a tremendous factor as the Athenians made the decision whether to hide behind their walls or go out to face the Persians at Marathon.[18] This susceptibility of olive trees to destruction made it imperative that Athens remain at peace for a prolonged period, at least long enough for the city to become powerful enough to protect them. Therefore the policy of Pisistratus and his immediate successors became the maintenance of peace at almost any cost.

In total, the economic policies and reforms of Pisistratus greatly increased the wealth of Athens and its citizenry. While Athens was not yet the military and economic power that it would become in later decades, by the time of Marathon it was richer and more powerful than most historians credit. As most hoplites were required to purchase their own armor and weapons, the creation of a wealthier peasant class automatically increased the numbers available to fill the army rolls. Moreover, it was this rapid economic growth that made it possible for Athens, which at the start of Pisistratus's reign had trouble defeating relatively insignificant Megara, to mobilize a force capable of defeating a large Persian army.

If protecting his economic miracle was not enough incentive to pursue a policy of being a good neighbor to all, Pisistratus's own experience was enough to convince him that it was dangerous to allow enemies to accumulate too close to home. He owed his return to power to Eretria providing him a base, Macedon sheltering him, Thebes sending him money, Argos sending soldiers, and Naxos offering him substantial military and economic support. As the men he sent into exile, particularly the always dangerous Alcmaeonidae clan (Megacles and his brilliant son Cleisthenes), were consistently intriguing for their return, it was imperative that he maintain good relations with all his neighbors. The tenacity and capacity of these exiles were not to be despised, and Pisistratus made it his first order of business that they never found succor in the cities or regions near Attica.

This task was not easy. Megara still harbored ill feeling over the loss of Salamis; close relations with the militarily powerful Thessaly tended to anger Thebes, which was already growing wary of Athens's growing strength; Aegina and Corinth became increasingly unfriendly as they continually found themselves on the losing side of expanding Athenian trade and industry; and finally, Pisistratus's close relations with Sparta could not be long held while he remained friendly to Argos. The strain of balancing all of these diplomatic arrangements must have been tremendous, but during his lifetime, Pisistratus was up to the task. Unfortunately for the legacy of his family, they proved unmanageable for his son and successor, Hippias.

Even though he maintained a policy of peace in the near abroad, on the other side of the Aegean, Pisistratus undertook a policy of imperialism. As we previously saw, this policy was propelled by the necessity to secure Athens's access to grain, as more and more of Attica's fertile land was transitioned to olive production. As a first step, Athens took the port city of Sigeum from the Mytilenians. This city was previously under Athenian control and was probably first seized during the war with Megara to hinder that city's trade in the region. Herodotus does not tell us how or when it was lost to Mytilene, nor does he tell us when it was retaken. He does relate, however, that Pisistratus installed his illegitimate son (of an Argive woman) Hegesistratos as tyrant and that this led to a long, bitter war with Mytilene.

The capture of Sigeum gave Pisistratus control of the southern shore of the Dardanelles; however, to completely control access to the Black Sea, Athens needed to control the north shore also. Fortunately, this was accomplished early in Pisistratus's tyranny. At the time, the Thracian tribe of the Dolonci controlled the Chersonese peninsula (the north shore of the Dardanelles) but were hard-pressed in a war with a tribe to the north, the Apsinthians. The Dolonci appealed to Athens for help, and Pisistratus was only too ready to agree and thereby extend Athenian influence into this strategic region. Pisistratus selected Miltiades (uncle of the Miltiades who would fight at Marathon), a leader among the powerful Philaidae clan, to take a force north and become the tyrant of the Chersonese, a position his family would hold until after the Ionian revolt.[19] Upon his arrival, Miltiades won or otherwise ended the war, built a defensive wall across the Chersonese peninsula, and became a close ally of Lydia's king Croesus. For Pisistratus, this single stroke removed a powerful potential rival from Attica, deprived what was left of the Party of the Plains of its leadership, and greatly enhanced Athenian power in a critical region.

Chapter 8

A STATE CREATED FOR WAR

Marathon would be, above all, a victory of Athenian arms. In fact, the advance guard of the most formidable military power in Greece—Sparta—did not arrive until the day after the battle. However, the truth is that in the decades prior to Marathon, Sparta played a decisive role in the development of Athens, both politically and militarily. Furthermore, in the two years just prior to the Persian assault, it was the actions of Sparta's army that made Athens's victory possible. In those two years, Sparta had all but annihilated the army of Argos, a city only sixty miles from Athens that was suspected of inviting Persian intervention in Greek affairs. Spartan arms also thoroughly cowed Athens's perennial enemy Aegina, which was also leaning dangerously toward Persia. Spartan troops would miss the Battle of Marathon, but they set the conditions that kept Athens from having to fight on multiple fronts. It is therefore fair to state that Sparta, knowingly or not, saved Athens from destruction. However, their temporary friendship came only after decades of conflict.

Sparta was different from any other Greek city-state. As a state it was born in war, and for several centuries it existed only for war. Alone among the Greek city-states, Sparta, during the centuries of its greatness, never built a wall around the five villages that constituted its core.[1] Modern historians are fond of stating that no walls were necessary, as Sparta was protected by the formidable Taygetus mountain chain, which rises nearly eight thousand feet at its peak. However, as all Greeks at the time understood, there was a far better reason Sparta lacked walls—its hoplites were the most formidable soldiers in the ancient world. Before it suffered crushing defeats against Thebes's brilliant general Epaminondas at the

Battles of Leuctra (371 BC) and Mantinea (362 BC), it was considered the height of folly for any Greek city to send its army into Sparta.[2]

As the cities of ancient Greece rose out of the Greek dark ages, populations soon began outstripping food supplies. Most cities addressed this problem by dispatching colonies to unpopulated lands. Sparta, however, eschewed colonies in favor of policy or military expansion, with the aim of subduing the entire Peloponnesus to its will.[3] Early Spartan conquests came from pushing the Argives back from the upper Eurotas valley and subjecting the local Laconian population to helot (serf) status. This early Spartan-Argive war was the start of a rivalry that was to plague the Peloponnesus for centuries afterward. Unsatisfied with this addition of Argive land, Sparta began to covet the fertile soil of Messenia in the southwestern Peloponnesus. Spartan soldiers first marched into Messenia in about 743 BC, but after that almost nothing is known but legends.[4] According to the Spartans, the dispute began during a celebration at the Temple of Artemis, in which both Spartans and Messenians were participating. In the midst of the Dance of the Spartan Virgins, some Messenian youth rushed the women and possibly tried to make off with them. When the Spartan king, Teleclus, tried to protect the virgins, he was murdered. The Messenians have a different version. In their telling, Teleclus had disguised fifty Spartan soldiers, armed with daggers, as virgins and was trying to sneak them into their territory. When the plot was discovered, Teleclus was killed in the ensuing scuffle. Still, war did not break out until Spartan anger was unleashed by a distinguished Messenian Olympic hero named Polychares, who took it upon himself to kill any Spartan who came his way as revenge for a Spartan having killed his son and stolen his cattle herd. This story probably reflects distant and long-lost tales of a period of intense border raids that could have easily escalated into all-out war.

For the next twenty years, the First Messenian War raged. The Messenians, although they may have won a few battles, were rarely a match for the Spartans in the field. They were, however, able to withstand interminable sieges behind their city walls and in their mountain fortresses, particularly Ithome. After enduring a number of frustrating setbacks, some decisive event occurred of which no source offers an explanation. All that is recorded is that in the twentieth year of the war, the fighting ended and the Messenians passed into servitude. As part of the peace settlement, the Messenians were forced to swear oaths that they would never rebel against Sparta and half of their agricultural produce would be delivered to Sparta as annual tribute. The Spartan general and poet Tyrtaeus records:

Like asses worn down by heavy burdens they were compelled to make over to their masters an entire half of the produce of their fields, and to come in the garb of woe to Sparta, themselves and their wives, as mourners at the death of a Spartan king.

For almost forty years, the Messenians endured the degradation of helot status. But in 685 BC, they revolted.[5] The Spartans advanced without proper preparations and were beaten in an indecisive battle. However, the Messenians took advantage of the Spartan retreat and raided Sparta. Here, they added insult to injury by offering a captured Spartan shield, rather than one of their own, at the Temple of Athena, deep within Spartan territory. In the midst of this crisis a new Spartan general, Tyrtaeus, came to the fore.[6] Although the Spartans suffered one more reverse at the Battle of Boar's Grave, in the third year of the war, Tyrtaeus turned the tide and defeated the Messenians, along with a number of their Peloponnesian allies, at the Battle of the Great Foss (Great Trench).

Tyrtaeus, besides being a general of formidable talent, was also a poet. In fact, he was the Kipling of his time, and his poems inspired the Spartans to one more supreme effort. When as a result of this crisis Sparta had transformed itself into the warrior state of popular imagination, the evening mess began with the singing of the holy paean, after which each member of the mess recited verses of Tyrtaeus's poetry. In one of the surviving texts, we find the ideal that motivated a Spartan army at war:

SPARTAN SOLDIER

Young men, fight shield to shield and never
succumb to panic or miserable flight,
but steel the heart in your chests with
magnificence and courage. Forget your own life
when you grapple with the enemy. Never run
and let an old soldier collapse whose legs have lost their power.
It is shocking when an old man lies on the front line
before a youth: an old warrior whose head is white
and beard gray, exhaling his strong soul into the dust,
clutching his bloody genitals in his hands:
an abominable vision, foul to see: his flesh naked.
But in a young man all is beautiful when he still
possesses the shining flower of lovely youth.

Alive he is adored by men, desired by women,
and finest to look upon when he falls dead in the forward clash.
Let each man spread his legs, rooting them in the ground,
bite his teeth into his lips, and hold.

After reducing half the Peloponnesus to helotry, the Spartans found it much more difficult to conquer the cities of the northern Peloponnesus. After a generation of continuous war, Sparta took a different tack. If it could not conquer the northern cities, then binding them into an alliance with Sparta as the dominant member was the next best option. For the war-weary northern cities, joining Sparta in a military alliance probably seemed a small price to pay if their political independence was assured. However, not every city in the Peloponnesus joined the alliance; most notably, the powerful city of Argos remained unswervingly anti-Spartan and was always outside of what became known as the Peloponnesian League.[7]

The Peloponnesian League is probably best viewed as a loose network of perpetual bilateral alliances. Each of the members swore to subordinate its foreign policy to the will of Sparta and to come to Sparta's aid in time of war. However, Sparta did not make any similar promise in return. So while Sparta could call on any member of the league in the event it went to war, none of the other members could make a similar claim on Sparta. In return, the members of the league supposedly received Sparta's protection, not least from Argos, which was viewed to be as avaricious in its demands on other Peloponnesian cities as Sparta was. The league had no permanent institutions, and the only time representatives of each city met as a body was when the Spartans called an assembly. Moreover, although every member had only one vote, Sparta appears to have controlled the votes of many of the smaller towns.[8] In any event, there was nothing in any of the league's agreements that enjoined Sparta to accept the dictates of the congress. Similarly, some of the major cities in the league, such as Corinth, maintained a large measure of independence. Later, Corinth's independent streak was to cause the Spartans considerable embarrassment in their military and diplomatic engagements with Athens in the years leading up to the Battle of Marathon. In fact, in the next century Corinth started a major war against its former colony of Corcyra without Spartan permission, starting the ruinous Peloponnesian War between Athens and Sparta.

Still, even with the Peloponnesian League behind it, Sparta did not feel secure. Argos, its perpetual enemy, remained much too powerful for

Sparta's liking. The start of the new round of Spartan-Argive enmity is lost to us and can be accounted for only as the natural result of two rising powers within a restricted geographic zone. With its frontiers at peace as a result of the advent of the Peloponnesian League, and the Messenian helots apparently docile, in about 545 BC, Sparta marched into southern Argos and claimed the fertile plain of Thyrea. Instead of engaging in a full-scale battle for the territory, both sides agreed to decide the issue by letting three hundred selected champions meet and fight to the death. The Battle of the 300 Champions took place in roughly 544 BC, and when it was over two Argives and one Spartan were left alive.[9] The two Argives, showing no great desire to close with and finish the dangerous Spartan, declared victory by virtue of their superior numbers and returned to Argos. The remaining Spartan then turned to stripping the Argive dead of their arms and armor and used the collection to build a victory monument on the battlefield. He then proclaimed himself and Sparta the victor on the grounds that he alone remained on and held the field of battle. With both sides claiming victory, a general battle was inevitable. When it took place, Argos was decisively defeated and did not rise again as a power for a generation.[10]

It is difficult to underestimate the effects this almost continuous warfare had on Spartan society. Prior to the Messenian conquest and its subsequent revolts, Sparta was similar to any other Greek city and there was no reason to suspect it would develop into a warrior state. But after the conquest of Messenia and the reduction of that populace to helotry, the Spartans were relieved of all economic responsibilities. The helots were forced to till this land, and set amounts of the produce were delivered to Spartan landowners. After these payments were made, the helots were permitted to keep any excess produce.

Although the helots were not slaves in the traditional sense of that word, the conditions of their lives were harsh. As a result, they were always ready to revolt whenever presented an opportunity. To counter this threat, Sparta was forced to maintain a constant high state of war preparation, which was possible only because its men no longer had to till fields or harvest crops. The state also created the *krypteia*, a secret police that enlisted the best of Sparta's youth. These young men were sent into the countryside with a writ to kill any helot they deemed a threat to Sparta or good order. To relieve these young men of the burden of "blood guilt" for these institutionalized murders, each year Sparta ritually declared war on the helots. Despite these precautions, revolts remained a regular occurrence and were typically repressed with unrestrained violence. This domestic situation resulted in the adoption of an extremely conservative policy when dealing with affairs outside of the Peloponnesus. So although the Spartans possessed the most feared and effective army in the Greek world, the continuous threat of a helot revolt made them supremely reluctant to send that army far from the Peloponnesus for any lengthy period.

As the Spartans were relieved of the necessity of earning a living, they were free to dedicate all their energy to affairs of state, and the state's primary affair was war. Spartan society and its institutions were relegated to the job of producing warriors, and every citizen was a soldier. Men performed this duty by fighting as hoplites in the battle line, while women performed it by rearing future soldiers. From the moment of birth, a person's worth was decided by his or her fitness to perform these sacred duties. Any infant found physically wanting was left exposed on Mount Taygetus to die of exposure or to be consumed by wild beasts. At the tender age of seven, boys were taken from their mothers and placed into the *agoge* (the upbringing).[11] Here a youth passed the next decade in brutal training designed to inure him to any hardship, create an unwavering discipline in the battle line, and push him repeatedly to the edge of human endurance.

At age eighteen (or twenty), a Spartan graduated from training and took his place in a "mess" as a full-fledged Spartan soldier. Selection to a mess was by vote, and a single no vote by any mess member was enough to blackball a candidate from that particular mess. If a Spartan was refused admittance to every mess, he was excluded from Spartan society. For recent graduates of the *agoge*, membership in a mess did not end their trial period. For the next decade they lived in barracks with their companions, and if any of them married, they could see their wives only during short, furtive visits. Only at age thirty did a Spartan become a *homoioi*, a peer.[12] And only at this point did he receive the privileges of full citizenship and earn the right to live in his own home. As one Athenian later said, "The Spartan's life is so unendurable that it is no wonder he throws it away lightly in battle."[13]

This Spartan discipline extended itself to the women. They were expected to be physically strong, able to bear many children, and imbued with the Spartan spirit. In his *Sayings of Spartan Women*, Plutarch gives some indications of what that spirit meant:

Damatria: After hearing her son was a coward and unworthy of her, Damatria killed him when he made his appearance. This is the epigram about her: "Demetrius who broke the laws was killed by his mother—she a Spartan lady, he a Spartan youth."

Unnamed: Another woman, as she was handing her son his shield and giving him some encouragement, said: "Son, either with this or on this."[14]

In most of Greece, the state of women was not far above chattel. In Athens, for instance, upon reaching puberty a girl would be locked away until marriage. Afterward, she would be kept out of the public as much as possible, and her husband would consider it a mortal insult to hear her discussed by any man outside of the immediate family. By contrast, in Sparta girls were encouraged to participate in physical exercise, often doing so nude and in contests with the boys. Spartan girls were fed much better than girls anywhere else in Greece and were even taught to read and write, a practice other Greeks ridiculed. Menander, an Athenian, quipped: "Teaching women to read and write? What a terrible thing to do! Like feeding a vile snake more poison."[15] Spartan women were also allowed to own property, were expected to speak their minds on public issues, and had the right to take another husband if the first was gone too long at war. Furthermore, when her husband was away, a Spartan wife was expected to look after her husband's property and protect it with any violence required, a job they were uniquely prepared for by both training and temperament. From the evidence still extant, one could easily get the impression that the only thing more dangerous then fighting the men of Sparta was fighting the women of Sparta.

By the middle of the sixth century BC, this system made Sparta the undisputed military superpower of the Peloponnesus and probably the rest of Greece. It was for this reason that Lydia's king Croesus sent for Spartan assistance against Cyrus in the early 550s and why the Ionians begged for their support against Cyrus's Persians and again when they later revolted against Darius and Persian rule. Sparta, with enough concerns at home, refused both entreaties.

Foremost among Spartan concerns were developments 150 miles to their north, in Athens. Throughout the period of Sparta's rise to dominance in the Peloponnesus, Athenian power was also growing. Athens's political institutions, however, were developing in a radically different direction from those of Sparta. Always slow to send its army far from the Peloponnesus, Sparta at first contented itself just with monitoring developments in Athens, though with growing unease. This hands-off policy ended with the rise of a new king, Cleomenes, who possessed a spirit of adventurism not typical of most Spartans. The start of Cleomenes' kingship marked the beginning of a fresh policy of active Spartan participation and interference outside of the Peloponnesus, particularly in Athenian affairs. Cleomenes himself is a difficult person to portray in much depth, but Herodotus appears to go out of his way to give him the worst press possible:

- Cleomenes son of Anaxandridas now held the kingship; he had obtained it not by virtue of merit and valor . . . [16]
- Because Cleomenes, it is said, was not right in his mind and lived on the verge of madness . . . [17]

Herodotus also states that Cleomenes did not rule for long, which is particularly interesting, as the historical record shows Cleomenes actively ruling as king for over thirty years, a remarkably long time for someone on the verge of madness since his coronation. The truth, which can be pieced together from other scattered segments of Herodotus's account, shows that the true Cleomenes was clever, unprincipled, cunning, ruthless, and determined. During his reign he bribed the Delphi oracle, deposed his fellow co-ruler, outwitted the ephors during a trial for his life, wiped out a generation of Argive manhood in battle, and played kingmaker in Athens.[18] It was a truly remarkable career, which, however, came to an inglorious end in the stocks, where he was either murdered or committed suicide.

For Cleomenes, controversy began before he was even born. After many years of marriage, his father, Anaxandridas of the Agiad royal house, had not had a child with his first wife.[19] The ephors, concerned for the continuation of the royal line, ordered him to put her aside and take another. In a very un-Spartan move, Anaxandridas took a second wife but refused to divorce the first, so in violation of Spartan law he became a bigamist. This second wife soon gave birth to a son, Cleomenes. However, shortly after this, Anaxandridas's first wife also had a son, Dorieus, followed by three more sons. When Anaxandridas died in 520 BC, there was a contested succession that Dorieus expected to win based on his performance in the *agoge* and in war. The tradition-bound Spartans, however, decided that Cleomenes' claim, as firstborn, was the stronger, and he became king. For Dorieus's part, he could not abide a Sparta that he did not rule. He and some followers left, and after several failed attempts to establish a new colony, he was killed in battle with the Phoenicians, who did not approve of him causing trouble in their backyard. Even with Dorieus out of the way, Cleomenes was not free to act as he desired, for the unique Spartan constitution called for two kings of equal power ruling simultaneously. One king, descended from the Agiad family line, was considered a bit senior to the other (descended from the Eurypontid family) but had no authority over him beyond that of his own force of personality. In 515 BC, Cleomenes' co-king, Ariston, died and was replaced by his son Demaratus. For most of Demaratus's reign, his claim to history consists primarily of his opposition to the policies of Cleomenes, until he was deposed almost on the eve of the Battle of Marathon. Demaratus ended his days in Persian service and accompanied Xerxes' army for the second invasion of Greece in 480 BC.

When Cleomenes was free to act, he spent much of his time either interfering in Athenian affairs or working to contain the growing power of Argos. In no small measure, his interference in Athenian internal matters greatly influenced and accelerated the growth of democracy. More important from our perspective, his continuous military interventions and threats propelled Athens to develop a military capability that was second to none, not even that of Sparta. Moreover, even his policy toward Argos was to profoundly influence Athens's ability to resist the coming Persian invasion. When Cleomenes finally tired of Argive insolence, he led a Spartan army that obliterated Argive military power, eliminating the growing threat of Argos allying itself with Persia. In effect, Cleomenes' thirty years of frenetic activity made the Athenian victory at Marathon possible.

Chapter 9

SPARTA VS. ATHENS

In 527 BC, Pisistratus died peacefully in his bed. He had guided Athens through almost two decades of peace and unrivaled prosperity. His sons, Hippias and Hipparchos, assumed power without any apparent challenge, with Hippias taking the leading role. However, even though Hippias had many of his father's personal qualities and talents, he found himself contending with a combination of forces that had never coalesced during his father's reign but were now coming together to his detriment. Moreover, the powerful Alcmaeonidae clan were unceasing in their intrigues to return to Athens.[1] For a time, Hippias did prove to be up to the challenge, but when the Alcmaeonidae found a new leader, Cleisthenes (son of Megacles), who was to make common cause with a temperamental and unpredictable Spartan king, Cleomenes, their combined might ended the reign of the Pisistratidae.

Hippias at first pursued the wise and generally peaceful policies of his father. But as Athens's economic and military power grew, the surrounding cities became increasingly apprehensive. Thebes had already defeated Thessaly and was now looking to expand its power throughout Boeotia. Cities looking to avoid being dragged into Thebes's orbit could turn only to distant Sparta or nearby Athens, a situation sure to arouse Theban jealousy. Moreover, Corinth and Megara were both reeling economically as expanding Athenian trade began to capture their traditional markets. When both cities entered the Spartan-dominated Peloponnesian League, their concerns became Sparta's, causing a fraying of Athenian-Spartan relations. In all likelihood, keeping Sparta as a friend would have been difficult for Athens under any circumstances. Growing Athenian power was sure to spark first the interest and then the jealousy of Sparta. That Athens was simultaneously trying to maintain close relations with Sparta's sworn enemy Argos further inflamed a deteriorating situation. Fortunately, for the time being, Sparta's growing wariness of Athens did not translate into immediate military action. Conservative Sparta, as always, remained slow to act, but that hesitation was ending now that Cleomenes had become king of Sparta.

The first opportunity for Sparta to make trouble for Athens came in 519 BC. Plataea, a small city-state just north of Attica and on the southern edge of Boeotia, came under heavy pressure to submit to Thebes's rule. In its search for a powerful ally, Plataea first turned to Sparta. For the Spartans, an invitation to expand their writ north of the Peloponnesus must have been tempting. Only the certainty of perpetual Theban enmity, which might become the basis of an effective anti-Spartan alliance with Athens and Thessaly, deterred it from making the deal. Acting with a cunning not typically expected of a Spartan, King Cleomenes advised the Plataeans to seek help from Athens, which being much closer to them could come to their support in a timelier manner.

The Plataeans took this advice, and the Athenians in turn offered them their protection. In a stroke, Cleomenes had placed his two most dangerous potential enemies (Athens and Thebes) at each other's throats. Predictably, upon hearing news of the new alliance, Theban hoplites immediately set out to conquer Plataea. The Athenians, their policy of peace at all costs now ended, marched to meet them. Before hostilities began, Corinth tried to mediate a settlement. The Corinthian mediators decided that Thebes should not coerce any city into its budding Boeotian League. Thinking the matter resolved, the Athenian army began marching for home. However, the Corinthian decision did not sit well with the Thebans, and they opted to roll the die and try to overturn the verdict through force of arms. Despite being surprised by the sudden Theban attack, the Athenians won the battle decisively enough to extend their borders into Boeotia.[2]

Unfortunately, this is all that Herodotus tells us of this affair. However, military historians can draw information from these scanty details of the battle that is critical to our full understanding of the Battle of Marathon. First and foremost, this attack wedded the Plataeans to Athens and accounts for the fact that they sent one thousand hoplites to fight beside the Athenians at Marathon. Just as interesting is that this is the first proof that Athenian hoplites had lost little, if any, of their military effectiveness in the years since the war with Megara and the long peace of Pisistratus. The Theban army was not a force that was easy to dismiss or vanquish. It must be noted that just the year before this battle, Thebes had decisively defeated Thessaly, previously the strongest power in Greece, at the Battle of Ceressus.[3] That the Athenians could administer such a thorough beating after being caught by surprise speaks highly of their discipline and martial prowess. Moreover, this battle took place twenty-nine years (or less) before Marathon. So a twenty-year-old hoplite fighting in his first battle would not yet have been fifty at the time of Marathon. As a Greek citizen was liable for military service until age sixty, one can assume that some veterans of this battle were still in the fighting line at Marathon. At the very least, most of the Greek generals at Marathon, including the polemarch (the overall commander), were almost certainly present. Commanders with thirty years' experience in war surely must have provided a steadying influence at Marathon. This is also the first, but far from the last, indication we have that the Athenian army was not exactly the force of unprofessional farmers of legend.

For the moment, Athens had come out ahead, and Cleomenes' first attempt to cause trouble by helping to tie it to Plataea had backfired. But in the long term, Hippias had made a fatal mistake. For Thebes, which had supported his father in his bid to return to power, was now a mortal enemy. Within months of being forced to withdraw their claims on Plataea, the Thebans opened their territory for the Alcmaeonidae to use as a base of operations. From here, the new head of the clan, the clever and determined Cleisthenes, gathered his forces and bided his time.

In 514 BC, an attempted assassination changed the character and nature of Hippias's regime and was to precipitate its eventual downfall. One of two homosexual lovers, Harmodius or Aristogeiton, had suffered an insult from Hippias's brother, Hipparchus, and determined to kill the tyrants. The two lovers chose the Great Panathenaic Festival for the murders, as during this festival Athenians appeared at the Acropolis fully armed. Moreover, they hoped that the mob would rise up in support and defend them from the wrath of Hippias's mercenaries. Only a few people were brought into the plot, but on the morning of the festival one of them was seen talking with Hippias. Believing their plan had been betrayed, the lovers ran from Hippias's location to find his brother, whom they murdered. Alarmed, Hippias moved rapidly in the face of this crisis. Harmodius was killed on the spot, but Aristogeiton was taken prisoner and later put to death. More critically, Hippias took the opportunity to disarm the

Athenians. Presumably, this was done by the many mercenaries in his employ. However, there is no indication that the Athenians resisted this move. For the time being, Athens was without a citizens' army of hoplites.

Embittered and increasingly paranoid after the murder of his brother, Hippias became despotic and malevolent. He ordered the execution of many citizens on the slimmest suspicion. Furthermore, he began raising taxes to exorbitant levels to pay for the mass of mercenaries he believed necessary to prop up his rule. All the time, the Alcmaeonidae clan was waiting, and it was not long before Cleisthenes judged the moment right for his clan's return. He ordered an armed incursion from their Theban base into Attica, and they established themselves in a fortified outpost near the frontier, at Leipsydrion near Paionia.[4] Presumably, they were hoping this would be enough of a catalyst to prompt a general uprising. But Cleisthenes had mistimed his adventure. The disarmed Athenians were not yet ready to risk all to depose a tyrant who was protected by a multitude of mercenaries. Moreover, Hippias, acting with his normal alacrity, sent his men against the Alcmaeonidae and inflicted a severe defeat on them. Chastised, Cleisthenes led his small army back into Thebes and began a new intrigue that was to prove more successful.[5]

After his military defeat, Cleisthenes understood that he could not win through force of arms unless he could entice another city into assisting in his private war. For this purpose he chose Sparta. To accomplish this, Cleisthenes enlisted the help of the Delphi oracle. In 548 BC, the oracle's temple was destroyed by fire. Cleisthenes committed his own remaining fortune and that of his clan to the rebuilding of the temple. This they accomplished to a degree of splendor far beyond that demanded by the specifications, thereby earning considerable goodwill from the servants of the god Apollo. Cleisthenes bought further goodwill through generous gifts to the Pythia, the priestess presiding over Delphi.

From this point on, Herodotus reports, every time the Spartans came to seek the advice of the oracle they were told, "First free Athens." At length, the Spartans decided it was wise to heed the words of the god and prepared a force to go to Athens and depose Hippias. It is difficult to know how much credence to give to this story. That the Alcmaeonidae would bribe the Pythia is credible, but their influence at Delphi paled in comparison with Sparta's. The best that can be said is that Cleisthenes knew that Sparta was already wary of Athens, which had recently defeated Thebes in battle, was destroying the trade of other Peloponnesian League members, and was cozying up to its mortal enemy Argos. Seeing the direction Sparta was already heading, Cleisthenes made the decision easier by presenting it with a religious sanction for a policy toward which it was already inclined. For its part, Sparta probably expected an oligarchy to take over from Hippias, and oligarchies were notoriously friendly to Sparta, particularly those it helped put in place.

The first Spartan force sent to Athens was a small one, and it went by sea under the command of an esteemed, but not royal, Spartan named Anchimolios. This force landed near Athens on the open shore of Phaleron. Here they found Hippias, his mercenaries, and one thousand Thessalian cavalry waiting for them. Warned of Sparta's invasion preparations, Hippias had already prepared the battlefield for cavalry operations. The Spartans, who probably believed the propaganda of Cleisthenes that they would be welcomed by the mass of Athenians, did not expect a fight and were mauled. Anchimolios was killed in battle, and the hard-pressed Spartans were pushed back to their ships without being able to retrieve their commander's body.

King Cleomenes could not tolerate this insult to Spartan arms and prestige. A large expedition was assembled, probably made up of the bulk of the Spartan army, and in 510 BC, Cleomenes and the Spartans marched through the Megarian passes and descended on Athens. Hippias with his mercenaries and Thessalian horsemen marched to meet them, but they were no match for the Spartan host. He was now paying the price for disarming Athens's hoplites. After being roughly handled, the Thessalians rode for home while Hippias retreated into Athens's fortified Acropolis, which, with his typical forethought, he had already stocked with provisions. Herodotus tells us that the Spartans were in no mood for a protracted siege and were preparing to march home when the fates intervened. Hippias's children were captured as they attempted to escape from the city, and to save them Hippias agreed to surrender and leave Athens within five days.

Hippias had prepared well for this eventuality. His half brother had ruled Sigeum for probably a couple of decades or more and had become close to the Persians, who now dominated the region. Moreover, Hippias, courting further favor with the Persians, had married his daughter to the tyrant of Lampsacus, who was known to stand in high regard with the Persian king. It should be mentioned that this tilt toward Persia was not missed by the Spartans, who saw it as a counterploy to their own growing

power, which it was. In fact, it may have been Hippias's pro-Persian incli-
nations that settled his fate, as Sparta consistently maintained an anti-
Persian policy during this period.[6]

Hippias went into exile. This was the end of Pisistratidae rule in Athens,
but it did not destroy the clan's power in either Athens or the rest of Attica. When Hippias departed, so did the Spartans, who left the Athenians
to handle their own affairs. The stage was now set for Cleisthenes to leave
his Theban base and walk onto the Athenian stage.

However, if Cleisthenes was expecting that as the deposer of the tyrant
he would be hailed as a hero, he was to be sadly disappointed. For with
the departure of Hippias, the old Solon constitution came back in force,
and with it came the strife that had plagued Athens before Pisistratus's
tyranny. Again there were three parties: the Plains (the old noble families),
the Coast (the Alcmaeonidae and their merchant-class supporters), and
the Hills (the remaining supporters of the Pisistratidae). The nobles of the
Party of the Plains had found a new dynamism under their leader, Isagoras,
who was able to enlist the support of the Party of the Hills, as they were
angry with Cleisthenes, whom they blamed for the removal of their man,
Hippias.

For several years, Isagoras and the nobles were able to hold the upper
hand, relegating Cleisthenes to a secondary role. Moreover, the period of
Isagoras's dominance was similar enough to an oligarchy (as he had to
maintain the support of other noble families) to please Sparta. But Isagoras and the other noble clans overplayed their hand. In an attempt to better control the Athenian assembly, they ordered sweeping changes to the
list of citizens. These revisions cost many of the poor (the Party of the
Hills) their right to vote in the assembly, which had been given them by
Pisistratus. It was a move that played right into Cleisthenes' hands, even
though, in a Machiavellian move, he may have supported the revision.
Now, after being continually outmaneuvered in his bids for power by
Isagoras, Cleisthenes turned to the newly disenfranchised mob. As Herodotus says, "The Athenian people had been spurned by their politicians, he
now brought them into his own faction."[7] This play for the support of
Athens's common people and of the countryside was a sudden volte-face
for the crafty Cleisthenes, who was now making a direct bid for the supporters of the Pisistratidae (Hippias's base), formerly his and his clan's
mortal enemy. For over a century, the Alcmaeonidae had resisted expanding the franchise to the lower castes. After all, they had failed to support
his father, Megacles, at the Battle of Pallene, when Pisistratus had marched

on Athens from Marathon. Moreover, they had also failed to rise in his support when he led his own assault out of Thebes just a few years before.[8]

As Cleisthenes was the only leading politician taking their side, the mob and countryside did indeed transfer their allegiance to him. With the support of the disenfranchised now firmly behind Cleisthenes, Isagoras and his noble supporters realized they were vastly outnumbered and could no longer hold on to power without assistance. Turning to a tried-and-true method, Isagoras called on Sparta to help. He may have been able to call on some friendship, as the Spartan king had once been a guest in his house, and Herodotus tells us that Cleomenes took that opportunity to sleep with Isagoras's wife.[9] Cleomenes, who was not happy with the nascent democracy being birthed in Athens, decided to come himself. He also followed Isagoras's advice and called on the Athenians to expel Cleisthenes and all of the Alcmaeonidae, claiming they were tainted with blood guilt and still accursed owing to their slaughter of Cylon and his followers over a century before.

Cleisthenes decided not to resist this turn of the tide and left Athens to bide yet more time. Soon after his departure, Cleomenes entered Athens with a small Spartan force, probably his personal bodyguard of three hundred or so hoplites. He promptly ordered the expulsion of seven hundred additional families known to support Cleisthenes. If Cleomenes, Isagoras, and the other Athenian nobles had stopped at this point, the situation might have stabilized in their favor. But, again, they overplayed their hand. Threatened by the move toward democracy, Cleomenes tried to rip it out at its roots and in the process overturn the constitution of Solon. With Isagoras's support, he ordered the Athenian assembly dissolved and replaced by three hundred supporters of Isagoras. Hearing of Cleomenes' plans, the assembly met and in a tremendous show of courage both refused to dissolve itself and called on the people to resist the invaders. The Athenian masses, who had now tasted the possibilities of real political power, heeded the call. The Spartans, along with Isagoras and his supporters, pressed by overwhelming numbers, retreated into the Acropolis and waited for the mob to disperse. But the mob did not disband, and for the next two days they maintained their order and continued to blockade several hundred elite and increasingly desperate Spartan hoplites. As the Acropolis had not been provisioned for a siege, the Spartans were soon in dire straits. On the third day, the Spartans negotiated a truce for themselves and marched out. As part of the humiliating terms of this surrender, the Spartans were forced to turn over their weapons in return for safe conduct. It was a humiliation Cleomenes would never forget. Somehow, they were able to smuggle Isagoras out with them, but his supporters were left behind. Herodotus reports that they were bound and confined to await their execution.

With Isagoras deposed, Cleisthenes and his supporters returned. Whatever his own predisposition, he now had to deliver on the promises he had made during his political struggles with Isagoras and the other noble families. He probably was also beginning to understand that it is easier for an adroit politician to manipulate the masses than it is to manage powerful competing factions. So as his first order of business, Cleisthenes turned himself to reforming the Athenian constitution.[10] His probable intentions were to break up the old political alliances, destroy the political power of the clans (families) and the four ancient tribes, and create institutions that he could control. It is doubtful that Cleisthenes foresaw that these changes, what Aristotle called "the mixing up," would within a short period convert Athens into the world's first true democracy.[11]

Cleisthenes made three key reforms to the Athenian political process:[12]

- Instituting ten tribes in place of the four original Ionic tribes.
- Creating a new five-hundred-man council (boule), consisting of fifty men from each of the new tribes, to replace the old four-hundred-man council.
- Creating the concept of ostracism, whereby a person could be banished from Athens for a period of ten years and then permitted to return.[13]

For our purposes, the most important change was the creation of the ten tribes, in which Cleisthenes enrolled all of the free inhabitants of Attica, along with resident aliens and even freed slaves.[14] It was in the organization of these tribes that Cleisthenes revealed his true genius. First, he organized all of Attica into demes (probably 174 in all). Roughly speaking, a deme was a geographic area based on the largest town and village within its borders.[15] Each deme was given the equivalent of a mayor and a small administrative organization, which enrolled everyone as a citizen of their deme. The demes of each of the three major regions of Attica—the Plains (the Philaidae), the Coast (the Alcmaeonidae), and the Hills (the Pisistratidae)—were divided into ten groups called *trittyes*. These *trittyes* were artificial organizations without any corporate existence, so they possessed no governmental organization or administrators.[16] This accomplished, each of the ten tribes received one *trittys* from each region.

The creation of the demes and new tribal structure wrecked the old system of clan loyalty in favor of loyalty to a specific geographic region. Similarly, through the creation of the *trittys* concept, Cleisthenes placed demes from each of the major regions within every tribe, thereby breaking down the old factional concerns and focusing everyone's attention on what was good for Athens and Attica as a whole. In a stroke, the power of the old parties (the Plains, the Coast, and the Hills) was shattered, as the new organization did not allow for regional or local political action.[17]

This new political organization was to have a profound impact on the organization and battle doctrine of the Athenian army. Each tribe (every one of which was named for a mythical hero selected by the Delphi priestess) was required to contribute one regiment of hoplites and a cavalry squadron for the common defense. In turn, each tribal regiment had a general, or *strategos*, of its own. These ten generals were elected annually by each tribe, and reputedly they rotated command of the entire army on a daily basis, although the third archon remained the overall leader, or polemarch, of the entire army.[18] Until this time, command of the entire army was vested in the polemarch, with no other generals involved in the command structure. Most other historians believe that the rotating command system was in effect at the Battle of Marathon. I believe that this command structure was put aside during times of crisis and that the polemarch remained the supreme military commander when Athens was at war. Any arrangement that left the supreme commander, the polemarch, without any real authority on a day-to-day basis would inevitably lead to a military calamity. As the Athenians were not unusually susceptible to institutional suicide, it is unlikely they would have long accepted military command arrangements that would cause chaos in practice.

While Athens remade itself, Cleomenes returned to Sparta. Still burning with the humiliation of turning over his weapons as the price of safe conduct out of Athens, he immediately began preparing his revenge. He called out the levies of the entire Peloponnesian League and ordered them to assemble for a spring campaign. Cleomenes, the master strategist, also began enticing other allies into his great crusade against Athens. Thebes, still smarting from its defeat at Athens's hands when it had marched on Plataea a dozen years before, had rebuilt its military forces, and it was eager to join in the Spartan attack. The Chalcidians, sensing an easy victory and desiring to participate in the spoils, also offered to contribute their few thousand hoplites to the common cause.

Cleisthenes, for his part, was well aware of the fact that it was one thing to humiliate a small Spartan force of three hundred men and quite another to take on the entire Spartan host. Desperate for allies, he sent emissaries to Sardis to meet with the Persian satrap, Artaphrenes, and ask for military assistance against Sparta. A remarkable event then ensued. According to Herodotus:

> When the envoys arrived in Sardis, and spoke according to their instructions, Artaphrenes . . . inquired who were these people who asked to become allies of the Persians, and where in the world did they live? When he heard the answer of the envoys, he gave them the brief answer that if the Athenians offered earth and water to King Darius, they would have their alliance, but if they did not do so, he ordered them to leave. The envoys, wanting to bring about the alliance, took the responsibility on themselves and consented to offering earth and water, for which they faced serious charges when they returned to their own land.[19]

Offering earth and water to Darius was recognized as the symbolic submission to Persian rule. Although Herodotus explains away the envoys' decision as something they decided on their own, it is virtually inconceivable that Cleisthenes thought the Persians would give him an alliance or march to Athens's aid unless the city submitted to Darius. This is almost surely an incorrect version of events developed during the five or six decades intervening between the event and his collecting the tale; in the wake of the victorious war with Persia and the great victories at Marathon, Salamis, and Plataea, the charge of Medizing (submitting to Persia) had become the worst epithet one city could lay upon another.[20] After such tremendous achievements, it did not suit the legend Athens had created about its own involvement in these events for it to be known that it had been the first to invite the Persians into Greek affairs. In all likelihood, the envoys had instructions from Cleisthenes to offer earth and water if necessary. He probably assumed that by the time they arrived back in Athens, there would be a Spartan army in the field and the Athenians would welcome help from any source, regardless of the price. That the envoys were rebuked upon their return reflects the fact that the situation in Attica was very different from what anyone could have predicted when they had left for Sardis.

In the spring of 507 BC, Cleomenes, probably with Isagoras in tow, led out the Spartan army and the full might of the Peloponnesian League against Athens. At the same time, the Thebans invaded Attica and seized the frontier demes of Oinoe and Hysiae, while the Chalcidians marched into Attica from the northeast. Neither the Thebans nor the Chalcidians felt themselves in much danger, as the Athenian army had massed itself against the main threat, Cleomenes and his Spartan hoplites. For its part, the Peloponnesian army got as far as Eleusis, where it did some damage but then halted. Before them, the Athenians, ignoring the Theban army that was ravaging their northern frontier, lined the ridge separating the Thriasian Plain from the Plain of Athens. If the Athenians could not halt the Spartans along this line, Athens would fall.

Heavily outnumbered, the ranks of Athenian hoplites waited for the inevitable assault. They could not have felt good about their chances, but still, they were prepared to offer stout resistance against the foreign invader. And then, to the Athenian hoplites, something of a miracle took place. Without a fight, the Peloponnesian army began to break up and march home. According to Herodotus, Cleomenes had not informed his allies of their objective when they had marched out, and when the Corinthians learned they were to make war against Athens, they first hesitated and then refused. Herodotus tells us that they considered it an unjust act, but it was probably more a matter of good policy. Corinth was a great trading city, whose principal rivals were Aegina and Megara, both sworn enemies of Athens. If Athens was destroyed or humbled, the full resources of these two cities would be free to turn on Corinthian interests.

With that, Demaratus, Sparta's other king, quarreled with Cleomenes about the practicality of continuing the invasion. When the rest of Sparta's allies witnessed the Corinthians marching home and learned that the Spartan kings were not in agreement, they too began to break camp and march away. As the Athenians held a strong position, even the Spartans hesitated before attempting an assault alone.[21] Their entire power in the Peloponnesus was based on the strength of their army. Any reverse, or even a victory that cost them heavy losses, might endanger that position or give the helots enough confidence to revolt. With no other choice, Cleomenes turned the Spartan army around and marched back to Sparta.

As a result of this debacle, Sparta passed a law that forbade both kings from being with the main army at the same time. They would not tolerate such dangerous dissension again.

As the Spartans marched away, the Athenians turned on their other two tormentors with a vengeance. We have no details of the fighting, except that they first fell upon the Thebans, who were trying to link up with the Chalcidians. All that Herodotus tells of the battle is that vast numbers of Thebans were slaughtered and seven hundred were taken alive. Immediately after mauling the Theban army, the Athenians, apparently on the same day, crossed over to the island of Euboea and routed the Chalcidian army. Herodotus states that the chains that held the Theban and Chalcidian prisoners were still available for him to view at the Acropolis, hanging from charred walls.[22] In time, the prisoners were ransomed for the standard two hundred drachmas each, and four thousand Athenian colonists (cleruchs) were established on Chalcidian territory.[23]

It is now about seventeen years before the Battle of Marathon, and we must closely examine the sparse evidence left to us by Herodotus to determine what these battles may predict about the future course of the war with Persia. First, they provide one more counter to the widespread contention that when the Persians arrived, the Athenians were amateurs in war. Without allies, they had stood alone along a ridge with the entire might of the Peloponnesian League arrayed to their front. Whatever their qualms, they did not waver and their courage did not fail. Athens's hoplites were fully prepared to follow the Spartan poet's advice "to bite their lips and hold," no matter what force was sent against them. Whether they could have won is not as important as the fact that they had the confidence to stand. That tells us something about their preparations. As every Athenian knew from the moment of Cleomenes' humiliation at the Acropolis, in the next campaigning season a Spartan army was certain to march upon them. It stands to reason that they would have spent the intervening months training and preparing for the expected assault.

Only a decade before, the Athenians had vanquished the Theban army that had marched on Plataea, and most of these veterans were still in the battle line. These Athenians knew what hoplite warfare was and would have taken the lead in preparing the army for the coming trial. Having humiliated a Spartan king, the Athenians could not have been under any illusion that retribution would not be harsh. While accepting Isagoras back might have been open to negotiation, it is doubtful that anyone in Athens believed it would be all that Sparta would demand. So throughout the fall and winter, the Athenians trained. They trained with the strength and determination of desperate men. I would contend that by spring there would not have been much real difference between the quality of the Athenian army and that of the Spartans. If the Athenian force had given any impression it was not ready or less than a fully professional fighting force, the Spartans would have attacked. I further contend that this display of professionalism played no small part in the Corinthians' decision not to participate any further in the campaign and was decisive in the Spartans' final decision to march off.

What happened next also buttresses the case that the Athenians were a highly professional and well-disciplined force. With the Spartans out of the fight, they marched across the breadth of Attica and went into an immediate assault on a well-trained and disciplined Theban army. Moreover, it appears they denied themselves a rest and attacked straight from the march. Then, without pause, the exhausted Athenians marched to the coast, boarded ships, made an amphibious landing, and engaged in another major battle in short order. As their future foes the Persians counted on the cavalry to win their battles, it should be noted that the Chalcidians possessed the most celebrated cavalry force in Greece. It did not matter, as their horsemen went down quickly under the rush of disciplined hoplites.

There is one last key point to make. The Athenians clearly possessed a military genius. Herodotus makes no mention of who commanded the Athenian army, his name is lost to us, but it is hard to believe that any of the above could have happened unless the Athenians possessed a soldier of rare talent. It is a well-known military maxim that an army is only as good as its leader, and the Athenian army was very good. Someone kept them at their tasks all winter, maintained their fighting spirit in front of the Spartan host, propelled them in what must have been an arduous forced march across Attica, and finally led them in two major battles possibly within twenty-four hours. Without putting too fine a point on it, no army could have accomplished this without a truly inspiring leader—one who possessed enough tactical brilliance to stymie a much larger Peloponnesian army and then decisively defeat two other armies while suffering apparently insignificant losses. Moreover, he had enough foresight and operational ability to keep his army concentrated, even under almost unendurable stress. He held his army in place before the Spartans even as Athens's northern provinces were being ravaged, although many of his hoplites must have had property and family to the north. Finally, he was enough of a master of warfare to plan the logistics required to move and fight an army on two widely dispersed fronts and also order that ships be on hand for an immediate amphibious assault.

So who was this genius, until now lost to history? It can only be a matter of speculation, but one strong possibility is Callimachus, the polemarch (Athenian commander) at the Battle of Marathon. He was almost certainly of the right age during this time, and when the Persians arrived he was placed in charge of the Athenian army, when that city was facing the greatest threat in its history. We must not underestimate this point. Every Athenian in 490 BC believed that their very survival was at stake. In such dire circumstances, they would naturally have turned to the man who had stared down the Spartans before destroying two other armies. That they would have given ten untested generals command on alternating days, as Herodotus would have us believe, so strains credulity that it must be discounted. An army with ten equal commanders would shortly rip itself apart. No army can long survive with divided leadership, and a city with Athens's experience in war would never make such a foolish mistake. From this point forward, it is best to think of the influence of the ten tribal generals along the lines of a council with no powers of command, although they may have alternated responsibilities as officer of the day, under the guiding hand of the polemarch.

Although Herodotus gives the bulk of the credit for the victory at Marathon to Miltiades, we must ask a couple of simple questions that the Athenians would also have asked themselves when they were deciding on a commander. There is nothing in the ancient sources to indicate that before Marathon Miltiades had ever stood in the battle line against an organized army. He was probably with the Persians when they marched into Scythia and may have even witnessed the Persians in battle. However, this qualifies him to be an adviser, not commander of an army. Is it likely that after two decades of continuous war the Athenians would give command of their army to an inexperienced and untested soldier?

Furthermore, very few Athenians trusted Miltiades. In fact, upon his arrival in Athens, he was put on trial for his life as a tyrant and suspected supporter of the Persians in the past. Although these charges were probably politically motivated, his trial would still have made a tremendous impression on the hoplites. They would know nothing of political maneuvering but would be all too aware of the fact that Miltiades was accused of being in league with the Persian enemy (which he most definitely once was). It must be judged as highly unlikely that the Athenians would give supreme command of their army to a man who had been absent from the city for twenty years and had spent all of that time as a close ally of the Persians.

So why was the polemarch Callimachus mostly forgotten by Herodotus? Foremost among the reasons was that Callimachus was killed during the Battle of Marathon and therefore was not there to ensure the survival of his place in history. On top of this, Miltiades was fortunate to have a son, Cimon, who would later rise to the pinnacle of power in Athenian politics. Cimon spent most of his adult life burnishing the reputation of his father and ensuring his place in history, even if that meant making sure history was written to his liking. When Herodotus was in Athens earning a living by reciting his histories, Cimon was already powerful (sharing power with Pericles). It would not have been wise for Herodotus to present a history that was markedly different from what Cimon wanted peddled. That of course assumes that after years of Cimon's patient remaking of history there was even an alternative viewpoint available to Herodotus.

Furthermore, Callimachus was from an area of Attica that had always been loyal to Pisistratus and his clan. By the time of Herodotus, the Pisistratidae were held in low repute, and there were probably few persons for the historian to interview who were willing to give a favorable report on any of that clan. In any event, Herodotus has very little to say about the man who was given command of the Athenian army at Marathon. Given his propensity to favor those whose descendants agreed to interviews and slight those whose descendants snubbed him, it may be assumed that this oversight was deliberate.

The most remarkable thing we note upon returning to Athens in the immediate aftermath of the defeat of Thebes is that Cleisthenes disappears from the pages of history. Historians have often remarked on a very weak tradition that he was a victim of ostracism and died in exile, while others note that he died of old age (he was about sixty-four). I discount these traditions as Pausanias, in his description of Greece, mentions he saw Cleisthenes' tomb among Athens's honored war dead.[24] There is no reason to doubt this, as many of the tombs of the period were undisturbed when Pausanias visited the location in the second century AD.[25] It is therefore likely that he was killed during the war with Chalcis and Thebes, for if he had survived these engagements, it is doubtful Herodotus would have failed to mention him again.[26] With or without Cleisthenes, the war with Thebes and the rest of their Boeotian allies continued, despite their shattering defeat in battle. In 506 BC, the Thebans asked the Aeginetans, longstanding enemies of Athens, for assistance but received only sacred images

that were supposed to aid them in battle. Inspired by the images, the The- ·
ban army with its Boeotian allies marched once more against Athens.
Again, Herodotus presents us with no details except to say that the Thebans were roughly handled. Disappointed with the mystical powers of the
images, the Thebans returned them and asked Aegina for more practical
support.

In answer, the Aeginetans sent their fleet against the Attic coast, burning the Athenian port at Phaleron to the ground and damaging many
coastal demes. Before deciding on how to respond to this "unheralded
war," the Athenians consulted the Delphic oracle and were told to wait
thirty years before avenging themselves on Aegina. They were further informed that they might win if they attacked before that time, but only
after a long war and much suffering. The oracle's answer was not to
Athens's liking, and it immediately began preparing to inflict vengeance
upon Aegina. Preparations were well along when word came that Sparta
was once again preparing for war, and Athens turned from Aegina to face
its most dangerous enemy.

Herodotus relates that the Spartans had only recently learned that
Cleisthenes had bribed the Delphic oracle to convince the Spartans to
march against their good friend Hippias. This, however, is likely another
fabrication presented to justify Sparta's intention to pursue an offensive
war. For as was already noted, Sparta maintained extremely close relations
with the priestesses at Delphi, and it is implausible that leading Spartans·
would not have known of these bribes at the time. Assumedly, Cleomenes,
still burning with the humiliation of his surrender at the Acropolis and
now with a failed previous campaign against Athens, was using the claim
as propaganda to stir up the Spartans and Peloponnesian masses. Moreover, many other leading Spartans were beginning to see that a powerful
democratic Athens was not in their best interest, and they conveniently
forgot what Hippias had done to anger them in the first place. Sparta, apparently without Cleomenes taking the lead, asked Hippias to leave
Sigeum and join them for a conference of the Peloponnesian League. As
far as Sparta and Cleomenes were concerned, the conference was a failure,
as once again the Corinthians took the lead in opposing plans to attack
Athens. So another threat to Athens dissolved.

It needs to be noted that Athens had just won another major battle
against Thebes and was preparing, with great confidence, for war with
Aegina. Furthermore, they turned from this plan to prepare for war with
Sparta without any indication of the fear such an encounter had filled

them with the previous year, when Cleisthenes was so worried that he sent for Persian help. For all practical purposes, Athens, during this period, was just as much a nation in arms as Sparta. Herodotus attributes the wondrous improvement in Athens's fighting capabilities to democracy, telling us that men fight harder and better for themselves than they will for any tyrant. For the more practically minded, the improvements could be accounted for by increased training and superb generalship.

Hippias did make one final plea before the Peloponnesian allies, asking them to come to his aid and return him to Athens. When the plea fell on deaf ears, he gave up and returned to Sigeum. Soon afterward, though, he traveled to Sardis and enlisted the support of the satrap, Artaphrenes, in his quest to return to Athens as its tyrant. Athens, upon hearing that Hippias was at Sardis, sent its own envoys to Artaphrenes to request that he ignore the supplicant. Instead, the envoys were told to accept Hippias back or prepare to suffer Persian wrath. When the envoys returned, the request was summarily dismissed and Athens became an enemy of the Persian Empire.

It was at this juncture that an Ionian Greek named Aristagoras arrived in Athens asking for support for the Ionian revolt then racking the Persian Empire. The angry Athenians, despite the Spartans' having turned Aristagoras away, offered to help, and soon thereafter they boarded hoplites on twenty ships and sailed to confront the awesome might of Persia.

PART III

PRELIMINARY MOVES

Chapter 10

PERSIA'S RETURN TO WAR

In 513 BC, Darius the "shopkeeper" returned to his true avocation—war. By doing so, he brought a halt to Persia's economic expansion, almost lost Persia's main field army, and set in motion the tide of events that would lead to war with Greece just two decades later. Historians have long debated what was behind Darius's invasion first of Thrace and then, more disastrously, of Scythia. The best explanation is that Darius had long looked toward the west as the next arena for Persian expansion. Now, with the empire's internal affairs finally settled and its other borders secured, it was time to prove he was every bit the conqueror Cyrus was. Moreover, Darius probably viewed Thrace as a secure base in Europe to support further Persian expansion to the west. Once Thrace was conquered, the march into Scythia seems a typical example of the mission creep that has found its way into almost every victorious campaign in history.

After crossing into Europe, Darius sent his fleet, almost all of it impressed from the Greek cities of Ionia, along the western coast of the Black Sea to the Danube River. Once there, the fleet sailed upriver for two days and constructed a bridge at the mouth of the Danube delta, where it waited for the arrival of the army. The tribes of southern Thrace, awed by the size of the Persian army, offered no resistance, and Darius's easy victories must have greatly encouraged him and his army. Only when they approached the Danube did they encounter the first serious resistance from the Getae. Of this tribe, Herodotus relates:

> The Getae, though they are the bravest and most just of the Thracians, adopted an attitude of foolish arrogance [to Darius] and were at once enslaved.[1]

With the Getae crushed, the Persian army crossed the Danube into Scythia.

Unfortunately, it is almost impossible to give more than the barest sketch of events that took place after Darius crossed the Danube into Scythian territory. To an even greater extent than is typical for most major events in ancient history, the course of the Scythian invasion is lost to us. What is absolutely known is that the expedition was a near disaster.

As his army marched away from the Danube, Darius left the Greek crews behind with their ships. Although Herodotus does not mention any Persian force being left behind, I find it unlikely that Darius would have marched off without leaving a loyal Persian force at the bridgehead to guard his baggage, protect the bridge, and keep a wary eye on the Greeks. It is almost inconceivable that a commander of Darius's proven ability would have left his base solely in the hands of the Greeks, the most unreliable element of his army.

The Scythians, alerted to a large army marching through Thrace, had plenty of time to mobilize a hot welcome for the Persians, who were probably overconfident after the easy destruction of Getae military power. Darius was probably caught by surprise at the size of the force the Scythians mobilized against him, the extent to which they had denuded the territory, and their elusiveness. Harried from the start by horse archers who could outrange his best bowmen, unable to gather supplies, and incapable of bringing his opponent to battle, Darius stubbornly persevered in his aim until he was threatened with his own annihilation.

It was at this point that one of the most important events in Herodotus's history takes place. With Darius's army in trouble on the north side of the Danube, a large Scythian cavalry force approached the bridgehead and bade the Greeks destroy the bridge, return to Ionia, and raise the banner of revolt. The Greeks were further informed that Darius and the Persians would be dealt with so that they could never make war on them again. According to Herodotus's version of events, the Greeks held a conference to discuss the proposal, whereupon Miltiades of Athens, who was then the tyrant of the Hellespontine Chersonese, initially persuaded most of the other Greeks to destroy the bridge. However, he was opposed by Histiaios, tyrant of Miletus. Histiaios reminded each of the Greek commanders that they were all tyrants of their own cities and held their grasp of power only through the support of Persian arms. If the Persians were overthrown, Histiaios told them, they would all be deposed. With their own best interest in mind, the Greeks voted to hold the bridge, although they did remove the portion within bow shot of the north shore. Disgusted, the Scythians departed, judging

> the Ionians as free men to be the most worthless and cowardly of
> the entire human race; but as slaves, to be the most fond of servility and the least likely to turn from their masters.[2]

Eventually, Darius and his haggard army reached the Danube. In the darkness, he was unable to see that only a portion of the bridge had been disassembled. With the Scythians closing in, there were a few panicked minutes before he realized the Greeks were still there and the bridge was being extended back to the north shore.

What makes this story important is that it is the first time Herodotus calls our full attention to Miltiades, who was later heralded as Athens's savior and served as a senior commander against the Persian army at Marathon. As we will see, upon his much later return to Athens, Miltiades was put on trial for his life, accused of being a tyrant and a supporter of the Persian king. The keystone of his defense was the claim that he had been the only Greek to advocate destroying the Danube bridge and therefore to leave the Persian army and its king to face certain destruction. It was a strong defense at the time and helped him pull off a surprise acquittal.

Historians have long puzzled over the truthfulness of Miltiades' account. How likely was it that he could have advocated stranding the Great King and then survived in power for almost another decade? One would assume such a traitor would have felt Darius's wrath soon after the king had returned to safety. This alone is sufficient reason to doubt Herodotus's account of what took place at the bridge and to believe instead that it is a fabrication Miltiades crafted to secure his acquittal.[3]

Most likely Miltiades fully supported the decision to hold the bridge for Darius. Word must certainly have reached the Greeks that Darius was in trouble somewhere deep in the Scythian hinterland. This news must have stirred the camp with excitement, and there were likely enough Greeks present to overpower whatever Persians Darius had left behind, although they could not be certain of success. The revolts of the Greek cities near the Bosporus, including Byzantium and Chalcedon, attest to the fact that news of the Persian army having met some kind of disaster in Scythia was spreading rapidly throughout the empire. It is unlikely these cities would have considered such a course if they feared the Persian army was still intact in nearby Thrace. However, the Greeks on the Danube lost nothing by staying in place a bit longer and risked much by sailing away. In the end, practical, selfish concerns won out and they stayed.

Several points of evidence lead us to conclude that Miltiades was lying at his trial. First, upon his return, Darius appeared to have been in a hurry to show himself alive and well in the heart of the empire. As the revolt in the Bosporus made it impossible to return by the most practical route, he instead crossed the Hellespont at Sestos, in the heart of Miltiades' domain. Darius, who returned to his western capital, Sardis, with only a small bodyguard, surely would not have been able to move through Miltiades' territory if his loyalty had been in doubt. Moreover, there were no Greek tyrants of this era who did not have enemies, and Miltiades had more than his share. In fact, some of his foremost rivals were at the bridgehead with him. If Miltiades had campaigned publicly for the destruction of the bridge, it would surely have come to Darius's attention. Given Darius's proven ruthlessness to his enemies, one would expect Miltiades' wellbeing to have suffered dramatically soon after Darius's return to the heart of his empire. Instead, Miltiades was soon back at the Chersonese, resuming his role as tyrant. Here he remained for at least the next fifteen years, a loyal supplicant of the Great King.

As Darius hastened to Sardis and eventually on to Susa, presumably to make sure reports of disaster did not spark a new round of civil war, he left a large force behind under a Persian general, Megabazos.[4] This force was charged with subjugating the rest of Thrace and was soon on the march. Although resistance was sometimes fierce, he was able to push as far west as the borders of Macedonia, which offered earth and water to the Persian king.[5]

That such a substantial Persian force still existed in Thrace is an indication that the Persian defeat north of the Danube was not as catastrophic as many historians have previously reported. However, it is also likely that the empire did not have any substantial forces in reserve for other duties, as it was at least two years before Megabazos's replacement, Otanes, could be sent with reinforcements to crush the revolts in Byzantium, Chalcedon, and other nearby Greek cities.

In the meantime, Darius had been rewarding those who had done him great service during the expedition. Among them was Histiaios, whom Darius credited with holding the bridgehead at the Danube for him.[6] When asked what he wanted as a reward, Histiaios requested and was granted the lands of Myrkinos in southern Thrace. As Megabazos was returning to Sardis with a portion of his army, he passed through this area and took careful note of the abundance of lumber-rich forests and silver mines in the region. He may also have noted Myrkinos's strong strategic position, as it was the key to control of the north Aegean islands and sat along all of the major east–west trade routes, including those leading to the gold-laden interior. Upon reaching Darius, he informed the king that Histiaios, once entrenched in this position, might make himself powerful enough to become a threat or at least a major inconvenience to the empire. Convinced, Darius sent for Histiaios and carted him off to Susa in gilded captivity as a royal adviser.

For at least the next decade, the mists of history enshroud events within the Persian Empire. We can assume that Darius presented his invasion of Thrace as a great success and returned his attention to consolidating his hold on power. Moreover, we know that Otanes was busy crushing revolts and bringing order to the northern frontier, which would keep the army occupied and distracted from mischief for most of this time. Beyond that, very little is known.

But stresses were building in certain portions of the empire, and in 499 BC, they boiled over in Ionia. Moreover, when the Ionians appealed to their brother Greeks to come to their aid against the Persians, the Athenians were quick to answer the call.

Chapter 11

IONIA REVOLTS

I n 499 BC, the Greek city-states of Ionia revolted against Persian rule, setting in motion the first great struggle between East and West. Herodotus has very little good to say about the conflict, describing the affair as an ill-considered enterprise doomed to failure from its inception. Given the final result, the revolt may well have been ill considered. However, as it took the Persians six years of near maximum effort to crush the revolt, Herodotus's claim that it was a doomed enterprise is doubtful.

The proximate cause of the revolt is easy enough to determine. The ruling party of Naxos, an Aegean island, was overthrown. The losers then went to Aristagoras, the tyrant of Miletus, to seek his help in regaining power. Thrilled at the notion that by helping the fallen oligarchs, he might gain control of what Herodotus describes as an island that "surpassed all other islands in its prosperity," Aristagoras asked the Persian satrap in Sardis, Artaphrenes, for permission to act. Artaphrenes was also enamored with the idea of seizing the richest trading city in the Aegean, which, as luck would have it, also provided an excellent jumping-off point for further conquests in Greece. But a major military expedition was beyond his personal authority, and he needed to consult Darius. After the Great King had given permission, Artaphrenes assembled an army and a fleet of two hundred ships. The combined forces, however, were placed under an awkward command relationship, where Aristagoras shared responsibility with Darius's cousin Megabates.

In all likelihood, a trading island like Naxos, with ships and trading agents in every port, would have noted preparations for such an extensive expedition as soon as they began. When the expedition arrived, its forces found the Naxians prepared and waiting. After a four-month siege, Aristagoras admitted defeat and departed.

Aristagoras was now in the unpleasant position of having commanded a fiasco. He undoubtedly understood that he would be on the losing side of any effort on the part of the Persians to find a scapegoat. According to Herodotus, at precisely this opportune moment, a message arrived from Histiaios ordering the rising of the banner of revolt.[1]

Histiaios's role in this entire affair is perplexing. He was the former tyrant of Miletus and the father-in-law of the current tyrant and failed military commander, Aristagoras. It will also be remembered that he was the Greek who had made the decisive argument at the Danube bridgehead to keep the bridge intact, making it possible for the Persian army to escape from difficulties ensuing from the ill-fated Scythian expedition. Initially, he had received the reward of the city of Myrkinos, but he was soon afterward ordered to Susa to become an adviser to Darius. Herodotus would have us believe that his decade of gilded captivity had chafed at him and that he had been working throughout most of this period to foment a revolt in his Ionian homeland. Later, when the revolt did begin, Histiaios supposedly convinced Darius that he could negotiate a peace if only he was allowed to return to Ionia.

Herodotus states that Histiaios's proposal to Darius was a ruse and that he always planned to take command of the revolt once he arrived in Ionia. Nevertheless, one wonders whether it is reasonable to believe that the man who held the Danube bridge for Darius, and who refused to rebel when he held a golden chance to destroy Darius and the Persian field army, would now seize a much more uncertain opportunity a decade later. Moreover, Histiaios, unlike most of his compatriots, had spent considerable time at the heart of the empire. He was in the unique position of being able to assess the might the Persians were capable of mobilizing in an emergency. It would take a very brave man or a fool to poke a finger in the eye of the man who wielded such power. The most likely case is that Histiaios made his offer to Darius in good faith, in hopes of further rewards and possibly reinstatement as tyrant of Miletus. However, upon his arrival in Ionia, he found himself trapped into rebellion by circumstances he had not foreseen.[2]

Accepting that Aristagoras, regardless of Histiaios's involvement, had personal reasons to lead a revolt and that he probably had the support of the army and fleet when it returned from Naxos, there is still one question Herodotus does not answer.[3] Why did Miletus and the rest of Ionia follow his lead?

Foremost among the reasons is economic decline. When the revolt broke out, the Ionian cities were most likely in a state of economic depression. They were trading cities, and their ability to trade was being severely curtailed. Sometimes this was the result of Persian actions, but most often it was due to changing circumstances. The rise of Carthage had closed off the western Mediterranean, while Phoenician traders, enjoying Darius's favor, were replacing the Ionians in many eastern Mediterranean ports. Moreover, cheaper high-quality wares from Egypt and the Black Sea coast were replacing many of the goods Ionia traded in.[4] Furthermore, Darius's conscription of ships and trained crews for various operations in Thrace and along the north shores of the Black Sea must also have been a constant disruption of Ionian trading activities.

The final factor was Darius's tax levy. By this time, it is likely that the Persian system for collecting revenue was operating with a high degree of efficiency. Considering their worsening economic plight, the Ionians must have found the four hundred talents demanded of them an excessive burden.[5] Darius's spending binge had ended long ago, and he now stored the bulk of these revenues in the royal treasury in Susa, while additional revenues collected in Ionia were spent well inland by the satrap in Sardis. As very little of these revenues ever made their way back into circulation in Ionia, the effect was to starve the Greek cities of liquidity. Soon enough, the entire Ionian economy seized up.

The Ionians blamed their dire economic condition both on the tyrants ruling their cities and on the Persians who kept them in power. They also would have been well aware of the tide of democratic ideas sweeping across Greece, which must have made an impression on them. Finally, we must throw in the effects of what we would call national feeling. Even after being under the Persian yoke for over fifty years, the Ionians must never have lacked adherents to the cause of freedom from the tyranny of an alien conqueror. This desire for independence must have been continually stoked or rekindled by the example of the free Greek cities just across the Aegean. Moreover, many Ionians interpreted the Persian defeat at Naxos as a sign of weakness. In the Ionian popular imagination, if the Naxians could hold the Persians at bay from behind their city walls, then they could do the same. Aristagoras may have lit the fuse, but the powder had been piling up for some time.

The leaders of the conspiracy met immediately after Aristagoras returned from Naxos. They voted unanimously to rebel, with the exception of the writer Hecataeus, who pointed out the vast wealth available to Darius compared with their own meager resources. After being outvoted, Hecataeus advised them to put their faith in controlling the sea, where the Persians were weak and by which means they could supply cities under Persian siege. He also advocated that the rebels immediately seize the great wealth stored in the temple to Zeus at Branchidae, to gain sufficient capital to wage a protracted war. Unwilling to commit such a great sacrilege, the rebel leaders voted down the proposal.

At first, things went well. The Persians, evidently surprised, failed to react immediately. The rebels overthrew the city tyrants but for the most part spared their lives and sent them into exile. The one exception was Koes, a strong supporter of Darius, whom the people of Mytilene stoned to death.[6] Aristagoras himself voluntarily laid down his position as tyrant and was immediately elected as a general. The rebellious cities made some efforts to coordinate their activities and did manage to create a standard currency from which to pay for soldiers and the maintenance of the fleet. However, they failed in two areas that later proved calamitous. The Ionians never created a combined field army under the command of a single general. Instead, each city opted to go its own way and provide as best it could for its own defense. The rebels compounded this error by failing to immediately expand the revolt into adjacent regions, particularly the Hellespont, the Bosporus, and Thrace. This was a major blunder, all the more remarkable as their actions in trying to involve mainland Greece in the quarrel make it obvious they understood that they could not hope to fend off or prevail against Persia on their own.

To make sure they did not have to go it alone, Aristagoras placed his brother, Charopinus, in charge and departed for Greece to enlist Sparta's aid. Upon arriving in Sparta, he met with King Cleomenes and initially interested him in an *anabasis* into the heart of the Persian Empire, which he portrayed as ready to crumble at the first push.[7] To help with his pitch, he brought a bronze tablet on which was engraved a map of the world. As he pointed at the map, Aristagoras explained the riches of Persia and how they were there for the taking. Cleomenes was almost sold, but he went off for three days to consider the matter further. When he met with Aristagoras again, he asked a practical question that had escaped him earlier: How far was it from the coast to Darius's capital at Susa? Upon being told it was a three-month march, Cleomenes hastily concluded the interview and went home. No Spartan king was going to lead an army ninety days from the coast and leave Sparta itself at the mercy of the helots or an attack from one of its many enemies in the Peloponnesus.

Not ready to give up, Aristagoras followed Cleomenes to his home and offered him the astronomical bribe of fifty talents to lead a Spartan army to Ionia. It was at this point that Cleomenes' daughter, the irrepressible Gorgo, told Cleomenes, "Father, your guest is going to corrupt you if you do not send him away immediately and stay away from him."[8] Pleased with his daughter's advice, Cleomenes left the room, and Aristagoras left Sparta. Gorgo is one of the few Greek women Herodotus mentions by name, and she is always described in flattering terms. She was later to become famous as the wife of King Leonidas, who led the Spartan three hundred in their last stand at the pass of Thermopylae. Plutarch also credits her with replying to the question "Why are you Spartan women the only ones who can rule your men?" with, "Because we are the only ones who give birth to men."

Aristagoras moved on to Athens. He arrived at an opportune time, as a Persian ultimatum had just reached the city. As will be remembered, when the former tyrant Hippias had left Sparta, after the failure of Cleomenes' second attempt to build a coalition to attack Athens, he went to the court of Artaphrenes at Sardis and enlisted the aid of the satrap. When envoys from Athens reached Sardis to convince Artaphrenes to ignore Hippias's entreaties, they were instead told that if they wanted to remain secure from Persian arms, they would have to accept Hippias, their former tyrant, back.[9] It was at this juncture that Aristagoras arrived and was permitted to speak to the assembly of Athenian citizens. Where he had failed with Cleomenes, he succeeded with a mob already angered by Persian threats. The Athenians voted to send twenty triremes and a small force of hoplites to Miletus, which, given the small size of the Athenian fleet at this time, was not an insignificant force.

In the spring of 498 BC, the twenty Athenian ships, joined by five triremes from Eretria, arrived in Miletus. Herodotus states that the Eretrians had sent the five ships unbidden to repay a debt they owed the Milesians, who had assisted the Eretrians in a war against Chalcis.[10] With this reinforcement, the Ionians determined to undertake the first offensive action of the war. After boarding their army on the fleet that had not yet disbanded following the attack on Naxos, they sailed north to Ephesus. From there they marched inland to Sardis, which they took without difficulty, except for the Acropolis, which Artaphrenes held with a large Persian force. Most of the houses in Sardis were constructed of reeds, and when one caught fire, by accident or design, the city went up in one huge conflagration. Almost immediately after the fire began, the Ionian army was set upon by Lydian and Persian forces "residing nearby" and had to make a fighting retreat to Mount Tmolus. Using the cover of night, they stole back to their ships.

Many historians have wondered how the Persians could have been caught so totally by surprise. The revolt was now many months old. What had the Persians been doing? In a much later history, Plutarch quotes an explanation from an otherwise unknown Greek writer, Lysanias of Mallus, that the reason the Persian army was not available to defend Sardis was that it was attacking the heart of the rebellion, Miletus.[11] Despite the unreliability of this evidence, most have accepted this version of events. Nevertheless, it is unconvincing. It is likely that Artaphrenes, in an attempt to crush the revolt in its infancy, would have sent all the forces at his disposal in a rapid assault on the rebel headquarters at Miletus. This would have been a hastily organized expedition that counted on overwhelming the rebels for success. Faced with the veterans of Naxos manning the walls, they would not have lingered long, as they would not have brought much in the way of supplies and were not equipped for a siege. They were also in all likelihood outnumbered and would not have been willing to stand in the open for a decisive fight. Moreover, if that army was still at Miletus when the Athenians arrived, it strains credulity to believe the rebel army would have sailed off to attack Sardis and hope that their own city would not fall while they were away. Knowing what we know about Greek methods of warfare and its hoplite tradition, if the Athenians arrived to find their enemy waiting to engage them, they would have marched out with the Milesians to offer immediate battle. At the time, it was the rare Greek force that could resist the call to decisive engagement.

So where was the Persian army when Sardis was burned? The answer must be that it was on hand. It is unlikely that the Greek army was forced to retreat to Mount Tmolus and had to sneak away in the night out of fear of some irate locals.[12] Furthermore, Darius states that the retreating Greeks were closely pursued by the Persians, who caught up with them at Ephesus. Here the Greeks turned to fight and suffered a sharp defeat. Herodotus states, "Many of them were slaughtered by the Persians. . . . Those who escaped from the battle dispersed as each one fled to his own city." In other words, the Greeks were routed. Even the Athenians sailed for home and refused any and all entreaties for further participation in the conflict.[13] The combined Athenian and Ionian force may have stolen a march on the Persians, who were caught napping. However, they were ready to react ferociously.[14]

Informed that an Athenian force had participated in the burning of one of his capital cities, Darius inquired about who they were. After being told, he

> took a bow, set the arrow on its string, and shot the arrow towards the heavens. As it flew high into the air, he said, "Zeus, let it be granted to me to punish the Athenians." After saying this, he appointed one of his attendants to repeat to him three times whenever his dinner was served: "My lord, remember the Athenians."[15]

Athens and Eretria may have retreated from Asia, not to return for a considerable period of time, but the burning of Sardis inflamed the imagination of the occupied lands in the Western Empire. The warlike Carians joined the revolt, along with Byzantium and many of the cities of the Hellespont. Moreover, Onesilos, the brother of one of the local tyrants in Cyprus, carried all of that island into revolt, with the exception of Amathus (a mostly Phoenician city), which he placed under siege.[16] The Persians reacted rapidly to the threat of losing Cyprus, which would have been a staggering strategic loss, as the island commanded the passages from Phoenicia and Ionia.

By now, the Persians, understanding the dimensions of the revolt and the immensity of the threat, had shaken off their lethargy. The full resources of the empire were mobilizing and were now aimed at Cyprus. Even as Onesilos prosecuted the siege of Amathus, word arrived that a Phoenician fleet and the Persian army were massing in Cilicia. Sensing their danger, the Cypriot rebels sent for help to the Ionians, who immediately dispatched their fleet to the island's assistance.

It was to no avail. While the Ionians were in harbor at Salamis (modern Famagusta), the Persians landed on the island's north shore and marched overland to Salamis. Simultaneously, the Phoenician fleet rounded the Keys of Cyprus and came on in full battle array. At sea, the Ionians had the better of the fighting, but Herodotus gives no details. As the Phoenician fleet does not return to the war for three years, one can assume that it suffered a crippling blow. But on land things did not go well for the rebels.

Onesilos drew up his forces somewhere on the central plain of that island, and the Cypriots likely had numbers on their side. However, they were facing a professional military force, fighting with the desperation of stranded men who knew defeat meant certain death for them all. After a desperate fight in which the rebels managed to kill the Persian commander, treachery resolved the issue. One of the local tyrants and his army deserted the battlefield, and the Cypriot war chariots followed their example. A general rout ensued, and soon thereafter the Cypriot cities each fell in short order. Only Soloi managed to hold out for five months before the Persians undermined its walls and sacked the city. The Ionian fleet, unable to influence events on land, had previously sailed for home.

Even as the Persians mobilized forces to retake Cyprus, other levies were called forth throughout the empire. It was now 496 BC, and these reinforcements were streaming into the theater of war. With these substantial new forces, Artaphrenes devised a strategy that would strip the Ionians of their recent allies, the Carians and the cities of the Hellespont. Three Persian generals, Daurises (son-in-law of Darius), Hymees (reputedly the commander who pushed the Greeks out of Sardis and defeated them at Ephesus), and Otanes (the general who replaced Megabazos in Thrace ten years before), were entrusted to undertake new operations.

The year's campaign began with Daurises leading an army into the Hellespont, where he met less than inspiring resistance. Five cities—Dardanos, Abydos, Perkote, Lampsacus, and Paisos—fell in as many days. But before he could finish his work in the region, Daurises received orders to march his army south to put down the Carian revolt. As he marched away, Hymees, who was operating farther to the east, had seized Kios, a key city on the south shore of the Sea of Marmara (the Propontis to Herodotus), and then marched his army into the Hellespont to subjugate the cities still in rebellion.[17]

Beating the Greeks was proving easy for Persia's professional warriors. However, the Carians were another matter, for they were the "wild geese" of their time. As G. B. Grundy states, "The Carians were not mere amateurs in the art of war, but numbered among them men who had seen fighting in many lands, the soldiers of fortune of their time. The race was infected with the strange fever which has at different periods driven members of some of the world's most virile peoples to seek their livelihood in quarrels not their own."[18] This was the type of man Daurises was now marching on, and he encountered their army on the banks of Marsyas

River. Herodotus reports that the battle was long and fierce, but the Persians eventually dealt the Carian force a shattering defeat, leaving ten thousand of their men dead on the field along with two thousand Persians.

The Carians reportedly retreated in despair, but after receiving reinforcements from nearby Miletus, they turned once again to face the Persians. This time, according to Herodotus, they suffered an even worse defeat, with the Milesians suffering by far the greatest loss. Herodotus's assessment of the results of these two battles is called into question by what happened next. The Persians, continuing their march toward the Carian cities, were caught by the regrouped Carian army in a night ambush. As Herodotus relates, "They stumbled into a trap and perished . . . so those Persians died."[19] Among the dead were many top Persian commanders, including Daurises. It was probably the worst defeat a Persian army had ever suffered in the field, leaving one to question how the Carians, having been bested in two fights to the extent Herodotus reports, could have inflicted so terrible a defeat. It is therefore not unreasonable to surmise that the Carians were defeated in two battles, but not as decisively as Herodotus states. Moreover, in the second battle the bulk of the casualties was probably sustained by the Milesians, leaving the Carians relatively undamaged. As both of these battles were hard contests, the Persians too must have suffered greatly. Herodotus does not provide a chronology for these events, but it is likely that a mauled Persian army would have taken some time to recover, which made it possible for the Carians to regroup and prepare a devastating welcome when the Persians once again continued their march.

Simultaneously with the operations conducted in Caria, Artaphrenes himself was with Otanes when his army struck due west to the Aegean. They soon captured the Ionian city of Cyme, which apparently did not offer serious resistance. This bold stroke cut Ionia in half. From this point, overland communications between the northern and southern Ionian cities became near impossible. For Aristagoras, the situation must have seemed desperate. All or most of the cities of the Hellespont and the Bosporus had returned to the Persian fold, and as Daurises' army had not yet been lost, matters did not look good in Caria, either. Moreover, horrible tales from the survivors of the Milesian force sent to Caria's aid must have greatly lowered the morale of the rebellion's leading city. With the rebellion foundering, Herodotus has Aristagoras play the coward and run off to Myrkinos, where he was killed in a battle with the Thracians. Modern historians, though, have been kinder to Aristagoras's reputation, claiming he probably went to Myrkinos in hopes of creating another strong-point for the rebellion, one well placed to supply food and silver to Ionia.

It was at this time that Histiaios (of Danube bridge fame) arrived in Sardis, after finally convincing Darius to send him to Ionia to negotiate a peace. In an audience with the satrap, Artaphrenes, he stated his astonishment that the Ionians would ever think of revolting against Persia's beneficial rule. Artaphrenes, unconvinced of Histiaios's sincerity, replied, "Histiaios, you stitched up the show and Aristagoras put it on."[20] If Artaphrenes had any evidence that this was the case, his close relationship with Darius would have availed Histiaios nothing. The Greek would have met his end then and there. Still, the accusation was alarming enough for Histiaios to flee the city for the coast. Upon arriving at Chios, he convinced the leaders, who were suspicious of his motives and feared he was an agent of the Persians, that he had supported the rebellion from the beginning.

Once ensconced in Chios, he attempted to correspond with some Persians in Sardis he believed were in favor of a negotiated settlement or willing to oppose Artaphrenes. However, his messenger was a Persian spy who delivered all of his letters to Artaphrenes, who directed them to be delivered and the replies returned to him. In short order, Artaphrenes had an accurate list of those ready to betray him and ordered a series of gruesome executions. This purge coupled with the destruction of one of their major field armies in Caria likely accounts for the lack of Persian military activity in 495 BC. The break in military operations does not, however, mean the Persians were inactive. Falling back on proven methods of dealing with an opponent who proved difficult to defeat in the field, the Persians bought off the exhausted Carians, who returned their loyalty to Persia and were thus allowed to seize and retain substantial holdings of their former ally Miletus. Even worse for the Ionian cause, Persia redoubled its mobilization efforts, rebuilt its field army, and assembled a great fleet in Phoenicia.

Thwarted in his attempts to make trouble in Sardis, Histiaios asked the Chians to support his return to Miletus. But the Milesians, just recently freed of the overbearing Aristagoras, were not willing to accept their former tyrant and closed their gates to him. When he tried to force them during the night, he was wounded in the scuffle. He then made his way back to Chios, but after finding himself unwelcome there, too, he went to Lesbos, which he convinced of his fidelity to the rebel cause. He was given eight triremes to command, but instead of taking these ships to the aid of the Ionian cities, about to face the greatest crisis of the war, he sailed toward Byzantium and became a pirate, doing much harm to the Ionian cause.[21]

Later, after the Ionians were defeated, the Persians captured Histiaios while he was leading a small force scavenging for food. He was brought before Artaphrenes, who, taking no chances that the Greek would convince Darius to spare him, had him immediately impaled.

While Histiaios caused what trouble he could in the Sea of Marmara, both Ionia and Persia spent 495 BC preparing for the climactic battle. Only eight Ionian cities led by Miletus and a few Aegean islands still fought on. Against them were ranged the combined fleets of the Levant, Egypt, Cilicia, and Cyprus: six hundred ships in all.[22] From Sardis marched the full strength of the Persian army, which had been mustering there in its multitudes for a year. No longer distracted by operations in the Hellespont or Caria, Artaphrenes concentrated his full might on his primary target—Miletus.

Through a supreme effort, the Greeks assembled the greatest fleet they had yet put to sea. Herodotus presents an exact tally of the contributions each of the parties made by those cities still carrying on the fight:

Miletus	80 ships
Priene	12 ships
Myous	3 ships
Teos	17 ships
Chios	100 ships
Erythrai	8 ships
Phocaea	3 ships
Lesbos	70 ships
Samos	60 ships
Total	353 ships

The small number of ships from some of the Ionian cities was probably the result of having to keep a large number of their men at home to guard each city's walls. Still, the Milesians, who were the most immediately threatened by the Persian army, knew that the decisive battle would occur at sea and managed to spare enough men from the walls to man eighty ships. With the Carians out of the fight, the Greeks did not attempt to place an army in the field, and each city saw to its own defense. All of their hopes therefore rested on the fleet, which made camp at the island of Lade (off the coast of Miletus) and waited.

The Persians came, but dealing with the Carians had taught them a lesson that would pay dividends for another two centuries—there were always a significant number of Greeks whom they could buy off. Fearful of the large Greek fleet that had decisively defeated them in their last encounter at Cyprus, the Persian force did not strike immediately. Rather, they had the deposed Ionian tyrants make contact with the forces of their respective cities and promise lenient terms if they were to desert the rebel cause. This carrot was offered alongside the threat of a gruesome stick in the event they fought on: "We shall lead you into captivity as slaves, and we shall turn your sons into eunuchs and drag your virgin daughters away to Bactria and give over your lands to others."

While the Persians waited for their bribes and threats to do their insidious work, they kept a close eye on the Greek fleet as it practiced its maneuvers. At first, they must have been impressed as the Greeks toiled long hours every day, but shortly the training regimen let up. If we are to believe Herodotus, the Greek crews, men who spent their lives at hard toil, wearied of practice and refused to train. They further claimed that it was wrong for them to follow the orders of the appointed commander, Dionysius of Phocaea, when he had brought only three ships to join them in the coming battle.

What are we to make of this? It is unlikely that the Ionians simply got tired of drilling, as Herodotus claims. To judge what was going on, one must look at matters from their viewpoint. After half a decade of war, they were further away from winning independence than ever. Now, despite having inflicted tremendous blows on the enemy's armies and fleets, the Persians had not become disheartened and given up the fight. Instead, they had patiently rebuilt their forces and come on stronger than ever. The Greeks were making one more supreme effort in the knowledge that defeat meant ruin, but with equal certainty that victory meant they would probably confront an even stronger Persian force the following year. Moreover, by this time the Persian army was probably besieging Miletus and controlled the shores. The task of feeding over fifty thousand unanticipated sailors would have been difficult under any circumstances, but with the Persians at the city walls it was impossible.[23] It would not have been long before the ships' crews were on short rations, which would account for their dissatisfaction with their appointed leaders. Moreover, the fleet remained crowded together in what must have been an unsanitary mass of humanity and a superb disease incubator. Under such circumstances, dissension was inevitable. Dispirited, dealing with gnawing hunger, and with sickness spreading, many began looking on the Persian offer with greater favor.

When the Samian fleet alerted its former tyrant that it was ready to desert, the Persians considered their work done. They sailed out to offer battle under the command of a Persian officer named Datis, who later commanded the Persian forces at Marathon, with a rising star, Mardonius, as his second in command. The 353 ships of the Greek fleet were waiting in a line that must have extended almost two miles. Aligned on the eastern wing, close to their own city, were the 80 ships of the Milesians. To their right were ships from Priene, followed in order by Myous, Teos, Chios, Erythrai, Phocaea, and Lesbos and with those of Samos anchoring the west wing.

As the battle lines closed, disaster struck. The Samians set their sails and made for home, using the same wind propelling the Persians forward to make good their escape. The Lesbians, seeing their flanks exposed by the Samians' treachery, also set their sails and escaped.[24] The remaining Greeks were doomed. Still, they fought hard and died hard, with the Chians particularly distinguishing themselves.

In the aftermath of battle, the Greek survivors made land at Ephesus, where the locals supposedly mistook them for raiders bent on seizing Ephesian women. Showing a ferocity they never displayed against the Persians, the Ephesian men sallied forth to slaughter the exhausted Chian crews. Interestingly, the Ephesians did not send any ships to join the Ionian fleet at Lade. It just might be that they had already made a deal with the Persians and thought that killing the Chian crews would gain them further favor with Darius. The tale of their mistakenly killing the Chians because they believed them to be raiders may then be considered a cover story created for a time when it was no longer wise to admit they had helped the Persians. Herodotus does report that the Greek commander, Dionysius, broke through the Persian battle line and with three ships eventually escaped to Sicily. Here he turned to a life of piracy but refused to plunder Greek shipping, opting to grow rich attacking only Carthaginian and Etruscan vessels.

The rest of the Ionian war is easily summed up. Miletus was taken by storm. As the leading city of the revolt, it was treated particularly harshly, and the majority of the inhabitants were either slaughtered or enslaved.[25] After Miletus's fall, all that was left for the Persians were mopping-up operations. In short order, each of the remaining Ionian cities either surrendered or fell by storm. At first, the Persians made good on their threats and enacted a policy of terror. According to Herodotus:

> For after they had completed the conquest of the cities, they picked out the most handsome boys and castrated them, making them eunuchs instead of males. And they dragged off the most beautiful virgins to the King. After they had carried out these threats, they also set fire to the cities and to their sanctuaries, too. Thus the Ionians were reduced to slavery for the third time, the first being at the hands of the Lydians, and then twice in succession by the Persians.[26]

Later tradition probably exaggerated the reprisals (except possibly in the case of Miletus), as in a very short time a level of normalcy returned. Just fourteen years later, Darius's successor, Xerxes, was confident enough of Ionian loyalty to place substantial levies on them for participation in the great invasion of Greece in 480 BC. In 492 BC, the Ionians must have been shocked when a new Persian military commander, Mardonius, the second in command at the Battle of Lade, replaced the recently reinstalled Ionian tyrants with democracies.[27] It is worth noting that these were democracies that were ruled by a king and his provincial governors. In this regard, they would be akin to the local democracies China allows many towns and cities, where voters are given a choice among various Communist Party members. Many times in history, appearance trumps reality. The Ionians may have been pleased with the appearance of democracy, but no one doubted who was truly running things.

Mardonius had under his command a new army, probably raised in the expectation that the Ionian revolt would continue another year, as well as numerous veterans of the earlier fighting who had not wished to be demobilized yet.[28] He took this army to the Hellespont and crossed into Thrace, which had broken away from Persian control during the Ionian revolt. The going was easy at first, and most of the cities and tribes in the region submitted without offering any resistance, including the Macedonians, who became, Herodotus says contemptuously, "slaves of the Persians."[29] Greek tradition says that Mardonius's true plan was to march into Greece in order to undertake the punishment of Eretria and Athens and that this aim was thwarted only by twin disasters that befell him in the fall of 492 BC.

While Mardonius's fleet was sailing around the treacherous waters of Mount Athos, a northeasterly gale struck it, wrecking three hundred ships and drowning many of their crews.[30] This disaster was followed by defeat on land, when his army was set upon by an unconquered Thracian tribe—the Byrogi—while it was encamped in Macedonia. According to Herodotus, the Byrogi "slaughtered many of them [Persians] and wounded Mardonius himself." It is likely that later Greek tradition magnified both of these disasters. Even Herodotus states that Mardonius did not leave the region until he had killed many of the Byrogi and enslaved the rest.[31] Given the lateness of the season, it would appear unlikely that Mardonius ever contemplated an invasion of Greece, and there is certainly no evidence that he had made any preparations to do so. The Greeks may have felt threatened by a large army so close to their northern borders, but it seems clear that Mardonius's only mission was to enforce Persian power in the lands that had previously submitted. In this, he thoroughly succeeded.

But Darius had not forgotten the insult that Athens and Eretria had offered him. All along the coast of the empire, ports were alive with shipbuilding activities, for Darius had ordered the construction of a great fleet, including special transports for his cavalry. Alongside this construction, the Persian general Datis began to gather the battle-hardened veterans of the Ionian revolt and Mardonius's expedition. As this irresistible force assembled, Darius sent forth his envoys to demand the tokens of submission from the Aegean islands and the Greek mainland cities. The answers came back: Many had submitted and sent back earth and water to Darius.

Sparta and Athens killed the Persian envoys.[32] For them, it would be war.

Chapter 12

SPARTA SAVES GREECE

After the Athenians abandoned their early intervention in the Ionian revolt, both they and the Spartans adamantly refused all entreaties to send reinforcements to their beleaguered Greek brethren. The ancient sources never make clear why both cities refused this aid, when it was obvious that the next object of Persian attention would be Greece proper. What appears to have happened is that the Spartans, deterred by the very size of the Persian Empire, refused to consider dispatching their army for a ninety-day march into Asia's hinterlands. As for Athens, there were many in the city who had always opposed an overt anti-Persian policy, and with the ruin of the first expedition, after torching Sardis, this party was in the ascendancy.

No doubt both reasons played a role in Athens's and Sparta's decisions to keep their armies close to home. However, there were more pressing reasons. For Sparta, the failure to rally its Peloponnesian allies for the attack on Athens years before was not just a diplomatic setback; it was a warning. Argos, Sparta's ancient and most dangerous rival in the Peloponnesus, was again on the rise, and it was beginning to flex its muscle. As long as the other cities in the Peloponnesus could turn to Argos for support and protection, they would always be able to thwart Spartan desires. Corinth made this explicit in 431 BC at the start of the Peloponnesian War, but it must have been a strong, if unspoken, factor in 496 BC, when the allies stood together and defied Spartan wishes. It was obvious to Cleomenes that if Spartan supremacy was to be made real, Sparta would have to humble Argos again, and it would have to be done with a purely Spartan army. As for Athens, it had troubles of its own. Thebes and Chalcis had sued for peace, but Aegina was still prosecuting its war against Athens. The Athenians could have dealt with Aegina, and would later do so decisively, but with a restive Thebes to the north and Spartan intentions uncertain, it could not focus on its immediate enemy. Moreover, Aegina was the preeminent naval power in the region, and it would be another decade before Athens could afford to assemble a fleet powerful enough to contest the seas.

The Persians were certainly aware of these Greek conflicts, and they were quick to employ their established diplomatic practice of playing potential foes off against one another during the run-up to war. In fact, Aegina was to offer earth and water and become a Persian ally in the year before the Battle of Marathon, and Argos (along with Thebes) Medized during the Persian invasion of 480 BC. As both Athens and Sparta understood the magnitude of the Persian forces that would march on Greece as soon as they had subdued Ionia, it was imperative for them to put their own houses in order. The odds of defeating the Persian Empire already appeared slim, but they would be much worse if the Spartan and Athenian hoplites also had to worry about being stabbed in the back by another Greek city. They needed to clear the decks before the Persian onslaught. It was at this point that Sparta made its great contribution to Greek independence.[1]

It had been fifty years since the Spartans and Argives had fought the Battle of the 300 Champions, which had led to a general engagement of both cities' main armies. This had resulted in the breaking of Argos as a military power and the ceding of Thyrea to Sparta. Argos had spent the intervening five decades restoring its military power, and by 494 BC it felt ready once again to contest Sparta for supremacy of the Peloponnesus. In keeping with Spartan tradition and piety, Cleomenes consulted the oracle at Delphi on the advisability of attacking Argos. For once, the notoriously ambiguous oracle was the model of clarity: Cleomenes would defeat Argos.[2]

In 494 BC, Cleomenes once again led the Spartan army out on campaign.[3] This time, there was no call for the Peloponnesian allies to come to Sparta's aid. Sparta would deal with this affair on its own. Cleomenes led the army to the banks of the Erasinos River, approximately three miles south of Argos, where he found the Argive hoplites massed, prepared to contest his crossing. Cleomenes ordered a sacrifice and the omens read. However, these were not found favorable, and Cleomenes was informed that the river would not care to be crossed at present. To this he responded, "How patriotic of it."[4]

Although he was reluctant to test the omen and tempt the fates, he was not ready to give up the campaign. In fact, Cleomenes appears to have been prepared to find the direct route to Argos barred to him. As the Argives, sheltering behind the Erasinos, had no knowledge of these bad omens, they remained at their posts as Cleomenes marched his army away from the Erasinos to the coast of Thyrea. Here, Aeginetan and Sicyonian vessels waited to ferry the Spartans across the gulf to Nauplia and into the rear of the Argive army. That the Spartans had massed these ships exactly where Cleomenes needed them indicates that this was a well-thought-out campaign many months or years in the planning. It also demonstrates that the march to the Erasinos may have been a feint, designed to draw the Argives away from the true direction of the Spartan attack. In this case, one may infer that Cleomenes might well have paid for the omens he desired, although that would go against what we know of Spartan piety.

When news of the Spartan landing reached the Argives, they force marched to Tiryns and deployed at Sepeia. For several days, the armies watched each other without engaging, until Cleomenes noticed the Argives had entered into a routine he could exploit. Day after day, both armies stood to arms from daybreak until the noon meal (there was no breakfast). Cleomenes noted that the Argives soon began mimicking his army and were using Spartan bugle calls to alert them when the Spartan army was about to break for the day. When Spartan bugles called for assembly, the Argives assembled and stood to, and when the bugles announced dinner, the Argives broke ranks and ate, just as the Spartans were doing. On the appointed day, Cleomenes had the bugles blow assembly as usual. All day, both armies baked in the hot sun as gleaming ranks faced each other. When the appointed hour arrived, the Spartan bugles made the meal call. Both armies began to break up and go to eat. But without warning or any signal, the Spartans hastily re-formed and advanced. Caught unprepared, the Argives could not reassemble their phalanx and were crushed.

Plutarch presents a different version. According to him, the Argives had asked for and received a seven-day armistice, but on the third night of that truce, the Spartans attacked. When someone later reproached Cleomenes for this violation of an oath, he said that he had made a truce for days but had said nothing about nights.[5] In this same passage, when asked why he had not slaughtered all the people of Argos, Cleomenes replied, "Oh, we will not kill them off, for we want to have some left for our young men to train on."[6]

The Argive survivors retreated into the sacred Grove of Argos, where the pious Spartans refused to follow. Instead, they blockaded the grove, and at length Cleomenes inquired of several deserters the names of some of the Argives huddled in the forest. He then had heralds call into the forest the names of these men, informing them that their ransom had been paid and they were free to go. As each emerged, the Spartans murdered him. Approximately fifty Argives met this gruesome end before the Argives discovered what was happening and refused to emerge from the forest. At his wits' end, Cleomenes ordered helots traveling with the army to pile brush around the grove and set it afire. In this way, any guilt (and accompanying curses) for the sacrilege of burning down a sacred grove would fall on the helots, not on the Spartans. When the hideous deed was done, some six thousand Argive hoplites had perished in the battle and fire. Sparta had broken Argive power. The city would not assert itself again for over a generation.

Sparta was now undisputed master of the Peloponnesus and the dominant military power in Greece. In acknowledgment of this fact, Athens in 491 BC sent envoys to Sparta to request help with their problems with Aegina.[7] By this time, Aegina was a member of the Peloponnesian League, as evidenced by its contribution of ships to assist Cleomenes' end run around the Argive army. However, it was also a trading city, with substantial interests along the coasts of the Persian Empire. Thus, when Darius's heralds arrived in the wake of the Ionian revolt's collapse, demanding earth and water, Aegina submitted. By now, the Athenians had become convinced that Mardonius's march through Thrace, in the wake of Ionia's defeat, was a prelude to a Persian descent on Greece. Even though that expedition had met with disaster off Mount Athos, the Athenians were acutely aware that Persia was already constructing a fleet and assembling an army in Ionia aimed directly at them. As far as they could see, Aegina's submission meant the Aeginetans planned to stab them (and Greece) in the back as they confronted the Persian foe. Even the Spartans became worried about Aegina's intentions, and Cleomenes decided it needed to be coerced back into line.

On his own (probably with his elite bodyguard), he went to Aegina and demanded hostages to ensure its good conduct. However, his co-king, Demaratus, once again wrecked his plans. He sent a message to Aegina's leader, Krios, that he did not support Cleomenes' action. Here we are left to wonder whether Demaratus hated Cleomenes so much that he would oppose any policy his co-king offered. Assuming he was a loyal Spartan, the only other explanation is that he believed Sparta could not stand against Persia's might.[8] Whatever his reasons, he succeeded in pulling the rug out from under Cleomenes. Krios asked if he had the full support of the other Spartans or if he was acting in this fashion because Athens had bribed him with silver. Lacking support at home and with few troops, Cleomenes gave up. But before leaving, he told Krios (which means "ram"), in a play on his name, "to gild his horns and enjoy his moment." In religious rites, the Greeks gilded a sacrificial ram's horns just prior to leading the animal to slaughter. Humiliated once again through the actions of Demaratus, Cleomenes returned to Sparta in a rage, determined to have Demaratus deposed.

When Demaratus was born, his father, Ariston, was told of the birth while meeting with the ephors. After counting out the months of his marriage on his fingers, he swore an oath: "He could not be my son." Later he decided the birth had been premature, but the seeds of doubt were planted. Now, Cleomenes used that doubt to claim Demaratus was not a rightful king. In this he received the assistance of Leotychidas, who was next in line for the throne and had other reasons to detest Demaratus.[9] At trial, Leotychidas both prosecuted the case and swore an oath that Demaratus was not the true son of Ariston. When the trial ended, the Spartans remained undecided. At Cleomenes' suggestion, they sent emissaries to consult the oracle at Delphi. Here, Cleomenes had already prepared the ground, so he was not surprised when the oracle proclaimed that Demaratus was not the son of Ariston. With that, the Spartans deposed Demaratus. Soon thereafter, after suffering intolerable taunts from Leotychidas, Demaratus left Sparta and took up residence in the Persian court. When he is next heard from, he is accompanying Xerxes as an adviser during the invasion of 480 BC.[10]

Cleomenes wasted no time returning to Aegina, this time with Leotychidas alongside him. Standing up to Sparta when it was of two minds on a matter was one thing. It was quite different to consider making a stand when confronted by the unified will of both kings. With no opposition, Cleomenes seized Krios and nine other Aeginetan leaders as hostages. However, he did not bring them back to Sparta. Instead, he turned them over to their mortal enemy Athens. Herodotus tells us that when Cleomenes returned to Sparta, the Spartan assembly discovered that he had bribed the oracle as part of his plan to depose Demaratus. Fearing punishment, Cleomenes withdrew from Sparta and went to Arcadia, where he began to stir up a revolt against Sparta. Since we do not know anything more than this fact, we may deduce that his likely intent was to raise a force sufficiently large to cause the Spartans to invite him back to resume his position rather than risk a major revolt of the helots. So when word came that Sparta wanted him to return, he must have thought his plan had succeeded. Once he arrived, however, the Spartans seized him and placed him in stocks, where he later committed suicide or was murdered. Herodotus tells us that the Spartans locked him up because he had gone insane from drinking too much unadulterated wine, whereupon he threatened a helot standing nearby until the panicked man gave him a knife, with which he mutilated himself. Whatever the cause of Cleomenes' death, it was an inglorious end for the man who made Sparta the greatest power in Greece.[11]

Soon after hearing of Cleomenes' death, Aegina sent a delegation to Sparta to denounce Leotychidas for turning over their leading citizens to the hated Athenians, despite the fact that Aegina was a member in good standing of the Peloponnesian League. Leotychidas, who was already under severe criticism for having gained the throne through deceitful methods, was put on trial. The Spartans found that Leotychidas did indeed inflict a grievous insult upon the Aeginetans and decided to hand him over to them for punishment. As the Aeginetans led their captive away, a Spartan of some distinction, Theasides, arose and said: "What are you planning to do, Aeginetans? Will you really seize the king of the Spartans now being surrendered by his own citizens? Even if the Spartans made this decision in anger, you, if you do this, will have to worry that they will later repent it and invade and utterly destroy your land."[12] Upon further reconsideration, the Aeginetans thought better of punishing a Spartan king and asked Leotychidas to go with them to Athens to plead for the release of the hostages.

When the Athenians refused to release the hostages, the Aeginetans retaliated by seizing a sacred vessel carrying many important Athenians returning from a religious festival. This led to a renewed round of warfare between Aegina and Athens on the very eve of the Persian invasion. As the war went against Aegina, they sent to Argos for help. After losing three-quarters of its hoplites at the Battle of Sepeia, Argos had little to offer. It did, however, allow volunteers to go to Aegina, and one thousand men went. Herodotus tells us that few of them ever returned, as they were killed by the Athenians in a great battle on Aegina. Besides recording some inconsequential fighting at sea, Herodotus tells nothing of this last phase of the war with Aegina, in favor of his starting the story of the Marathon campaign.[13]

What are we to make of this? For one thing, we know the Athenians invaded Aegina and won a battle decisively enough to kill most of the thousand Argives present, which would indicate that the Aeginetans must have suffered great losses as well. As the Athenians referred to this stage of the conflict as the "War of Reprisal," we have some indication of how incensed they were over the Aeginetans' attack on their religious leaders. It also provides some insight into the frame of mind of the hoplites who landed on Aegina. One can assume that the Athenians freed the hostages seized by the Aeginetans, while continuing to hold on to their own hostages.

We are also presented further proof, if more is required, that the Athenians who fought at Marathon were much more than simple farmers. And once again we see the hand of a supremely talented military commander at the tiller. With virtually no notice, someone (one can assume it is Callimachus) organized a large amphibious expedition, invaded a well-defended island, defeated a reinforced Aeginetan army, and returned in time to prepare to meet the Persians. As for the quality of the veteran Athenian hoplites, they appear to have had no trouble crushing the Aeginetan army in short order.

While Athens was embroiled in the war with Aegina, Miltiades returned home from the Chersonese. Despite the likelihood that Miltiades' reputation as the general who led Athens to victory at Marathon was a result of later propaganda, there is no denying that he figures prominently in every account of the battle from Herodotus to the present. It is therefore advantageous to relate some of the details of Miltiades' remarkable career. His uncle Miltiades the Elder had been sent to the Chersonese by Pisistratus to rule as a tyrant and protect Athenian interests in that strategic location. Miltiades the Elder was succeeded by his stepbrother Cimon's son Stesagoras. Miltiades the Younger (of Marathon fame) in turn replaced Stesagoras.

Miltiades' father, Cimon, was a powerful member of the Philaidae clan who apparently got involved in the succession struggle following the death of Pisistratus. It appears that he was a dangerous enough rival to warrant assassination, probably on the orders of Hippias. However, Hippias, after securing a firm hold on power, treated Cimon's son Miltiades well and even had him sworn in as an archon in 525/524 BC. In 516 BC, he sent Miltiades to rule the Chersonese, after the murder of his brother Stesagoras during a war with Lampsacus. Miltiades seized power in the Chersonese in a coup and then secured it by marrying the daughter of a Thracian king and surrounding himself with five hundred mercenaries. Although he apparently did his best to protect Athenian interests, the expansion of Persian power into the region circumscribed his ability to act independently. In 514 BC, he led a contingent in support of Darius's Scythian expedition and according to his personal testimony was a key participant in the debates over whether to destroy the bridge over the Danube and leave the Persian army trapped in Scythia. As noted earlier, the role he presented for himself was likely a fabrication. At some point during the Ionian revolt, Miltiades took advantage of Persia's distraction to seize the Persian-held islands of Lemnos and Imbros in Athens's name.[14]

When the Ionian revolt finally collapsed, Persia rewarded those who had remained loyal (or cut a deal during the war, as the Carians apparently did) and punished the others. Owing to his seizure of the two islands, Miltiades was definitely on the list of those who no longer enjoyed Darius's favor. As a result, as Mardonius pushed north with the Persian fleet, recently victorious at the Battle of Lade, Miltiades prepared his escape. After loading four ships with his personal goods and treasure, Miltiades fled. The Persians overtook one of the ships and captured Metiochos, one of Miltiades' sons. Metiochos was taken to Darius's court, where he was kept in honorable condition as a "guest" of Persia for the remainder of his life.[15]

Athens did not greet the tyrant of the Chersonese warmly. In fact, his arrival precipitated a political crisis. Although Cleisthenes was no longer on the scene, his Alcmaeonidae clan still controlled the government. Now, Miltiades—a Philaidae and a relative of Isagoras, whom Cleisthenes had deposed—was in their midst and making a grab for power. Miltiades' family connections and social rank made him a favorite of the nobility, while his advocacy for expanded trade made him attractive to tradesmen and merchants. On the other side, the government (Alcmaeonidae) could count on the multitudes of farmers and the previously disenfranchised for support. Moreover, when he arrived, Athens was in the throes of a great debate as to whether to submit to Persia or resist. Miltiades was firmly in the camp of the resisters, while the Alcmaeonidae government was tilting toward submission. In any event, Miltiades won election as a general of his own tribe, Oeneis, and began to increase his power base.

Those who were comfortable with the status quo and saw no place within it for Miltiades now put him on trial for his life. They charged him with being a tyrant in the Chersonese, but it is hard to see how this was a capital offense in Athens or even how it was a crime to rule over Thracians. In all likelihood, as a Thracian tribe (the Dolonci) had invited him back after the Scythians had driven him off, he could legally have been viewed as a Thracian tyrant ruling over Athenian colonists. Fortunately, Themistocles, the future hero of Salamis and the man who rallied Greece to resist Xerxes in 480, was the archon that year. As he came to wealth and power as a result of the reforms of Pisistratus, he was considered a "new man." He was also rabidly anti-Persian. For him, Miltiades' political allegiance was secondary to the fact that he was reliably anti-Persian.[16] With Themistocles' strong support and influence, the Athenians acquitted Miltiades.

It was not a moment too soon, for the great Persian invasion force was already weighing anchor and heading for Greece. When they arrived, they would find both of their Greek allies, Argos and Aegina, humbled by Spartan and Athenian arms. Moreover, both Sparta and Athens, after a long period of brutal political infighting, had at the last moment achieved a tenuous alliance.

PART IV

WAYS OF WAR

Chapter 13

GIANT VS. LILLIPUTIAN

In the fifth century BC, Persia was the sole superpower. Its landmass covered 7.5 million square miles, reaching from the Aegean to India, and its population was probably in excess of 40 million. Measured against that standard, Athens was feeble.[1] All of Attica consisted of less than 4,000 square miles, and in 490 BC probably only about 150,000 citizens lived on this land.[2] No wonder so many historians considered Athens's stand a hopeless cause and its victory akin to a miracle. What is therefore no less remarkable is that Athens, with a full understanding of Persian power, still decided to stand against the titan. Or did Athens know something that has been overlooked by later commentators?

The first thing to understand about ancient empires is that the latent power that appears available from a cursory examination is, in fact, illusory. Not discounting the organizational achievements of Darius, it is fair to say that the Roman Empire centuries later possessed a superior organization. Despite this, Rome, even at the height of its power, normally maintained less than 2 percent of its empire's total population under arms and could sustain only 3 percent mobilization for limited periods of time.[3] It is safe to assume that because of its inferior organization, the Persian Empire would strain to maintain 2 percent of its population under arms. Moreover, throughout most of history, at least until the Industrial Revolution, the bulk of the population survived at the barest subsistence level; even the slightest change in conditions could bring on famine. These societies required every hand in the fields, and only a small proportion were available for military uses.[4] Two percent of the population of Persia still equates to eight hundred thousand men. But this is a high estimate of

Persian capabilities, and there is reason to believe that the Persians failed to approach these levels.

Darius, who had come to power by way of a military coup, knew better than anyone the danger of maintaining large standing forces without an external enemy to hold their attention. Therefore Persia's permanent military establishment was always small and depended on local levies in the event of war. One has only to look at how long it took to mobilize sufficient forces to crush the Ionian revolt, or the expectation of all involved that the Persian Empire would collapse if it lost its field army in Scythia, to see how dependent it was on local levies.

This was not the end of Persia's problems, though, as its frontiers were not secure. Thrace remained restive, and beyond the Danube, the Scythians were still waiting for opportunities to attack the empire, while their kin on Persia's northeastern borders were always ready to sweep down on the empire's fertile plains. Keeping these enemies in check required well-garrisoned fortresses as well as a mobile field force large enough to effectively counter any major incursion. Moreover, all the other frontiers of the empire also required permanently stationed troops. Furthermore, the Ionian revolt was a reminder, if one was needed, that a number of subject peoples within the polyglot empire were looking for any sign of weakness to make their own bid for independence. To forestall this, Darius had to keep numerous large royal garrisons in major cities and at key geographic locations.

Finally, one must never lose sight of the cost and logistical difficulties of sending an expeditionary army far from the center of power. Again, the Roman example is instructive. When Caesar began the conquest of Gaul, he had only six legions, with probably an equal number of auxiliaries, for a total force of about 35,000 men. It is doubtful that he ever had more than 50,000 legionnaires during the entire war. Similarly, Crassus, when he set out to conquer the Parthian Empire, led out only 45,000 legionnaires. Even the more resilient and aggressive early republic had great difficulty sending substantial forces far from Italy. Although republican Rome could maintain over 100,000 troops facing Hannibal in Italy for sixteen years, it strained every resource to maintain a mere 30,000 in nearby Africa for the decisive campaign that finally vanquished Hannibal at the Battle of Zama. In summary, if the most efficient and warlike empire of the ancient world could sustain only 50,000 troops on distant campaigns, can one reasonably expect the Persians could do much better? That they managed to double this number for Xerxes' 480 BC campaign reflects the fact that the Persians spent almost half a decade preparing and that they expected this to be a lightning campaign, which would allow for the demobilization of most of the army in a short period of time.[5] More than any other factor, the inability of Persia to maintain a large expeditionary force for more than a single campaigning season accounts for Xerxes' departure with probably half the army before it had suffered any major setback on land.

When judging how much power Darius could throw against Greece, one must never lose sight of the fact that the Persian Empire had just finished crushing the Ionians, after enduring what must be judged as catastrophic costs. Victory had taken over half a decade, and in the process Persia had lost two fleets and probably had one more extensively damaged at the Battle of Lade. Furthermore, the Carians had annihilated one field army, and thousands more Persians must have fallen in other operations. On top of this, a substantial part of the empire—previously the richest portion—lay in ruins. As it was from this region (Ionia) that the Persians expected to draw the bulk of the matériel support required for an invasion of Greece, its ruin was a severe drag on preparations.

On the other side of the equation, the Persians could probably forgo the calling up of new and untried levies. The veterans of the Ionian campaigns (probably with a number of defeated Ionians among them) and Mardonius's campaign in Thrace were still available, and Athens offered rich booty. As very few of these men would have been survivors of the Carian disaster, this army would have never tasted defeat. Inured to hard conditions and familiar to combat, these men represented a formidable foe.

Given all this, and extrapolating from the best available estimates as to the size of Persian armies during the campaigns in Thrace and Ionia, a supreme Persian effort could have fielded at best forty thousand troops and possibly as many or a bit more sailors for a campaign in 490 BC.[6] It is almost inconceivable that the Athenians—living in the period, having experienced personally the difficulties of campaigning, and having a number of citizens (not least of whom was Miltiades) with substantial experience with the Persian army—were not aware of these factors and limitations. Still, forty thousand troops and a similar number of sailors was a huge force. In fact, it was several times larger than the entire hoplite class of Attica. Thus the great question remains: What advantages did Athens have that convinced its citizens that making a stand would be more than a forlorn hope?

The most important factor was that Athens was going to fight this war on its home ground and would therefore be able to mobilize a far higher percentage of its population than Persia. If we accept a total population of Attica of 150,000, that would mean there were approximately 30,000–35,000 men of combat age.[7] Of these, Athens could probably afford to equip 14,000 of them as hoplites, possibly a few thousand more, depending on the amount of war booty they had collected in previous years. Consequently, the fact that there were only 9,000 Athenian hoplites at Marathon requires an explanation. Most probably the hoplites at Marathon did not represent all who were available to Athens, although they may have been the best of them. Moreover, the road from Marathon, guarded by the bulk of the Athenian army, was indeed the easiest route to Athens, but not the only one. Other roads and even paths (the Persians proved at Thermopylae that access to a goat path was enough for them to inflict a nasty surprise on an enemy) required strong garrisons. The same was true of key positions along the coast, in order to prevent the Persians from making an amphibious end run around the Athenian encampment.

But could Athens afford 14,000 Hoplites? The answer is yes. During this time, a hoplite was expected to supply, at his own expense, his armor and weapons. This cost was not insignificant and was a strong limiting factor in the size of the armies of many Greek cities. However, a number of factors would have made it easier for many Athenians to afford the hoplite panoply. Foremost among these were the land reforms of Pisistratus. By breaking up the nobles' large estates, he had provided thousands of the poor and landless with enough property to produce a surplus of food for sale in the city. This surplus was sufficient for thousands of yeoman farmers to purchase armor and join the privileged ranks of hoplites.[8] As Attica transitioned its fields from grain to olives, the surplus created by trading would have been even greater. Revenues from an olive-based trade would also have enabled a number of city and coastal dwellers to enter the hoplite class. Furthermore, although the Athenians discovered the richest veins in the Laurion silver mines a few years later, the mines still produced sufficient silver for the government to subsidize some hoplites if necessary. While there is no record of the state giving or loaning cash to purchase armor, there is substantial evidence of numerous loans for farming and other business activities, which amounts to the same thing. It would be odd indeed if a city that had been almost constantly at war for two decades did not do all within its power to increase the size of its main fighting force.

These constant wars had led to at least three battles that Athens won decisively. Although it is hard to estimate the total numbers of enemy casualties, we know that seven hundred Thebans were captured in one battle, and consequently one may safely assume that twice that number were killed. Moreover, the Athenians had beaten Chalcis's army so severely that the city immediately withdrew from the war. As Athens no longer rated Chalcis a threat, it must have demobilized most of its military establishment—that is, turned over its armor and weapons. Megara, a city about the same size as Chalcis, was able to field three thousand hoplites in 480 BC, so that is probably a fair estimate of the size of Chalcis's army. Finally, one thousand Argive hoplites and an unknown number of Aeginetans were killed in battle against the Athenians in the year before Marathon. A conservative guess is that over the years, Athens easily collected enough armor from its enemies to outfit approximately eight thousand hoplites. From this, it would seem that the normally expensive hoplite panoply was probably available in Athens at drastically reduced prices.[9]

However, this is not the end of Athens's mobilization. As the Battle of Marathon was fought after the harvest, the rest of the male population of Attica was also available for military duty. These were mostly the *thetes* class of poorer citizens and often used as light troops.[10] Herodotus does not mention these light troops as being present at Marathon, but it is unlikely they would have remained behind, particularly as an even lower class—slaves—did fight in the battle. Like the contemporary accounts of medieval battles, which habitually left out the contributions of peasants and foot soldiers in favor of the deeds of the heavy cavalry (knights), Herodotus probably did not believe the participation of these citizens of any account. Yet any reasonable reconstruction of the events of the battle requires their presence and active participation in critical roles.

Although slaves were normally forbidden from participation in combat, they were present at every major battle, and in emergencies they could be freed and permitted to fight in the ranks.[11] Under any circumstances, slaves would have been present to prepare food, rescue wounded men, serve as attendants, and most important act as baggage carriers and caretakers for the hoplites' armor.[12] However, if Athens ever faced an emergency, Marathon was it. It is likely that in this crisis the Athenians would have released at least a portion of their slaves for combat duties, and evidence for this exists. Pausanias states that during his travels he saw the common grave of the Plataeans and "servants" killed at Marathon.[13] There is no way to know the number of slaves and recently freedmen who

traveled with the army, but several thousand would seem a reasonable estimate.

So in practical terms, Athens could field a fighting force at least nu-
merically equal to what the Persians were capable of throwing at Greece
in 491 BC. Most important, the core of the Athenian army consisted of
nine thousand heavily armored hoplites. The key point that deserves em-
phasis is that this was a veteran force. In recent years, it had humbled
Thebes, Chalcis, and Aegina and faced down a Spartan army, which in itself was no mean achievement. For almost twenty years Athens had been
a nation in arms, surrounded by enemies waiting to pounce—the Israel of
its age. One should not underestimate the confidence this would have
given the average Athenian hoplite. Furthermore, the Athenian army's
high level of training allowed its leaders to plan a maneuver even the Spartans would have found difficult, if not impossible—one that would make
them victorious at Marathon.

The Athenian victory was indeed stunning. However, any reasonable assessment makes it clear that as long as Athens stood on the strategic defensive, the deck was not as stacked against it as is typically assumed.

Chapter 14

PERSIAN WARFARE

Mesopotamia was more than the "cradle of civilization." It was also the "cradle of war." From the moment humans first settled into organized communities, civilization and warfare have found themselves inextricably entwined. Along the Tigris and Euphrates rivers, great empires rose and fell based on the fortunes of battle and the tides of war. Unfortunately, most of the tales of these three millennia of unrelenting carnage have disappeared into the mists of history. But despite all that has vanished, the story of one empire still reaches across the chasm of three thousand years as the embodiment of what can be built through a policy of blood and iron and maintained through war and savage cruelty—Assyria.[1]

Even at the zenith of its power, with all of the great Mesopotamian states under its dominion, Assyria remained continuously at war either against new threats on its expanding frontiers or putting down revolts among the restless people within its empire. Between 900 and 650 BC, the height of Assyrian power, the empire engaged in no fewer than 108 conflicts as well as innumerable punitive expeditions against neighboring peoples and to punish for internal revolts.[2] Their brutal method of warfare is best described by their own words. King Sennacherib (704–681 BC) describes a battle with the Elamites in 691 BC:

> At the command of the god Ashur, the great Lord, I rushed upon the enemy like the approach of a hurricane. . . . I put them to rout and turned them back. I transfixed the troops of the enemy with javelins and arrows. . . . I cut their throats like sheep. . . . My prancing steeds, trained to harness, plunged into their welling

blood as into a river; the wheels of my battle chariot were be-
spattered with blood and filth. I filled the plain with the corpses
of their warriors like herbage. . . . As to the lords of the
Chaldeans, panic from my onslaught overwhelmed them like a
demon. They abandoned their tents and fled for their lives,
crushing the corpses of their troop as they went. . . . In their terror they passed scalding urine and voided their excrement into
their chariots. Attack by foot soldiers, using mines, breaches as
well as sapper work. I drove out of them 200,150 people, young
and old, male and female, horses, mules, donkeys, camels, big and
small cattle beyond counting, and considered them booty. Himself I made a prisoner in Jerusalem, his royal residence, like a bird
in a cage.[3]

When Cyrus began his campaigns of conquests, he did not have anything approaching the financial or material resources required to build a
professional organized force along the Assyrian model. Rather, he had the
kara, which loosely translated meant the warriors of his tribe, his friends,
and any other warriors his kin were able to gather. However, soon after
Persia absorbed the Median Empire, Cyrus immediately reorganized the
kara along the lines of the professional Median army (called the *spada*).
By integrating the Persian *kara* into the Median *spada* and adopting most
of the Medes' battle methods, the Persians became the inheritors of all the
Assyrians had learned of warfare.

Cyrus's new *spada* consisted of cavalry, horse archers, foot archers, and
infantry. This appears to be the same organization that the Median king
Cyaxares had copied from the Assyrians, who were the first to organize
regiments based on their specific arms.[4] Moreover, by taking advantage of
Assyria's experience and knowledge in terms of how to take a fortified
city, the Persians built and maintained a superb siege train for use in any
prolonged campaign. Although not mentioned in Herodotus's account,
this siege expertise and technology was instrumental in crushing the Ionian revolt, as it made short work of the Ionian walls. This army sufficed to
conquer a sprawling empire, but after having seen firsthand the combat
power of the Greek phalanx, no later Persian army was complete without
a formidable core of Greek mercenaries.

For victory in battle, the Persians relied on archery, from both foot
archers and those on horseback, and their excellent cavalry. The infantry
was less important and generally found its most worthwhile employment

in finishing off an enemy force already decimated by the archers and scattered by the cavalry. As their approach to war did not require it, the Persians never built a truly effective heavy infantry force. Some would immediately object and claim that Persia's elite ten-thousand-man Immortals fit this bill.[5] However, this force wore only light protection and was never able to stand toe-to-toe with heavily armored hoplites. Herodotus describes the Persian Immortals as follows:

> They wore soft felt caps on their heads, which they call tiaras, and multicolored tunics with sleeves covering their bodies, and they had breastplates of iron fashioned to look like fish scales. On their legs they wore trousers, and instead of shields they carried pieces of wicker, which had quivers hung below them. They were armed with short spear, long bows, and arrows made of reeds. From their belts they fastened daggers, which hung down their right thigh.[6]

Herodotus further tells us that this "elite" Persian force tended to make campaigning as easy as possible on itself:

> The most impressive dress and equipment were displayed by the Persians. . . . Their dress and equipment was conspicuous because of the lavish amount of gold that they wore. And they had brought along covered wagons which carried their concubines and large retinues of well dressed servants.[7]

Herodotus further relates that the Persians armed their cavalry like the infantry, except that some wore bronze helmets. According to Xenophon, they also carried two javelins. Other elements of the Persian army fought with their traditional equipment and weaponry.

The Persian army, weighed down with baggage, moved slowly, and it did not march or fight at night.[8] When it eventually did come up against a foe, it relied on the coordinated action of its combined arms, centered on massed archery, to inflict sufficient losses to shatter an enemy's cohesion. The infantry would form on the center, with the cavalry on each flank. Once arranged, the infantry would stick their shields into the ground to create a field-expedient palisade, behind which the mass of archers would shield themselves. As the archers pinned down the enemy force and thinned its ranks, the cavalry would start moving off in a series of flanking or encircling movements. As long as the enemy remained unbroken, the cavalry would keep its distance and join the foot archers in pouring arrows into the enemy formation. Periodically, masses of more heavily armored knights would charge in and discharge a volley of javelins. This would continue until their opponents could stand it no longer and their lines began to waver.

This was the signal for the heavily protected Persian shock cavalry, armed with spears and swords, to close with the enemy. While unbroken infantry could hold off cavalry indefinitely, once an infantry formation began wavering, it was useless. A thousand pounds of charging flesh with a screaming rider wielding a deadly spear or sword was a terrifying sight. Under such an attack, a decimated line that was already stepping back always broke. At this point, the infantry, which had remained standing at the wicker palisade to protect the archers from a sudden rush, started forward. Armed with their *akenakes* (short swords) and short spears, they delivered the coup de grâce.

This army comprised a hodgepodge of national identities, fighting styles, and equipment that made it impossible for Persia to forge a fully integrated fighting force—one trained on the same weapons, doctrine, and tactics. Throughout the two hundred years of the Achaemenid dynasty, the Medes and Persians remained the army's fighting nucleus, with tenuous support provided by a relatively unsophisticated mob. If this Persian core faltered, the army was in serious trouble regardless of its size. As Persia's enemies on the Asian plains were themselves relatively unsophisticated, the Persians were under no disadvantage on any Central Asian battlefield. In Asia, the elite Persian core was the decisive instrument of war. However, when it faced Greek hoplites, it foundered. This is most easily explained by Persia's inability to develop first-class heavy infantry. Armed only with short swords and spears, they were unable to outrange the longer spears of a Greek phalanx. Moreover, the Persians never anticipated having to fight a close battle against organized infantry, as they expected their archers would break up enemy formations long before they could close for a hand-to-hand fight. Arrows were particularly ineffective if the enemy sprinted through the kill zone and closed rapidly—the Athenian tactic at Marathon. Arrows never made much of an impression on a phalanx that maintained its order and discipline. It is instructive, in this regard, to take note of the Spartans at the Battle of Plataea in 480 BC. Here the Spartans stood motionless under showers of arrows, while their leaders made repeated animal sacrifices in the hopes of eventually getting good omens.

As the Persians never expected to fight a hard, close battle, they would be at a decisive disadvantage once the hoplite battle line was upon them. The Persians themselves, at least, wore some scaled armor for protection. But most of their polyglot army did not have even this much. There were the Sagartians, who fought with lassos; some of the Indians went into battle carried on donkeys; the Colchians wore wooden helmets and carried short spears; the Thracians wore fox on their heads and fawn pelts on their feet; and so it went for the entire army. It was a mark of Persian military genius that they could weld these disparate troops into something approaching a coherent force.

In any case, the protection provided by scaled armor paled in comparison with that offered by the Greeks' bronze breastplates. And there was no comparison between the heavy Greek shield and the wicker of the Persians. These Persian shields, apparently constructed of sticks threaded through a wet shield of leather, were almost the height of an average man and just a bit wider than the human frame.[9] They may have sufficed to stop or slow an arrow, but against a charging hoplite they were close to useless, as they could not stop a spear thrust.

Much worse for the Persians was the fact that as they expected to be fighting an already shattered infantry, they had no training on how to handle a formation that fought as a single unit. A Greek phalanx was a single fighting formation, and if still intact on impact, it would have no trouble cutting its way through any Persian force to its front. As Herodotus relates about the Battle of Plataea:

> The Persians were not inferior in courage or strength, but they did not have hoplite arms, and besides, they were untrained [in this kind of warfare] and no match for their opponents in tactical skill. They were dashing out beyond the front lines individually or in groups of ten, joining together in larger or smaller bands, and charging right into the Spartan ranks, where they perished.

In head-to-head combat during this era, the only thing that could hope to halt a Spartan or Athenian phalanx was another phalanx.

However, the most formidable weapon the Persians had was the cavalry, mounted on superb Nesaian horses. As Paul Rahe states: "For control of their realms, vast plains and steppes, the Achaemenids depended less on their archers and charioteers [and infantry] than on their cavalry—the last including horse archers capable of firing volley after volley as they circled the enemy, knights in light armor who hurled javelins into the enemy ranks, and shock cavalry equipped with spears and sabers."[10] Caught in the open, a Greek phalanx would have found itself doomed against such a force, unless it could find a way to keep the cavalry at arm's length. This it usually accomplished by the employment of slingers, archers, peltasts, and its own cavalry—or, as Alexander did at Gaugamela, by placing heavy infantry in reserve to cover an exposed flank.

It is important to note that the Greek phalanx possessed an overwhelming advantage on a narrow front in a battle fought in a box—a perfect description for the Plain of Marathon. For there is one thing that a horse will not do: It will not run head-on into a wall of spear points. Some historians make much of the fact that medieval knights often ran down infantry. This is the case only because the infantry wasn't disciplined, unbroken, or armed with pikes. Even as late as Waterloo, the allies gained victory only because even the most courageous of French horses would not throw themselves on a bayonet. So when the British troops formed squares with bristling bayonets facing in every direction, they became impervious to the swirling masses of French cavalry.[11] When it comes to cavalry charging a phalanx, human bravery counts for nothing. It was the courage of the horse that mattered, and in this case Persia's fabled Nesaian mounts proved no braver than any other horse.

Through recent popular books and movies such as *300*, the Persians, and particularly their rulers, have entered the public imagination as a collection of particularly obnoxious effetes. As a result of Greek writers such as Xenophon and orators such as Isocrates, who in the decades after Marathon fed their audiences a constant diet of tales of Persian feebleness, even the ancient Greeks believed the Persians were inferior warriors. If the Persians did lose some of their warlike character in the later days of the empire, it certainly was not the case in the empire of Darius and his immediate successors. As Herodotus describes, "From the age of five to the age of twenty, they teach their sons just three things: to ride horse, to shoot the bow, and to speak the truth. . . ."[12] The Persian forces that the Greeks fought at Marathon and then again, a decade later, at Thermopylae and Plataea were not soft. They were seasoned warriors within a culture that prized warriors above all else. The example began with Darius himself, who despite his undoubted achievements in consolidating the administrative infrastructure of the empire was most proud of the fact that he was a king on horseback—a true warrior.[13]

It is important to understand that the Persian army the Greeks faced at Marathon was considerably different from the typical Persian force generally depicted. First of all, it was a veteran army, inured to hardship and the terror of battle by six years of fighting in Ionia and Thrace. While no Persian army ever approached Greek levels of tactical integration, this one probably came the closest. Six years of war would have seen to that. Over time, national differences within the army eroded, as common experiences and the natural adaptation that takes place on the battlefield brought about a convergence of fighting methods and equipment. Furthermore, this force was superbly disciplined and probably possessed a high level of tactical flexibility as a result of training and fighting together over a long period of time. The only time Persians may have ever seen massed hoplites was when the Milesians marched to the assistance of the Carians, and the Persian army possessing that experience was massacred in a later ambush.

It was also predominantly an infantry force, although the Persians appear to have brought a thousand or so cavalry to Marathon. Still, it would have used the typical Persian methods of battle as outlined earlier. This was because at no time during the Ionian revolt did this force face an organized hoplite army. It therefore never found it necessary to make any of the adaptations required to face a phalanx.

The army sent to Marathon was a supremely confident force that had never suffered defeat. It was a skilled force, capably led, with overwhelming numbers, and full of confidence. This was not the soft Persian force typical of later generations. It was a veteran army, slimmed down for war. It was a force to reckon with and could not be taken lightly. No one in Greece could have liked the Athenians' chances in the upcoming fight.

Chapter 15

HOPLITE WARFARE

U p until 650 BC, warfare had been the job of aristocrats, as only they could afford the implements of war, particularly horses. However, as Greece recovered from the collapse of the Bronze Age, the population grew at a steady rate (probably approaching 3 percent a year).[1] This growth in turn led to dramatic changes in agriculture as the Greeks converted land from pasture to farming. Moreover, as the population continued to rise, this farming became progressively more intense. As the population continued to expand, increasing food requirements pressed marginal land into agricultural service, and even the poorest tracts of territory were now worth defending.[2] As farming intensified, large tracts were divided into small family-owned plots, which came to dominate the landscape. These two transitions, in turn, had led to the development of a unique style of conflict—hoplite warfare—by 650 BC.[3] Now that farmers needed to protect their holdings and could do that only as part of a collective, the concept of a hoplite was born. In turn, this collective action came to be centered around the polis, or city-state.

No one has ever figured out how this took place in practice, but medieval history may provide a clue, as it had a strikingly similar developmental curve. As in ancient Greece, the mounted warrior (the aristocrat) had been the dominant military force. Toward the end of the Middle Ages, town-centered economic changes whittled away at the political dominance of the knight. Unwilling to cede their hold on power, the mounted nobility fought to hold their gains. In one notable instance, the French king sent an army to subdue what amounted to a revolt of townspeople in Flanders. The resulting Battle of Courtrai pitted heavily armored mounted knights against an infantry formation.[4] Similar to a Greek phalanx, the Flemish townsfolk were well disciplined, closely packed, and eight deep, with spears extending to the front. Against them came the flower of French chivalry. When the battle was over, the flower of French chivalry was reduced to "dung and worms."[5]

Western Europe was on the edge of a technological revolution that was about to radically change the character of war, if not its nature. However, had technology and gunpowder not intervened, this steady Flemish infantry would have been well on its way to establishing a military order very similar to that of the Greek phalanx.[6]

While a spear stuck in the ground or protruding forward was sufficient to stop a charging horse, it was insufficient against a similarly armed force of infantry. As each city-state developed a phalanx, its rivals were forced to follow suit, as there was no other way to hold one's own in a pitched battle. As the character of war changed from aristocrat centered to crowded fields of massed men rushing at one another with extended spears, it quickly became apparent that the better-protected and better-drilled force had a distinct advantage. To further protect themselves from opponents stabbing at them with spears, these warrior farmers progressed to adding breastplates, greaves, and the distinctive *hoplon* shield to their panoply.[7] Similarly, the difference in quality of men who drilled together over those who refused to practice soon made itself felt, and regular drilling became a requirement in many cities.[8]

As small city-states could not typically afford to maintain a standing army, the most practical and efficient means of defense was to have a large body of men with a vested interest in defending their soil on immediate call to rush to the city's defense.[9] As these part-time soldiers had many other concerns and commitments, war tended to become a ritualized process, and rules developed over time.[10] These rules can be summarized as follows: One side would declare war and march its phalanx into the territory of another; its opponent would mobilize its phalanx; and finally, both sides would agree on a level place on which to fight. After the proper sacrifices were made, each side made straight for the other and a climactic crash ensued. It was all over in a morning or afternoon, and one side or the other would retreat off the field. Both sides accepted the verdict of the battlefield, and the losers either gave up the strip of land claimed or (if the aggressors lost) gave up their claims and marched home. Rarely were battles costly in terms of personnel losses, nor would wars continue past this climactic engagement.[11]

For the past century, historians followed the ancient evidence and what appeared to be common sense. The poor land of Greece could barely sustain the population in good times. Thus no city could afford to hole up behind its walls while an invader laid waste to its lands, as that would mean economic ruin and famine. Moreover, farmers practicing intensive agriculture could not afford to be away from their farms for prolonged periods, either sheltering behind walls or besieging them. Considering these circumstances, each side in a conflict had a strong interest in ending a war as rapidly as possible. The climactic head-to-head hoplite battle appeared to fit everyone's needs.

However, by the time of Marathon, the whole ritualized system was breaking down. For example, Sparta in its battle of annihilation against the Argives at Sepeia, and Athens in the decades prior to Marathon, appear to have fought with the intention of winning decisively enough to change the political landscape permanently. By the time of the Peloponnesian War, all that was left of the former system of warfare was the phalanx itself.

This Greek way of war made little sense to the Persians. Herodotus quotes the thoughts of the Persian general Mardonius on the matter: "The Hellenes are in the habit of starting wars without the slightest forethought, out of obstinacy and stupidity. For whenever they declare war on one another, they seek out the finest and most level land and go there to fight, so that the victors depart the battlefield only after much damage has been done [to themselves], and I won't say anything at all of the defeated, as they are completely destroyed . . . if they must wage war against one another, they should seek out the place where either of the two sides would be the most difficult to subdue and try to fight there. Thus the Hellenes do not employ intelligent strategies."[12]

Greek warfare was much simpler than that fought by the Persians. Two armed bodies of men would form into a solid phalanx of bristling spears and then advance at the double and collide with one another on an open plain.[13] Here, they stabbed, pushed, screamed, and kicked until one side gave way. Every hoplite went into battle carrying a large round shield (hoplon) that covered his left side as well as the right side of the man to his left. According to Thucydides, this caused a phalanx to move at an oblique angle as it advanced, as each man covered as much of the right side of his body as he could behind his neighbor's shield. These densely packed hoplites could not maneuver easily, so an engagement soon resembled a rugby scrum, the difference being that each side was trying to kill the other.

Moreover, the men of the Greek phalanx had no respect for light troops, which made up the bulk of the Persian army. As Euripides commented in one of his plays:

> Archery is no test of manly bravery; no! he is only a man who keeps his post in the ranks and steadily faces the swift wound the spear may plough.[14]

Although every man who could afford the full hoplite panoply was expected to so equip himself, many peasants could not afford such an expensive purchase. It is unlikely that these peasants and urban poor were denied a chance to aid their city in time of war. In many cases, they probably played a critical role, but being despised by those of higher social standing (the hoplite class), they rarely received their due. In this regard, the Spartans at the Battle of Plataea brought seven helots for every hoplite, all of whom were armed and apparently joined in the battle. Herodotus, unfortunately, did not consider their accomplishments worthy of recording. It can be assumed, however, that thirty-five thousand or more armed helots accomplished quite a lot that has been lost to us.

Still, the core of any Greek city's army was the phalanx, which came into existence for only one reason: to fight decisive, pitched battles. Unfortunately, as with almost everything else in ancient military history, one finds that there is no general agreement on how they did this. The debate currently breaks down into only two schools of thought, the orthodox and the heretical.[15] The orthodox school maintains a traditional picture of the phalanx consisting of a dense formation of interlocked shields with typically eight or more ranks pushing one another forward in a tight mass. The heretics claim that this is an impossible way of fighting, as the crush of men would have made it impossible for individual hoplites to wield their weapons. They argue that instead of the compact mass, the phalanx fought in an open order like the Roman maniple, where every hoplite was given enough space to engage in individual combat. However, the heretics are substituting their imaginations for an overwhelming body of literature and archaeological evidence that supports the traditional view.

None of this should suppose that the phalanx did not sometimes fight in open order. The purpose of the phalanx push—the *othismos*—was to break open an opposing phalanx, and one can suppose that such an act could easily lead to individual fighting as one or both phalanxes began to lose cohesion. In fact, the center of the Greek phalanx at Marathon almost

broke under the pressure of facing overwhelming numbers and had to resort to individual combat for a time. However, when phalanxes engaged
each other, individual combat in the Homeric tradition was the exception
rather than the rule. The simple truth is that all of the time available for
training a citizen army was spent on collective training as part of a phalanx, to make this formation as invincible as possible. Except for the Spartans, most Greeks did not have the time required to also hone individual
fighting skills to a degree that would have made it practical to attempt it
on the battlefield against an unbroken enemy.[16]

In summary, hoplite warfare amounted to a brief brutal encounter that
put a heavy toll on the courage and discipline of the individual. Any moral
weakness within the phalanx would destroy its cohesion and make it easy
prey for the enemy. For this reason, those suspected of showing any sign
of cowardice were severely punished. The Spartans, for instance, required
a coward (trembler) to wear a beard on only one side of his face so that
everyone knew he was only half a man.

Chapter 16

THE WESTERN WAY OF WAR

Victor Davis Hanson and his supporters view the development of the phalanx and its employment as a shock instrument as the beginning of the "Western way of war." He has theorized that the Western way of war has been far superior to the war-making ethos of any other culture and society for the last twenty-five hundred years and marks the Battle of Marathon as the first example of this superiority. Others, rallying around the standard of Professor John Lynn, say that the historical record is so fractured that no enduring influence is possible over time.[1] It would be unforgivably neglectful to write a book on Marathon and fail to weigh in on this debate.

When I first read Hanson's writings on the topic, I was not entirely convinced. After all, how could the Western way of war be declared superior to all others when it was bested by the Mongols and the armies of Islam, to name just two groups that have been more than a match for Western armies over the centuries? However, after years of reflection on the matter, I have become a convert and now stand in the minority of historians who find themselves in general if not complete agreement with Hanson.[2] I should also admit that I enter this discussion with some trepidation, as it has become a rather uncivil battlefield itself. One former West Point history professor, Robert Bateman, has even gone so far as to refer to Hanson as the "devil" and called his work "a pile of poorly constructed, deliberately misleading intellectually dishonest feces."[3]

According to Hanson, the Western way of war rests on five principles that first manifested themselves at Marathon:

1. The use of superior technology to compensate for inferior numbers.
2. The exaltation of discipline, which turns individuals into organized units capable of unified action and sustaining horrendous levels of punishment.
3. An aggressive military tradition that seeks decisive battle.
4. The ability to change, adapt, and innovate over time and as required by changing circumstances.
5. The creation of dynamic financial systems able to accommodate the expense of this type of technologically intensive and highly destructive warfare.

It is hard to quibble with this analysis, because for the most part these principles have held up in every military conflict through most of the last twenty-five hundred years of history. Unfortunately, there are a number of places where the historical continuity appears to have been broken or where Western armies were decidedly inferior to those of other societies, such as against the Mongols or in the early decades of the Arab conquests. Hanson recognizes these gaps but never really confronts them or their implications in his writing. He believes that for every setback in battle Western armies suffered, he could list a hundred examples where the reverse was true, and therefore in the "big picture" rare counterexamples are mostly irrelevant. That, of course, is one of the problems with writing "big history" or creating a sweeping context in which to place twenty-five hundred years of warfare. There are always dozens of instances where the big picture is not correct in every particular or circumstance. However, that does not mean the theory is wrong on a macroscale. Although the comparison is not exact, I liken this to a person saying that quantum physics has proven Isaac Newton wrong in many particulars. This may be so, but Newton's theories still explain almost everything observable to the human eye: Apples do still fall to earth when dropped.[4] Likewise, I could hand a betting man a list of a hundred major battles between Western armies and those of other civilizations and tell him to pick the winners. Even if he did not know one whit of military history, he would win most of his bets by blindly checking off the Western side of each pair. If he was to use the same approach for wars and not just battles, he would get rich even quicker. For even when defeated in battle, Western states have shown a remarkable ability to absorb horrendous losses and in a short period of time reconstitute their armies and reenter the fray.

Lynn defines Hanson's Western way of war (and I believe Hanson would accept this assessment) as follows: "In its mature form . . . [the] Western Way of War theory asserts a unique and continuous military culture that is dependent for much of its character on a societal and political culture that is equally unique and continuous. The conjunction of the two supposedly created the singular lethality of Western culture at war in comparison to the other traditions that grew up in Asia, Africa, and the Americas. In short, it made the Europeans the 'most deadly soldiers in the history of civilization.' "[5] Hanson might qualify that statement by adding that they were the deadliest "on the battlefield," as many cultures proved just as adept as the West at the mass slaughter of innocents.

Lynn counters this argument with "claims that a Western way of warfare extended with integrity for 2,500 years speaks more of fantasy than fact."[6] He presents numerous examples of this continuity being broken, starting with the differences between the Roman Empire and classical Greece. From there, he lays out how difficult cultural transmission would have been in the Dark Ages and through the Middle Ages. However, to me this line of argument misses some key points. First, Lynn agrees with Hanson that the way a society's military fights reflects its culture, as it is adapted to the particular circumstances of the moment. The question should therefore be, is there a Western culture and has it had continuity over the last twenty-five hundred years? For if there is a distinct Western culture that has given rise to a particular societal framework, then by extension there must be a Western way of war that grew up alongside it. Simply put, the answer again has to be yes. Rome may have been different, but the Romans looked back to Greece for many aspects of their civilization, including for their early military system. The same holds true for every Western historical epoch since then, which have all looked back on Greco-Roman antecedents for guidance and direction. How, then, does one argue that Western art, philosophy, and literature can trace their roots back to Greece and Rome, but Western military institutions are not permitted to do so?

In truth, any society, nation, or civilization is at its root a collection of its stories. Military institutions have always glorified their past, and they devote considerable time reflecting back on both their own accomplishments and those of others. On a basic level, soldiers spend countless hours regaling one another with "war stories." This is how units pass on the traditions and ethos of their organization from one generation of soldiers to the next. It is a process that has remained unbroken for thousands of years.

It is fair to say that many older Goths who had crushed a Roman army at Adrianople told stories to new warriors about what it was like to see and fight legionnaires in the field. Many of these Goths, in turn, participated in the sack of Rome itself in AD 410, while their sons stood side by side with the Romans when they fought Attila's Huns at the Battle of Chalons in AD 451. Over generations, traditions were built on the backs of these stories and the millions of others that came after them. This, indeed, is how cultures are built over the ages. It is how our Western military culture was built and maintained over two thousand years.[7]

These stories are passed on in many ways, and they can obviously be distorted in the telling. Despite this, central themes persist over time and form the basis of our distinct Western civilization and culture just as other stories in other places form the basis of other civilizations. As a point of observation, in 2003 the author had the privilege of traveling with the American army that invaded Iraq. Those soldiers knew little about Marathon, but they were maintaining a tradition set back in 490 BC— seek out the enemy and engage him in a decisive battle of annihilation. Moreover, even as this book is being written, 150,000 Americans are fighting in the lands that make up a substantial part of the narrative of this book. Of that number, a conservative estimate would allow that well over half of them have seen the movie *300*, which presents a new version of the Greek-Persian war of 480 BC. Whatever its historical inaccuracies, *300* has allowed the story of the Battle of Thermopylae to enter into the consciousness of a new generation of soldiers.

Furthermore, professional soldiers are often voracious consumers of military history. Even during the Middle Ages, those leaders who knew how to read had almost all perused Vegetius's fifth-century work *The Military Institutions of the Romans*, looking for hints on how they could mimic Roman arms. Interestingly, Renaissance commanders, looking for ways to reform their armies in the wake of the gunpowder revolution, continued to turn to Vegetius for guidance. Even today, Vegetius's work remains in print, and a fair number of professional soldiers have taken the time to read it.[8] Moreover, Thucydides' history, *The Peloponnesian War*, written almost twenty-five hundred years ago, remains on the reading lists provided by the U.S. Army and Marine Corps and is taught in the war colleges of all our services.

Lynn, however, discounts this passing on of tradition when he argues that the barbarians broke the developing traditions of the Western way of war because of the vast cultural differences between themselves and the

Romans they supplanted. For Lynn, the barbarian invasions and the onset of the Dark Ages is a great cultural divide. Nothing after the fall of Rome is as it was before. Few historians doubt that much was lost when the Western Roman Empire collapsed, but not everything. While I do not join those historians who see the end of the Roman Empire as a smooth transition from one political system to another, there is no doubt that the barbarian invaders attempted to keep the ideal of Rome and its institutions alive for a long time.[9] Even during the bleakest years of the Dark Ages, the idea of Rome and all it represented was never lost. Moreover, when Europe began its economic and cultural recovery, it turned to Roman and Greek antecedents for the basic building blocks of its knowledge. In fact, the widespread acceptance of the Aristotelian worldview by medieval scholars is commonly cited as the great intellectual handicap that needed to be overcome before the Enlightenment could truly begin.

In truth, it appears to me that Lynn, in *Battle*, often undercuts his own argument. The entire theme of his book revolves around the fact that militaries and their way of fighting are determined by their society and culture—something Hanson would agree with. If that is true, then Western militaries, their traditions, and their methods of war are a result of a unique Western civilization. Since Lynn himself admits that "Greek and Roman precedent has provided us with ideas, myths, and a vocabulary of war," one is left to ask what Lynn believes a civilization's culture consists of.[10] Most would agree it is the result of the very transmission of ideas over time that Lynn agrees took place.

And what are these ideas that have made the West different and therefore our military tradition unique? They were identified and commented on by the great Persian king Cyrus over twenty-five hundred years ago, when he told a Spartan envoy: "I have never yet feared any men who had a place in the center of the city set aside for meeting together, swearing false oaths, and cheating one another."[11] What Cyrus treated with contempt—open markets and the free exchange of ideas—has through fits and starts remained the driving dynamic of Western civilization. In turn, this dynamic has shaped and formed a distinctive Western military tradition.

In the twenty-first century, there remain two open questions. Is the Western way of war as defined here and by Hanson still an appropriate model for waging wars, and are Western societies still capable of conducting war in this tradition? After two horrendous bloodlettings in the last century, many believe Europe's near Kantian peace has made it incapable of defending its interests.[12] At the same time, our enemies have adopted forms of warfare, such as terrorism, designed specifically to negate the weapons and organizations designed to fight and win decisive battles. The fact remains that whenever Western soldiers do enter into a stand-up fight with any of our current opponents, the result is always foreordained. In the test of battle, Western military forces are still supreme. Unfortunately, this brings to mind the opening exchange of Harry Summers's book on what went wrong in Vietnam:[13]

> **American:** You know you never beat us on the battlefield.

> **North Vietnam official:** That is true, but it is irrelevant.

Today, America and the West remain supreme on the battlefield. Whether its leaders can develop a strategy that can turn battlefield victories into war-winning strategies remains to be determined.

Still, while our enemies have demonstrated that they are capable of launching devastating attacks on our homeland, they still have not become, as of yet, an existential threat on the level Athens faced at Marathon. Although such a monumental crisis may never again arise, the growing rift between the West and the backward-looking forces that are rising in the Arab-Persian world means a future war between civilizations cannot be ruled out. I remain confident that if faced with such a threat, the West will remember its twenty-five hundred years of tradition, much to the detriment of any possible foe. Having said that, we must all hope our leaders are wise enough to forestall any threat of this magnitude before it manifests itself. Because the Western way of war is brutal. If it is ever again unleashed in all its decisive barbarity, it will be many generations before our enemies recover.

PART V

BATTLE

Chapter 17

THE PERSIANS SAIL

Although the Persian expedition that Mardonius led into Thrace at the end of the Ionian revolt had probably not been intended as a prelude to an immediate assault of Greece, it is safe to assume that he was expected to secure a base for a future invasion. Darius, therefore, could not have been pleased to hear about Mardonius's losses against the Thracian Byrogi tribe or the loss of the fleet off Mount Athos. Still, he remained as determined as ever to punish Eretria and Athens for their effrontery during the Ionian revolt. The burning of Sardis had sullied his honor and the prestige of the empire. Retribution was required, and Darius was probably not inclined to postpone his vengeance any longer than necessary. But if he was leaning toward a postponement, the constant entreaties of an aged Hippias, then residing at the Persian court, would have kept his determination from waning. At length, Darius relieved Mardonius of command. Whether he did this because of the failure in Thrace or because Mardonius was still recovering from wounds is unknown. One suspects the latter, as Mardonius returned to royal favor rapidly and was the military commander of Xerxes' much larger 480 BC invasion.

To replace him, Darius chose Datis and Artaphrenes. Artaphrenes was Darius's nephew and the son of the satrap Artaphrenes, who had crushed the Ionian revolt. However, he was young and inexperienced, and it is doubtful that he was placed in overall command. More than likely he was the royal representative and as such a symbol of the importance Darius placed on the success of this mission. Datis was a Mede. He was also a battle-hardened leader and likely the commander of the Persian fleet at the Battle of Lade, after which he oversaw the reduction of the Ionian cities that remained in revolt.

Both men left Darius's court and proceeded to Cilicia. They brought with them a small core of elite Persian infantry, possibly also some Persian cavalry, and a Saka contingent of cavalry.[1] Along the route, particularly once in Ionia, they collected more troops. One can assume that the levies raised to fight the Ionian revolt and for the invasion of Thrace were eager for additional paydays. At any rate, the two commanders arrived in Cilicia with a large host, where they met up with the 600 ships of the Persian fleet.[2] Among these ships were specially constructed transports for horses.[3] If we accept these numbers, it is possible to make a reasonable estimate of the size of the Persian army. Datis would have known from spies and reconnaissance that Athens had 70 triremes and Eretria had somewhat more. Given that the Eretrians had likely mauled a Persian fleet early in the Ionian revolt, they had to be taken seriously. Furthermore, although it did not happen, Datis had to be prepared for the possibility that both fleets would combine to face him. Given the Persian predilection to always outnumber their potential foes, Datis would have wanted at least 300 combat ships to meet 150–170 Greek vessels. We can only guess at the number of horse transports, but as the Persians had been building them for over a year, 50 is a reasonable estimate and may be high. That leaves 250 ships available for carrying supplies and troops.

Each trireme would require a full complement of 170–200 sailors, in case of a battle. This would have left room for 30 soldiers or marines. The transports would use mostly sails and would need few rowers, leaving room for probably 80–100 soldiers, assuming they shared space with supplies. The cavalry troops would likely have shared space with their horses. As these vessels would also need to hold substantial amounts of fodder, they probably could have carried 20 horses at best. Putting all of this together indicates that the Persians had close to 35,000 infantry/archers and 1,000 cavalry. There would also be over 50,000 sailors with the expedition. Of course, these numbers are open to debate, but it is noteworthy that they agree with the estimates presented earlier of what Persia was capable of accomplishing in 490 BC.[4]

Mindful of the possibility of storms, the fleet at first kept close to shore and sailed up along the Ionian coast. From there it set out for Naxos. It will be remembered that Naxos had precipitated the Ionian revolt when it successfully resisted a Persian assault and siege, thereby driving Aristagoras into rebellion. As Datis approached, it remained unconquered, but it knew it had no chance against the massive expedition sailing off its shore. Remembering Miletus's fate, the Naxians abandoned their city and took to the hills. The Persians, with vengeance on their mind, took the time to comb the countryside and kill as many of them as possible before burning the city to the ground. Vengeance done, the Persians sailed on.

As they approached Delos, that population, forewarned by events on Naxos, also took to the hills or sailed to nearby Tinos. However, Datis, with no need to avenge an earlier setback, adopted a different policy toward Delos. He kept his fleet out of the Delian harbor—across the bay at Rheneia—presumably to make sure his men did not take it upon themselves to do some looting. He sent for the Delian priests, who served Apollo's temple, and told them that Darius had forbidden him to do harm to them, their island, or the temple. He then bade them return home, and to prove his sincerity, he offered three hundred talents' worth of frankincense on Apollo's altar.[5] With Delos pacified, the Persians made a circuit of the nearby islands, enlisting troops for their army and taking hostages to ensure good behavior. Only Karystos, on the south coast of Euboea, refused to turn over hostages or march against their friends and neighbors. So the Persians, as Herodotus states, "besieged their city and ravaged their land until the Karystians adopted the Persian way of thinking."

With the Aegean quiescent, Datis turned his attention to his first assigned target, Eretria. The time had come for them to pay for their part in burning Sardis. The Eretrians were under no illusion as to what was about to befall them. After all, they had the example of Naxos's fate to instruct them. Everywhere in the city there was confusion and terror. They had sent to Athens for help, but as yet no word had come. Some in the city wanted to follow the Naxian example and head for the hills; others advocated shutting the gates and manning the walls to the end. This was not a bad strategy to adopt, as Datis was unlikely to have brought a siege train with him, and a successful defense of even a couple of weeks would have provided precious time for Athenian hoplites to prepare and possibly even for Spartan help to arrive. However, this was true only if there was no one in the city willing to betray it. Unfortunately, there was.

While Athens debated coming to the assistance of Eretria, it ordered four thousand of its colonists, settled at Chalcis, to march to Eretria's aid. The colonists marched out so promptly that they must have been expecting the order for some time. But as they approached, information arrived of dissension within Eretria. Giving the city up as doomed, the colonists crossed the narrow straits to Attica. This is the last Herodotus mentions of these hoplites, probably all veterans of the wars against Thebes. Athens, however, would not have forgotten them. In truth, despite their disappearance from Herodotus's account, it would be completely nonsensical for the Athenians to neglect such a large and experienced force at its direst moment. As they were not at Marathon, they were likely ordered to close off the possibility of the Medes escaping from Marathon to the north and to keep an eye on Thebes, which had gone over to the Persian side (Medized). Herodotus's neglect probably reflects the fact that he was writing for an Athenian audience at a time when tensions between that city and its former colonists were running high.

Even without the support of the Athenian colonists, Eretria was not defenseless. It had strong walls and three thousand hoplites to defend them. This was not enough men to meet the imposing Persian army in the field, but if they remained resolute, it was more than enough to hold the walls. When the Persians arrived, they wasted no time before trying to carry the city by assault. They failed, as they were to fail for the next six days. The fighting was fierce, and many fell on both sides. But on the seventh day, two prominent citizens, Euphorbos and Alkimachos, betrayed their city and allowed the Persians entry. History is silent about the fate of the traitors, but the Persians plundered the city, set its temples afire, enslaved its remaining citizens, and then prepared them for transport to Persia.

Their first objective accomplished, the Persians lingered on the island for several days. Assumedly, they needed a period of time to recover from the damage the Eretrians had done to them. Furthermore, by this time they would have been on the move for many weeks and the supplies with which they had started were probably exhausted. Before they could begin the next phase of the expedition, they needed to gather stores, while the horses required time to adjust their systems from fodder to grass.[6] Datis had now accomplished half his mission, but the real prize was just across the narrow gulf. Although he was confident of success, he was also an experienced commander. He would not rush.

But the Persians had made one massive and irredeemable mistake at Eretria. By destroying the city and enslaving the population, they had sent a message to the Athenians. It was precisely the wrong message, because just as in Eretria, there was considerable dissension in Athens as to what course to take against the Persian threat. For the moment, those pushing for resistance had the upper hand, but there were many who wanted to find some accommodation with the invader. Eretria's fate ended Athenian dissension. In a moment of folly, Datis had alerted the Athenians that despite the fact that their old tyrant Hippias was with his army, accepting him back in return for peace was not an option. Their city was to be burned and a large number of them were to be shipped to Persia as slaves of the Great King.

When Datis's Persians met Athens's hoplites, he encountered a force unified behind a single policy—conquer or die. All knew that defeat meant doom not just for themselves, but for their families as well.

Chapter 18

THE PLAIN OF MARATHON

Early in August 490 BC, the Persian army landed at Marathon. The site was chosen for a number of reasons. Probably the most important was the advice of Hippias, who was now near eighty and making a final bid for power.[1] He surely had memories of being a young man and landing on this same coast with his father, Pisistratus. At that time, the hill people had rallied to his father's cause and joined him on his triumphal march into Athens. No doubt Hippias expected a similar welcome on this occasion and promised as much to the Persians. It must have come as a shock to him and a depressing surprise to Datis that much had changed in Attica since Spartan arms had sent Hippias packing. The hill people may still have had complaints, but they preferred to address them through democratic councils rather than count on the possibly fleeting goodwill of a tyrant.[2]

Rather than march immediately on Athens, the Persians tarried on the coastal plain for an extended period.[3] How long is uncertain, but it was long enough to allow the Athenians to mass on the only practicable exit. Some have argued that the Persians halted to await the followers of Hippias, whom they expected to rally to his cause. Others claim the Persians waited in hopes that those Athenians supporting an accommodation with Darius would carry the day and the Persian army could march into the city unopposed. Both answers appear to be faulty. Datis was an experienced commander and would have made his plans or dispositions based on military realities, not on the uncertain hope of a popular uprising. There is a simple military explanation for the Persian delay: Even a modern amphibious landing is a scene of almost unparalleled chaos.[4] Unloading thousands of men, tons of supplies, and possibly a thousand horses from unsteady wood ships, beached or lying in the shallows, would have been a nightmare. At the least, it would have taken the better part of the day to unload and get organized. With that done, or while it was ongoing, the Persians would have had to build a fortified camp as a base. Behind this, they would have had to construct palisades along the beach to protect their ships when they marched off to Athens. If they failed to do this, the Athenians surely had enough troops to dispatch to the beach and set the ships afire, leaving the Persians trapped in Attica.[5]

On top of this, another simple explanation must be added: Although the Athenians could not have known where the Persians would land, the Plain of Marathon must have been on the top of their list. After all, it had a lot to recommend it. As Herodotus says, the plain was an excellent piece of ground for the employment of cavalry. Moreover, it had a promontory that stuck out almost ninety degrees from the shore that provided the fleet a large degree of protection from the elements—a natural port. It was also far enough from Athens to ensure the Persians could land without fearing the Athenian army would be upon them before they completed unloading, but close enough for them to reach Athens in a single day's hard march, if the gates were open to them.

However, the doors remained closed. The Athenians had not been at war almost constantly for the past twenty years without learning anything. The Plain of Marathon may have had a lot of advantages for the Persians, but it also had a very serious disadvantage: There was only one exit from the plain that was suitable for the rapid movement of an army.[6] It is almost inconceivable that the Athenians would not have strongly outposted this exit, as it had been the road used by the last successful invader of Attica—Pisistratus. The reason the Persians did not march off the Plain of Marathon was that there were several hundred determined hoplites standing behind a fortified wall across the southern road.[7] They could not have held this Thermopylae-like position indefinitely, but they did not have to. By the time the Persians had assembled sufficient forces to be certain of overrunning the Greek position, the rest of the Athenian army had arrived.[8]

The Athenians would have been alerted to the Persian landings, probably by smoke signals, within an hour of the first ship making shore. Herodotus tells us that they marched immediately to meet the threat, and there is no reason to believe it took them very long to muster their forces. The army would have begun mustering on the Persian approach across the

Aegean and had likely been standing ready since Eretria fell.[9] All it needed
was a direction in which to march and the order to go. That they would
march had been decided by the Athenians some time ago. Although we
are not privy to the debates over whether it was best to march out and
confront the enemy or to follow Eretria's example and try to hold the
walls, we are certain they took place. Both Aristotle and Plutarch make
reference to such deliberations and credit Miltiades with convincing the
Athenian assembly that their best choice was to fight on the open field.[10]
If there were any lingering uncertainties about forgoing the safety of
Athens's walls, the fate of Eretria must have sealed the case. Moreover,
marching out for a direct confrontation was always the natural inclination
of a Greek city-state. Also, any decision in favor of fighting from behind
walls would have come with a significant cost, even if the Persians were
held at bay. At least two-thirds of the population of Attica could not fit inside the walls and would have been at the mercy of the invader.[11] Moreover, it was close to harvesttime, and the grain was vulnerable to fire.[12] If
the Persians destroyed it, Athens could not be sure of replacing it, as the
Persian fleet was now positioned to blockade Athenian trade routes. Furthermore, if the Persians destroyed Attica's olive trees, they would under-
mine the region's economy for a generation.[13] It is, however, interesting to
speculate on the plight of a Persian army busily besieging ten thousand
Athenian hoplites when fifteen thousand Spartans and their Peloponnesian allies marched into their rear.

For the Spartans had already been sent for.

At the same time the Athenian army had marched to Marathon, the
Athenians had sent one of their day runners, Pheidippides, to Sparta to enlist the support of the finest army in Greece.[14] Pheidippides arrived in
Sparta the next day and announced to the magistrates, "Spartans, the
Athenians beg you to rush to their defense and not look on passively as the
most ancient city in Hellas falls into slavery imposed by barbarians, for in
fact Eretria has already been enslaved, and thus Hellas has become weaker
by one city." The Spartans would have been under no illusion as to their
eventual fate if Athens fell, so they resolved to help. Unfortunately for
Athens, they were celebrating one of their many religious festivals and
could not march until the full moon. Many commentators have interpreted this procrastination as reflective of a secret desire to see Athens defeated. However, the Spartans were a notoriously pious people, so this
explanation is believable. Furthermore, there is no evidence that anyone in
the ancient world doubted Spartan veracity on this matter. The fact that

the first two thousand Spartans arrived as soon after the full moon as they did demonstrates that they were massed on the edge of the Spartan border before the festival ended and had force marched the entire distance. There is one further possible explanation for why the entire Spartan army did not march immediately or why, when it did, only two thousand hoplites were immediately sent. Plato says that the Spartans were late for Marathon because at the time they were engaged in a war against Messene (a helot revolt).[15] There is enough other evidence to make a convincing case that the Spartans were having troubles at home, but it is impossible to gauge their extent.[16]

The Athenian vanguard would have arrived at Marathon in less than half a day and was probably there before sunset. Assumedly, the ten generals (one from each tribe) and the polemarch, Callimachus, were among the first to arrive. From the hills, they watched over thirty-five thousand Persians deploy across the plain and tens of thousands more sailors lounging near the shore, preparing an evening meal. One wonders if the clever old soldier Callimachus surveyed the ground and smiled. The Persians had placed themselves in a bottle, and he was the cork. All he had to do was bide his time; nature would do the rest.

To understand why this was so, we have to discuss the most important element of war, and the one most ignored by many classicists who have written about Marathon: logistics. The Persians had begun this campaign over a month earlier. What supplies they started with were used up. They may have been able to get some replenishment in Eretria, but it is doubtful the city offered them much after being besieged for a week, at a time when their grain supplies would already have been low, as the new harvest was still in the fields. The eighty thousand men of the Persian force (soldiers and sailors) would have required at least 225,000 pounds of grain and 50,000 gallons of water a day just for the men. The horses would have needed another 25,000 pounds of feed (assuming they could not go out grazing in the presence of the Athenian army) and 10,000 gallons of water per day. The Persians might have supplied the water with some difficulty from a local stream, some wells, and possibly the Great Marsh at Marathon, if it was not overly salty. However, it is unlikely these sources could have provided all of the water needed. Moreover, it should be assumed the Athenians would have dammed up the stream as it left the hills and may even have poisoned it with a few dead animals.

In any case, the food problem was almost insurmountable. There was no possible chance that the Persians could have set up anything ap-

proaching an effective commissariat with which to draw supplies from the
local area. It is almost certain that strong garrisons and roving patrols of
light troops and hoplites were all along the mountains and even in the hinterland to prevent the Persians from foraging. Besides, no foraging party
could have left the plain without being observed by the Athenians posted
in the hills. From that point forward, the life expectancy of the foragers
would have been drastically shortened.[17] Moreover, even if the fleet could
have been organized to ferry supplies from nearby islands, one can assume
that the food stores on these islands would also be running close to empty
as the harvest season approached. Even at half rations, the Persian army
would be starving in a matter of days.

If logistics are often neglected, there is one other topic that is never
mentioned by historians and frequently forgotten by soldiers. Delicately
said, the amount of fecal matter an army can produce in a very short time
(on full or half rations) is, to put it mildly, amazing.[18] Given the sanitation
practices of ancient armies, as many as eighty thousand men trapped in a
restricted space would have found conditions unlivable within a remarkably short time. Tarrying too long not only would be unpleasant, but
would have given time for the inevitable to happen. That great killer of
ancient armies—disease—would have struck, and the Persian army would
have vanished in the twinkling of an eye.

Datis needed a quick decision or he would be forced to withdraw in defeat. Callimachus knew this, of course, so it is fair to wonder if he smiled
as he considered the possibilities. If the Persians advanced for a decisive
fight, they would find his army arrayed in a fortified position, on ground
of his choosing. If Datis ordered a withdrawal, there would be a moment
when they would have some troops loaded and others milling on shore.
The same chaos that reigned on landing would repeat itself as the Persians
boarded their ships over an open beach. In that moment of vulnerability,
Callimachus would order the phalanx forward. In the meantime, the
Athenians could train, prepare, and await the Spartans.

The Athenian army marched along the south road to Marathon,
through Pallene, and skirting the south side of Mount Pentelicus, to enter
the plain from the southeast. There was a second route that went through
the hills to the north of Pentelicus and entered the plain from the west,
at the village of Varna.[19] However, this second road was little more than a
shepherd's path and unsuitable for the movement of a major army or its
logistics. Upon arrival at the base of the plain, the Athenians made camp

in the sanctuary of Herakles. Here they were joined by a thousand Plataean hoplites. The site the Athenians had chosen was a strong one. The sanctuary possessed an extensive grove, and in ancient times the surrounding area was still heavily wooded. There is also evidence that there was a wall on the site, but this is not likely to have been extensive. Taken as a whole, though, the site provided excellent protection against cavalry and was easily defensible against infantry.[20]

Before them stretched the Plain of Marathon and the Persian army. All around the plain were hills of sufficient size to hem in the Persians, even if they were not strongly outposted with Athenian hoplites. The Chardra River (a large stream, really) bisected the plain, and the northern half was dominated by the Great Marsh, which was almost impassable for any significant force. At the northern edge of the marsh, the Kynosoura peninsula stuck out at ninety degrees from the beach, providing a perfect shelter for the Persian fleets beached along a narrow strip of sand between the sea and the Great Marsh. Between the marsh and the Athenian position was an almost barren plain, with some sparse tree growth at points.

Herodotus tells us of the Athenians' arrival at Marathon but leaves us guessing as to what they did at that point. We do know that several days went by without either side engaging. But from Herodotus it would seem that the only notable event during that period was a debate among the ten tribal generals and Callimachus, the overall Athenian commander, on the advisability of attacking at all. In Herodotus's account, each of the ten Athenian generals had command for one day on a rotating basis. As far as he was concerned, Callimachus's role as polemarch was mostly honorary, and he had no more authority than any of the other generals. I strongly contest the accuracy of this viewpoint.

Herodotus relates the dispute among these generals:

> The Athenian generals were divided in their opinions: some were against joining battle, thinking their numbers were too few to engage the forces of the Medes, while others, including Miltiades, urged that they fight.[21]

The ten generals remained evenly divided on the matter, so Miltiades asked Callimachus to make the tie-breaking vote. Herodotus has him do this through a fine piece of oratory that convinced Callimachus to vote for battle:

It is now up to you, Callimachus, whether you will reduce Athens to slavery or ensure its freedom. . . . If you add your vote for my proposal, your ancestral land can be free and your city the first of Greek cities.[22]

After this, the four generals who supported Miltiades handed over to him the days they were to command the army so he could attack when he pleased. Miltiades accepted the extra command days, but Herodotus reports that he did not launch the attack until it was his day to command.[23]

There are a number of good reasons to disbelieve Herodotus's account. First off, Herodotus states, incorrectly, that the Athenians selected the polemarch by lot. He probably assumed this was the case from later Athenian practices and the fact that there was a council of generals who ran military matters in Athens during peacetime.[24] However, in 490 BC, the assembly still elected the polemarch, and once appointed, he was the commander in chief. As noted earlier, in this dire hour the assembly would naturally have turned to a man of proven combat experience, and they certainly wanted a man who had won battles for them in the past. As Herodotus never gives us the name of the man who defeated the Thebans, the Chalcidians, and the Aeginetans and stood down a Spartan army, we can only guess at possibilities. Assuming the Athenians possessed one whit of common sense, which they most assuredly did, they would have turned to this man now.[25] So Callimachus was not just a man of some political importance. He was also a soldier and general of no small repute. As such, he would have commanded the respect of the other generals present as well as that of the army.

One would also suspect that the decision to fight had already been made in Athens, and this was confirmed when the army marched. Therefore it was unnecessary to have this discussion at Marathon. It is much more likely that the debate was over how to engage and not whether to engage. Some have argued that the Athenians were stunned by the size of the Persian force and began reconsidering their decision to fight. This is unlikely to be the case, as the Athenians would have already received numerous reports about the size of the Persian force all during their advance across the Aegean and particularly when they were camped on nearby Eretria. In fact, based on the long history of reports on the size of enemy forces since the beginning of warfare, these reports were probably greatly inflated. If anything, the Athenians were probably surprised to find fewer Persians at Marathon than they had feared. Besides, the Athenian army at

Marathon had previously stood down a Peloponnesian force that greatly outnumbered it and was filled with dreaded Spartan warriors. Why would the Athenians turn coward now?

So what are we to make of Herodotus's version? First, no army places ten generals in charge. Based on the workings of almost every army in history, what Herodotus presents is a "council of war" empowered to give advice but not to command. Callimachus may have asked their advice, as many commanders throughout history have done, but the power to decide was his alone. The Athenian generals, upon their arrival at Marathon, had much to take in and debate. However, whether to fight or not was not among the decisions they were called on to make. The Athenians had already made that decision, and if tradition is correct, Miltiades may have been instrumental in getting the assembly to commit to battle. One might also note that conducting a withdrawal in the face of a superior and unbroken enemy is the most difficult of all military operations. If the Persians caught the Athenian army in a state of disorder (as happens to almost all withdrawing armies) on the Attic plain, they would have annihilated it.

The Athenians had come to fight. What they did not yet know was how or when to attack. It is here that Miltiades was instrumental, as he was the only one who could lay claim to having experience in dealing with a Persian army. That Callimachus was willing to listen to his advice is to his credit, but it is also no less than what is expected of a first-rate commander.[26]

There is one strong piece of evidence from the period that supports the contention that Callimachus was the supreme leader and true hero of the battle. In 490 BC, the Athenians erected a memorial to Callimachus on top of the Acropolis, a high honor indeed. They never did that for Miltiades, who was then languishing close to death in prison.[27] The inscription:

> *Callimachus of Aphidna dedicated me to Athena:*
> *I am the messenger of the immortals who have their thrones on Olympos*
> *Because he was victorious, when he was Polemarch,*
> *in the festival of the Athenians.*
> *And fighting most bravely of them all he won fairest renown*
> *For the Athenian men-at-arms and a memorial of his valor.*[28]

At least in 490 BC, the Athenians had no doubt as to who was in command, who distinguished himself in heroic combat, and who led them to victory. It is unfortunate that Callimachus died on the Marathon battlefield and was not present to protect his reputation and place in history. Unfortunately for history, a generation of Philaidae propaganda and the unceasing toil of Cimon (Miltiades' son) to resurrect his father's reputation took their toll on the truth about Marathon.

As for the other generals turning over their days of command to Miltiades, the most logical explanation is that although Callimachus commanded, the other ten generals rotated as something approaching the modern concept of officer of the day. In that position, they would have been responsible for ensuring the accomplishment of the camp's daily activities, including training and mustering the force for the probable daily show of force. As only Miltiades had experience with the Persians, his advice on battle tactics and how best to train for fighting a Persian army would prove critical to success. It was therefore efficient to place Miltiades in charge of training and preparations for successive days. In fact, he may have been thought of as a chief of staff or deputy commander under Callimachus.

This also helps to explain why the Athenians delayed in launching their attack upon their arrival at Marathon. Of course, the primary reason was that the Spartans had promised to come to their aid. There was no reason to go it alone if by waiting just a few days there was a chance you could have a few thousand murderous Spartans pitch in with you. But waiting did not mean the Athenians were idle, as has been assumed by many historians.

It is a mistake to assume that because Herodotus does not tell us what the Athenian army was doing during this delay, it was doing nothing. Armies that sit idle quickly lose their edge. No competent commander would have allowed the Athenian hoplites to lie about, thinking and worrying. Besides, it should never be forgotten that this was a veteran army that knew what had to be done and what its commanders expected of it. Upon their arrival, the Athenians would have established a camp and probably fortified it. This more than anything else accounts for why the Persians did not move to the attack themselves. Coming straight at a phalanx would have been a dangerous enough proposition without having to deal with a fortified position at the same time.

Furthermore, each morning the hoplites would have mustered for battle in front of the camp. At the least, this was an important psychological device to build confidence and show the Persians that the Greeks did not fear them. The Persians would have done the same thing, and for long hours both sides would have stood there throwing taunts at each other, building up their courage, and baking in the hot sun. But these displays also paid an important dividend to the Persians. They removed all guesswork about how the Athenians would attack. Ten thousand hoplites of nonvarying quality would form up in a dense formation and come straight at them. It appears odd, then, that the Persians were so unprepared to meet the charge. But despite what knowledge Miltiades could supply, there was still much about the Persians the Athenians did not know.[29] But they were learning.

One pictures Callimachus, with Miltiades at his side, watching each day as the Persians assembled. Callimachus's practiced eye would have taken in much. He would have noticed the Persians always aligned themselves in the same order with their best troops, the Persians and Saka, always in the center. He would have watched for where the cavalry deployed. He would have seen that some units were slower than others to get into formation and which ones lacked the discipline to stand fast in the line as they stood in the hot August sun. He could not have missed that enemy units farther away from the elite center were decidedly less disciplined. He saw what others missed.

The Persian flanks were weak and unsure.

A plan began to form in Callimachus's mind. The old general, the polemarch of Athens, knew how to defeat the Persian army.

Chapter 19

THE DAY BEFORE

Datis could not wait any longer. After five days, he was out of food, and conditions in the camp were becoming intolerable. He probably considered attacking the Greek position, but it must have been a daunting prospect. Every day he could see the Greeks assembled in front of their camp, their shields glistening and spears bristling, daring him to attack. But as he studied the ten thousand disciplined hoplites massed behind fallen trees, with thousands of light troops crowded behind them, he always thought better of it. Without a large body of reliable heavy infantry, he simply had no way of pushing the Greeks out of their fortifications. If only he could do something to make the Greeks march out into the plain and attack him, where away from their protective cover they would be easy prey for his archers. Unfortunately for Datis, the Athenians had not yet shown any tendency toward suicide.

With no other options, Datis gave the next day's orders—break camp and return to the ships. It was the most dangerous operation conceivable, one that invited attack. It would take all night to break camp and move the ships into place. The job was made more difficult by the necessity of hiding these preparations from the Athenians. From past experience, Datis knew that getting the cavalry on board ship would be the hardest part of the job, so they would have to board before daybreak, working in the early morning hours as the rest of the army stood guard. If that went well, he would collapse his perimeter back toward the narrow strip of beach where the marsh protected one flank and the ocean the other. Here his elite Persians and Saka could hold the line, under the protection of thousands of archers, while the rest of the army boarded ship. It was dangerous, but it was the only option left. As Datis studied the line of men whom the Great King had ordered destroyed, he must have thought one more time: If only the Athenians would attack.

That night, the Athenians heard unusual sounds coming from the Persian camp. Callimachus must have guessed what was happening, but he needed to be sure. He sent out spies, and soon enough confirmation came back: The Persians were preparing to depart.[1] The Greek generals understood that they must not allow the Persians to depart unhurt. If they did so, their next action would be both unpredictable and dangerous. A number of options were available to the Persians. From the Athenian perspective, none of them were pleasant. They might sail north to Thebes, which was never a friend of Athens and had offered earth and water. From there, they could have enlisted the support of Theban hoplites to supply the heavy infantry they lacked and together march on Athens. Alternatively, they could land at another point and march on Athens before the hoplites could assemble or hit numerous points along the coast to scour Attica with damaging raids. Even more dangerous, they might find common cause with Aegina and winter on that island, recouping their strength for another descent on Attica the following year. Even joining with Argos and first removing the Spartan threat was a possibility. With all of these possibilities, it became clear to Callimachus that if Athens was going to survive, the Persians needed to be injured as much as possible before they left the shores of Marathon.

Callimachus knew the Spartans had set out and were marching hard to his aid. But time had run out, and Athens could not keep its men under arms forever. It was now or never. He called together the ten tribal generals and gave his orders. The army would muster before dawn for battle. Previously, he had briefed them on his novel plan for victory, based on his observation that the elite of the Persian army was always placed in the center of their battle line. This was the force Callimachus aimed to destroy, for only it was irreplaceable. The Athenian hoplites would also need to stretch their line as far as possible to avoid being outflanked by the more numerous Persians, but they could use even this to advantage. The Athenian line would be eight deep on each flank and only four deep in the center. The plan called for the flanks to win, while the center drew the elite Persians deep into a trap. It was a tremendous risk, for if the center broke before the flanks had done their job, disaster was all but certain.

It was a brilliant plan, but Callimachus was a brilliant general.

Chapter 20

BATTLE

Ever since 1851, when Sir Edward Creasy published his reconstruction of the Battle of Marathon, historians have created dozens of other learned reconstructions and many hundreds of less informed attempts.[1] What follows is my best estimate of the sequence of the battle. This reconstruction is based on the oldest and most reliable primary sources available. Still, it is a unique reconstruction and one often distinctly at odds with the descriptions of the battle offered by other historians. Rather than break the flow of the narrative by addressing competing interpretations of the evidence, I have addressed all of the "great debates" about the battle in the following chapter.

Few slept that night, as even veterans found it difficult to doze off on the night before battle. Slaves kept themselves busy polishing shields and armor to a high shine. Slingers engraved their lead pellets with obscene phrases.[2] The few archers present in the Athenian ranks prepared their strings and arrows. All around, hoplites repeatedly and nervously handled and sharpened their weapons, while the generals made their rounds. They stopped at each group, told a funny story or two, offered some encouragement, called attention to someone's past heroism, and did what they could to soothe pre-battle jitters. But mostly they went over the plan time and again. Victory on the morn depended on three things: courage, every man knowing the plan and his part in it, and iron discipline.

Before dawn, the Greeks mustered. As usual, the men ate no breakfast.[3] Instead, they turned silently to the task of donning their armor. Then, after hefting heavy *hoplon* shields onto their shoulders, they singularly or in small groups made their way through gaps in the defensive barrier. The full moon had passed, but there was still enough light to make it possible for each man to find his place in formation. Men took their places noiselessly. Only the sounds of thousands of shuffling feet and the periodic clang of *hoplons* striking each other broke the silence. All along the line, veterans whispered encouragement to younger men about to engage in their first fight, urging them to keep close and shelter themselves as much as possible behind their neighbor's shield. Here and there, someone would, as a Greek playwright said, "let the water run down his legs" or even void himself uncontrollably. Men would chuckle about that later, but for the moment little was said. Fear was natural. It was forgiven, as long as the man stayed in the line.

Dawn broke.

The holy paean was sung.

The order came—advance.

Peering through the tiny slits in their helmets, men could see a bit better now and could make out friends—or in some cases enemies, who for today put aside their quarrels. In the center was the Leontis tribe, commanded by its general, Themistocles, later to become the savior of Greece when Xerxes returned to finish what Darius had begun. Beside him was the general of the Antiochis tribe, Aristides. Both men already despised each other, and Themistocles would soon have Aristides ostracized from Athens, only to see him recalled just in time to command the Athenian army at the Battle of Plataea in 479 BC. But for today, their tribes stood arrayed adjacent to each other, both tasked with the day's most difficult and dangerous mission. Any chance the Athenians had for victory rested on the valor of both generals. In the event, they met the challenge, as Plutarch comments: "[Both] ranged together fought valiantly."[4] On the far right, with their flank on the ocean, stood the Aiantis tribe. Here, Stesileos stood beside his father, Thrasylaos, the tribe's general. Stesileos would not survive the day, dying within arm's reach of his father. With the men of Aiantis marched the polemarch, who was one of them and by virtue of his position stood on the far right of the army. He was also fighting his last battle, as he would die at the climax, pierced by so many spears that his body did not fall. Also standing in the ranks of the Aiantis men was Greece's greatest dramatist, Aeschylus. Today he would fight bravely but also witness the savage death of his brother Cynegeirus, struck down just as the final victory was won.[5]

As dawn broke, the Greeks were clearly visible to the Persians, as had been the case for several days previously. Today, though, the Greeks were silent. There were none of the taunts of previous days. Did Datis, preoccupied with the job of getting his boats loaded, note the silence? Maybe not. The night loading had not gone well. How could it, as his men had never tried it before? The camp was mostly broken down, but the collected booty had still not been removed. The Persians, at least, had managed to get most of their ships into the water, but by dawn the horse loading was only partially complete.

But Datis was an experienced commander. He must have seen that the Athenian lines were tighter today, more disciplined. Possibly he could see that the shields and body armor were polished to a higher shine than in previous days. Did that mean anything? If he or any of the other Persians actually sensed anything was different, it did not cause them to change their daily routine. As they had done every morning since landing at Marathon, they formed to face the Greeks. There seemed no reason for haste. After all, they still had three times the Athenian numbers. Even the Greeks were not crazy enough to attack against such odds.

In unison, the Greeks began to sing the holy paean. The Persians looked on, befuddled.

When the song ended, the hoplites stepped off. For the first few steps they walked, but then the pace picked up, first to a fast walk and then to a trot. The hoplites crushed together, shoulder to shoulder and shield to shield, as each covered as much of his exposed right side behind his neighbor's shield as possible. Dread and fear melted away now that the army was advancing. Men who had soiled themselves in the line drew strength from the surging men surrounding them. At six hundred yards' distance, the mass of men began to scream their fierce and nerve-shattering battle cry: *Alleeee!*

The Persians could not believe what they were seeing. The Athenians had no cavalry or archers. This attack was madness. But the Athenians were coming on, and they were coming fast.

Hastily, the Persian commanders aligned their troops. Men holding wicker shields went to the front as thousands of archers arrayed themselves in the rear. In another moment, these archers would release tens of thousands of deadly bolts into the sky, and that would be the end of the Athenians. Despite the speed of the Athenian attack, the Persian army showed no panic. They, too, were professionals, victors of dozens of bloody battles. What they saw coming at them was new, but none of them doubted they would make short work of the charging hoplites.

The Persian spearmen were on line now. Patiently, they waited to release the hail of arrows that would darken the sky and decimate their foe. That done, the infantry would advance to slaughter the shattered remnant.

But a different kind of war was charging down on them now. And it was arriving at almost incomprehensible speed, for at two hundred yards' distance the Athenian trot became a sprint. Athenian hoplites had learned the art of war against other hoplites, and their kind of war was not decided by a hail of arrows. A collision of wooden shields and deadly iron-tipped spears wielded by heavily armored warriors settled matters. It was a horrible and terrifying confrontation of pushing, screaming, half-crazed men who gouged, stabbed, and kicked at their opponents until one side could bear the agony no longer and broke. Then the real slaughter would begin, as men released of fear would feel the surge of bloodlust propelling them forward in murderous pursuit of the fleeing foe.

Finally, the Persian archers let fly. But to no effect. Never having seen such a rapid advance, many of the archers mistimed their shots. Masses of arrows missed their targets entirely. Most of those that did strike the Athenians bounced off shields and heavy armor. Hastily the archers reloaded, as the shield bearers and protecting infantry, seeing that ten thousand metal-encased killers were almost upon them, uneasily began inching backward.

The screams of *Alleeee!* were ear-shattering now, but even that could not compare with the incredible noise of thousands of shields clanging off one another as the compressed Greek ranks came within striking distance.

In a shuddering instant, the hoplites smashed into the lightly protected Persians and convulsed their defensive line. Wicker shields were trampled down, and the first rank of Persian infantry died in an instant. Most of the spears did not shatter on impact (unusual for a hoplite battle), for the Persians were without serious armor. Again and again, Athenian spears lunged forward, more often than not finding targets. Men screamed, fought, and died. But soon enough, the hoplites had passed through the protecting infantry and gotten amid the archers.

Now the real killing began.

The flanks, where Callimachus had massed his hoplites eight deep, made rapid progress. In a very short time, the Persians facing the men of Aiantis on the Greek right and the Plataeans on the left lost their cohesion and will to resist. In places, unprotected archers drew their short swords and daggers and made a stand. But they made little impression on the locked shields of the Greeks. Like a heavily armored tank, the phalanx rolled over the opposition, killing as it came on. Some in the Persian army fell, only wounded. The front line of Greeks stepped over them, intent on killing or maiming those still standing to their front. They knew that other hoplites coming behind them would dispatch the wounded men by raising spear points high and then plunging the metal spikes at their spear's base into their prostrate victims. Any Persian who survived would be stabbed to death by the swarm of light troops following in the phalanx's wake. When the Persian flanks could no longer stand the horror of hoplite warfare, they broke and ran desperately to the rear in hopes of reaching the safety of the ships.

In ancient battles, this was where the bulk of the casualties were inflicted on the losing side. Panicked men on the run are incapable of any defense. In turn, their pursuers, propelled forward by an instinctual bloodlust, would almost always lose their formation as they rushed to cut down the fleeing enemy from behind. And for approximately a hundred yards, this was just what the Athenians did.

But then they did the impossible. At least it would be impossible, if the Athenian army had actually been a mass of unprofessional rustics as tradition posits.

Callimachus, seeing the Persian left routed, ordered the bugle blown.[6] Instantly the Athenian right flank halted. For a moment the killing stopped, as the Athenians reordered their ranks and turned ninety degrees. Behind them swept a mass of light troops, armed similarly to the Persians but with the inestimable advantage of being in pursuit rather than running away in panic. These light troops would not be decisive, but they would keep the pressure on and protect the Athenian flank while Callimachus closed the jaws of his trap. For on the other flank another bugle was blown, and here too Greeks and Plataeans instantly began re-forming their ranks and turning toward the center of the battlefield. These actions cannot be passed over too easily. What the Athenian army had just accomplished could be done only by a professional force as part of a preset plan, so the men were prepared for the order to change directions when it came. Moreover, such a maneuver required the Athenians to possess an iron combat discipline found only in veteran units.

While the Athenian flanks carried all before them, things had not gone as well in the center. Here, the hoplites were arrayed only four deep, and the men of the Leontis and Antiochis tribes lacked the mass to overwhelm their opponents. They were also facing the more heavily armored and dis-

ciplined elite core of the enemy army, the Persians and Saka. The first impact had sent the Persians reeling, but after that, numbers told. After an
exhausting charge, there was a limit to how long the front-rank Athenians
could fight. To keep the pressure on, the Greeks did what they could to
move fresher hoplites forward, but the press of the Persian counterattack
made that difficult.[7] The only advantage the Greeks in the center had was
that Callimachus did not expect them to go forward, but simply hold.
Even that was proving difficult.

Despite the exhortations of the intrepid Aristides and Themistocles,
the Athenians were nearly fought out. Nearing exhaustion, they could no
longer resist the weight of Persian numbers and began slowly stepping
back. Under normal conditions, for a line as thin as the Athenian center,
stepping back presaged disaster. But the Greek veterans did not rout.
Rather, they fell back with deliberate slowness, still killing their enemies
even in retreat. Behind the thin line ranged a mass of *thetes*, men too poor
to purchase hoplite armor, throwing javelins and slinging stones into the
Persian host.

As the Greeks bowed back, they entered the woods near their camp.
The broken terrain caused the phalanx to lose its cohesion. Gaps opened
between the shields, and hoplites began to fall. The men of Antiochus suffered heavily, and Aristides must have known his men were close to breaking. In another moment, the Athenians would be swept aside and the
Persians would win the day.

Then, salvation.

Having reset their lines, the flanks of the Athenian army stepped off
again. This time, they were aimed at the exposed flanks of the Persian center. An ancient battlefield was a confusing melee, filled with screaming,
horror, and blinding dust. So it is likely that the Persians and Saka, locked
in mortal combat with the hoplites to their front and sensing imminent
victory, did not even see the looming threat.

When the crash came, it must have been a complete shock. Two steam-
rolling killing machines now bore down on the exposed Persian center,
snatching away the victory the Persians had glimpsed only a moment before. Any Persians who could, ran. Many, however, were trapped and died
where they stood.

Datis could see what was happening to his center and must have cursed
the fact that he did not have enough organized troops to launch a counterattack. But it was all he could do to collect stragglers with enough fight
left in them to hold back Athenian light troops. Datis also knew that when

the Athenian troops finished massacring the Persians and Saka, they would re-form and come at him again. He must have worried over how long his staggering men could hold the line against another phalanx charge. Behind him, thousands of panicked men were wading into the water, looking for any ship that could take them aboard. Datis needed to buy these men time. If he could get enough of them away, there might still be a chance to launch one more daring strike for victory.

Datis's time ran out. The phalanx came on again. This time, the shine of the Athenian shields was obscured by collected dust, and the gleam of the spear points was dulled by drying blood. As for the men holding those spears, they were dirty, drenched in sweat, and splattered with blood. But despite their exhaustion, they knew they had won and were advancing with fresh determination. For Datis's men, given what they had just been through, the sight must have been horrifying. But they knew there was no place to retreat, and through personal example, Datis held them to their duty.

This time, the tired Greeks came on with deliberate slowness. Spared the crashing shock of a phalanx impacting at a run, the Persian line did not immediately break. The battle near the ships became fierce as desperate men grappled at close quarters. Here is where Callimachus fell, mortally wounded, and Aeschylus saw his brother's hand chopped off as he grabbed hold of a Persian ship. After a long, hard fight, the Persians gave way, and the Athenians swept across the narrow beach. But Datis's line had held just long enough for most of his ships and surviving soldiers to escape. In the end, the Athenians were able to capture only seven ships as the surviving Persians moved out to sea.

As the Persians sailed into the Aegean, the Athenian hoplites rested while the light troops hunted down and killed any Persian stragglers left behind, particularly the mass of men hiding in the Great Marsh. When the Athenian generals took stock, they found that 192 Athenian hoplites lay dead.[8] Most of these losses had been from among the men of the Antiochis tribe, who had been pressed hard in the center, and from the men of Aiantis, who had suffered serious losses in the desperate fighting near the ships. Still it had been a great victory, for over 6,000 Persian dead littered the battlefield.

With the victory won, a messenger, Pheidippides, was dispatched to Athens. According to the traditional story, he ran the entire distance in full armor, shouted, "Hail, we are victorious!" and promptly fell over dead. This is the historical legend on which today's marathon races are based.

*The Tumulus of Marathon, the burial mound of the 192 Athenians
killed at Marathon. The mound was erected soon after the battle
on the location where most of the Athenians fell.*
The Art Archive/Gianni Dagli Orti

Interestingly, Herodotus does not mention any messenger being sent from
the battlefield and does not credit Pheidippides with the run. The first
mention of any runner in the historical record is given by Plutarch approximately six hundred years later. Then it is not mentioned again for almost another hundred years, this time by Lucian.[9] Plutarch says the
runner's name was either Therisippos or Eukles, while Lucian credits
Pheidippides and has him exclaim, "Joy, we win!" as he drops dead. As
both writers are further away from the Battle of Marathon than current
readers are from the Spanish Armada, some historians have cast doubt as
to whether the run ever took place.[10] It is inconceivable, though, that after
winning such a glorious victory, the Athenian hoplites would have failed
to relay the news home. Back in Athens, the women, old men, and children were waiting for news. The Athenian commander surely did not keep
them guessing for one minute longer than necessary. So while the true details of the story are lost in the mists of time, I believe it can be judged a
certainty that someone was sent with the message from Marathon. As
Athens had a corps of professional runners for just this purpose, it is also
rather certain that the messenger ran the entire distance. So there almost
certainly was a first Marathon run, although it was a bit less than the modern 26.2 miles. Who made that run remains anyone's guess. However, by
the time the Battle of Marathon was won, Pheidippides had had time to
recover from his run to Sparta and back, and it is possible that he may

have been given the honor of reporting the great victory to a waiting Athens. As far as the runner using his last gasp to announce a victory, we will never know for sure.

As the messenger winged his way to Athens, exultant hoplites looked out to sea in horror. The Persian ships were heading south, and everyone realized the battle was not over yet. Athens was undefended, and the Persians would be landing on the beaches of Phaleron, just a couple of miles from the city, before the sun had set. For a few dazed moments the hoplites stared uncomprehendingly, wondering if the battle had been for nothing. Soon, though, a new leader, possibly Miltiades, took over for the dead Callimachus and began issuing orders.

All along the beach, exhausted hoplites steeled themselves for one more great effort. They hefted spears, shouldered their *hoplon* shields, and re-formed their regiments. The bloodied Antiochis regiment was left to secure the battlefield and the tremendous booty found in the wrecked Persian camp. The other nine tribal regiments set off on a race against time, for it was almost twenty-six miles to Athens and the Persians had a head start.

When Datis eventually arrived off the coast of Phaleron, he saw that through an almost superhuman effort, the Athenian hoplites had beaten him there. All along the ridge overlooking the beach were arrayed thousands of determined warriors ready to contest his landing. After suffering over six thousand losses and with his force still disorganized, Datis had had enough. The Persian ships turned back out to sea.

Athens had won.

The next morning, two thousand Spartans arrived. They had missed the fighting but still wanted to see the battlefield, probably wanting to confirm that the victory was as great as the Athenians claimed. Later in the day, after touring the battlefield, they praised the victors and marched for home.

With Callimachus dead, Miltiades was the hero of the hour. Making good use of his political ascendancy, he demanded that the Athenian assembly give him troops and control of Athens's seventy-ship fleet for an expedition into the Aegean.[11] Setting out almost immediately after Marathon, in

fall 490 BC, he began a circuit of a number of Aegean islands. Most submitted on his approach, but several had to be taken by assault.[12] All of
them were ordered to pay an indemnity to Athens, to help offset the cost
of the Persian War. It was not until he approached Paros, in the spring or
summer of 489 BC, that he ran into trouble. Paros had sent a trireme to assist the Persians at Marathon, so Miltiades set a particularly high indemnity for them—one hundred talents.[13] The Parians refused to pay and
closed their gates.[14]

Miltiades laid siege to the city and had driven it to the point of capitu-
lation when a forest fire started on the far side of the island. The Parians
had previously sent for Persian assistance and now interpreted the distant
glow as a signal from the Persians that they were on their way. Buoyed by
this expected reinforcement, the Parians broke off surrender negotiations.
Miltiades, suffering from a wound or severely broken leg, could not maintain the siege any longer and sailed for home.

He had been away too long, and upon his arrival he found his political
enemies arrayed against him. His failure at Paros had given them their
chance. Miltiades had promised success and treasure. Instead, he had given
Athens a humiliating failure and drained the treasury. Once again, Miltiades found himself on trial for his life. Owing to his continued popularity
with the mob, he managed to avoid a sentence of execution but was
handed a ruinous fine of fifty talents. Not that it mattered to Miltiades, as
the wound he had suffered on Paros had gangrened, and he died soon after
the trial ended.

Chapter 21

THE GREAT DEBATES

A s I mentioned at the start of the previous chapter, the reconstruction of the battle is mine alone and is based on rather sparse evidence.[1] The following questions are not my own. They are culled from the dozens of reconstructions of Marathon written by the greatest classical scholars of the past century.

Where Was the Persian Cavalry?

The Persians considered their cavalry the decisive force on any battlefield. However, Herodotus never mentions the use of cavalry at Marathon, causing historians to debate the presence of cavalry at the battle for at least the past two centuries. What we know from Herodotus is that Darius ordered the construction of special vehicles to carry horses and that these horses were unloaded at Eretria.[2] However, he never discusses this cavalry being moved to the Greek mainland, although he does state that one of the reasons the Persians selected Marathon as their landing site was its suitability for cavalry operations.[3] In the absence of evidence, historians have speculated widely. Some claim the horses had not yet crossed over from Eretria. Others feel they were off grazing to the north of the Great Marsh and were unable to return in time for the battle.

For my part, I believe the cavalry was at Marathon. My reasons are simple. First, the cavalry was the dominant Persian military arm and held the central place in their battle doctrine. The Persians were horse warriors and simply did not fight without cavalry present unless there was no way to avoid it. Next, Herodotus states that Datis brought cavalry on the expedition. Therefore I believe it is unlikely that he would have gone through the tremendous bother of carting unwieldy horses across the Aegean only to leave them behind on another island when he was face-to-face with the Athenian army. It is just possible that with fodder running short, and grazing area sparse on the Plain of Marathon, Datis may have sent the cavalry north of the Great Marsh. However, protecting them from Athenian light infantry when they were so far from his main base would likely have presented an insurmountable problem. Besides, it is hardly feasible that the cavalry could not have returned the couple of miles from their grazing point to the battle in time to have made an impact.

Although the literary evidence for cavalry being at Marathon is lacking, and what does exist was written centuries after the battle, there is archaeological evidence that tilts the balance in favor of the cavalry being present. Soon after the battle ended, the Athenians commissioned a painting of the battle—the *Stoa Poikile*. Although this painting no longer exists, archaeologists are almost certain they have found copies of portions of it on a Roman sarcophagus, displayed at Brescia's Santa Giulia Museum, and on one of the friezes of the Nike Temple atop the Acropolis.[4] Both depict a vicious fight near the Persian ships, in which cavalry is clearly present.

Given that evidence, I believe it is certain that cavalry was present during the battle, and the reason Herodotus never mentions it is that his audience was well aware of this fact. They did not require a reminder. In the reconstruction presented in the previous chapter, the cavalry enters the battle near the ships, as this follows the tradition clearly visible in the extant archaeological evidence of the battle. Earlier, I built a case around the proposition that it was Persian preparations to depart from Marathon that propelled the Athenians to attack when they did. It is only a small logical leap from that point to state that the Persians would have loaded the horses first. Anyone who has witnessed a horse race knows that it requires some expertise just to lead a horse into the starting gate. In many cases, a skittish horse absolutely refuses to enter or hurts itself in a panic. One could imagine how much harder it would have been to load a thousand or more horses over an open beach or in shallow water by trying to coax them up narrow gangplanks.[5]

Once the Athenian attack began rolling, one easily pictures the cavalrymen rushing to organize what horses were still left on the beach, while still others pushed horses overboard into the shallow water. They must have raced to assemble a force sufficiently large to make a difference, but by the time that was done, the Persian flanks had collapsed. Moreover,

Datis, knowing that cavalry was useless against an unbroken phalanx, would have held them back for the last stand near the ships.

There is one more possibility that cannot be ignored, although it is not part of my reconstruction. The Persians and the Saka were the finest cavalry Darius possessed, and both hailed from the far eastern regions of the empire. Herodotus tells us that Datis left Darius's presence for Ionia with a large force, probably these very same Persian and Saka troops. One can argue that both Datis and Darius wanted a core of Persian infantry with the attack. However, would he have converted the Saka, who knew only how to fight from horseback, to an unaccustomed role as infantrymen, in which they would have been much less effective? Further, why go through the trouble and great expense of marching this Saka "infantry" across the length of the empire when, in the wake of six years of war, there was plenty of infantry available in Ionia?

Given this analysis, it is possible that Herodotus does tell us that cavalry participated in the battle. When he states that the Persians and Saka were in the center of the Persian line, his audience may have taken it for granted that he was speaking of the cavalry. However, as the surviving representations of the *Stoa Poikile* show the cavalry fighting by the ship, my reconstruction has discounted this interpretation. If the cavalry was at the Persian center, it is possible that a number of cavalry cut their way out of the closing jaws of the Athenian trap and were available for the fight at the ships. It should also be noted that it was Persian practice to place their cavalry on the flanks, not in the center. It is possible, however, that they thought it best to keep the horses clear of the sea and away from the hills, from which light troops could descend with little warning.

If the Persian cavalry was in the line that day, what difference would it have made to the battle or its outcome? The answer is probably very little. First, Callimachus would have known it was present and would have made plans to deal with it. Light troops carrying brush, or *abittis*, would have protected the flanks, and here torches would have been invaluable. Herodotus does tell us that when the hoplites reached the Persian ships, they began shouting for "fire." One might assume, therefore, that there were men with lit torches nearby. Also, no matter how brave the cavalrymen, a horse will not stand its ground once soldiers begin stabbing at it with spears. It would have taken only a short time for the phalanx to throw the Persian cavalry, which had no room for maneuver on the small plain, into confusion. Moreover, as long as the phalanx held its cohesion, there was nothing the cavalry could do to make an impression on it.[6]

How Far Can a Hoplite Run?

Herodotus states that when the Athenians started their attack, they were eight stadia from the Persian line, or just a little less than a mile. He further states that when the Athenians attacked, they ran the entire distance. Virtually every historian who has studied Marathon has dismissed Herodotus's account of the run, stating that it was physically impossible for hoplites in full panoply to run that distance and still have the energy to fight. Those who have not dismissed it out of hand have moderated the historians' version along the lines that they may have advanced at a quick pace and then picked it up toward the end.

It is worth looking at the exact words of Herodotus before we go further:

> The lines were drawn up, and the sacrifices were favorable; so the Athenians were permitted to charge, and they *advanced on the Persians at a run.* There was not less than eight stades between the two armies. The Persians, seeing them coming at a run, made ready to receive them; but they believed that the Athenians were possessed by some very desperate madness, seeing their small numbers and their *running* to meet their enemies without support of cavalry or archers. That was what the barbarians thought; but the Athenians, when they came to hand-to-hand fighting, fought right worthily. *They were the first Greeks we know of to charge their enemy at a run. . . .*[7]

Clearly, Herodotus thought the run was a remarkable event worthy of special notice, as it was the only time he was aware of the Greeks attacking in such a fashion. Remember, he would have been reading his work in front of Athenians who had grown up hearing the story of Marathon repeated ad nauseam. In fact, no small number of the "Marathon Men" would still have been alive to hear his recitation. For them, the memories of such a run would be seared in their minds. This observation leads to several questions, starting with how reliable are battlefield memories. Science provides a partial answer. It turns out that a rush of adrenaline imprints a clear memory of events that will last a lifetime.[8] This is why people forget the mundane moments of their past but tend to remember every detail of a traumatic event, no matter how distant. As any veteran will tell you, there is nothing like hostile fire to release just such a surge of adrenaline.

Still, that does not mean the memory is a correct one. I experienced this myself when interviewing many dozens of soldiers on their combat experiences during the invasion of Iraq in 2003. I conducted these interviews an average of eighteen months after the event, but in many cases I had transcripts of interviews a number of these soldiers had given within days of capturing Baghdad. Interestingly, there were often divergences in the stories that different participants had of the same event, which reflected their individual perspectives on the fighting. However, where a soldier was describing events he had participated in, there was no difference between his first version and what he recounted more than a year later.[9] Given the imperative to close the distance before the Persians could fully prepare to meet the attack, and the extra impetus of getting through the kill zone of the archers as rapidly as possible, it is clear the Athenians had every reason

Hoplites running into battle, from a vase dating from the sixth century BC. A number of historians have doubted Herodotus's claim that the Athenians charged at a run at Marathon. This contemporary vase shows the hoplites running into battle. It leaves open the questions of how far they would run and how fast.
The Art Archive/Musée Archéologique Naples/Gianni Dagli Orti

to run. It should therefore be judged a certainty that if ten thousand hoplites "remembered" running toward the Persians, they did.[10]

One question remains: Can men outfitted in full armor and carrying heavy shields run close to a mile? At least one paper claims this is a physical impossibility based on tests run at Pennsylvania State University.[11] Researchers there took physical education majors, outfitted them like hoplites, and had them run a mile. They failed. However, this is hardly convincing proof. As every athlete knows, exercise is specific. If you want to do a lot of push-ups, you have to practice doing push-ups. All the weight lifting in the world is not going to prepare you for a push-up contest. Furthermore, if you were to take a well-conditioned physical education major and place him with a U.S. Marine or 101st Airborne Division squad in Iraq or Afghanistan, he would collapse of exhaustion inside of an hour doing what those young men do all day, every day. Hours of conditioning in the gym or on a track just cannot prepare an individual to go out in 125-degree heat on a combat patrol while carrying a hundred-pound combat load.

Here, I would like to fall back on personal experience. When I arrived at the 82nd Airborne as a twenty-two-year-old second lieutenant, I was chagrined to find out that my battalion commander, Lieutenant Colonel Frank Akers, thought it great fun to take his officers on formation runs with full rucksacks that ended with a series of sprints up and down the stairs at the local stadium. I can assure you, based on that miserable experience repeated many times over two years, it is quite possible to keep up a pretty brisk pace for five or more miles carrying a heavy load.[12] And for those who argue that men cannot run any great distance with a shield, I have often witnessed units running in close order carrying rifles at port arms for mile after mile. Is it easy? No. But for men trained to the task, it can be done.

If we keep in mind that the Athenians at Marathon were a nation in arms for most of the previous decade, then we can assume that they took training seriously.[13] And did they train to run at the enemy? Well, they had an Olympic event for just that—a sprint in full hoplite panoply with shield. However, I will relent on one matter: A mile sprint, while just barely possible, would wreck the cohesion of the phalanx and leave the hoplites too winded for immediate combat. What the Athenians remembered as a run was probably a double time for most of the distance, followed by a real run once they were within range of the archers. In their minds, there would have been no difference between the two. As I remember it, we did not go very fast when Lieutenant Colonel Akers took us out for some exercise with rucksacks, but among ourselves, we always described them as runs.

I think it is worth closing this segment with the thoughts of a foremost scholar of ancient Greece: "In the Sunday *Times* of 26th June, Harold MacMillan wrote that 'no one who fought at Ypres [as he did] can ever forget the road from Poperinghe to Ypres' in 1917; in 445 BC the march from Marathon to Athens in 490 BC must have been equally unforgettable for the veterans. I take it then that the salient facts in Herodotus' narrative are completely unimpeachable—namely, the landing of the Persian expeditionary force at Marathon, the Athenian march from Athens, the days of waiting, the rapid advance, the victory on the wings, the defeat in the centre, the combined attack of the wings on the centre, the immediate and close pursuit to the shore, the capture of seven ships . . ."[14]

Why Did the Athenians Not Wait for the Spartans?

After waiting over a week for the Spartans to arrive, why did the Athenians suddenly attack on their own when they must have known the Spartan advance guard was less than a day away and force marching to their aid? The answer to this can never be known. Beyond doubt, the two thousand Spartans who arrived the next morning would have been a welcome addition to the force. And if they had waited for the entire Spartan army to arrive, there is a strong possibility that the combined Greek force could have annihilated the entire Persian army. As the Athenians knew that a Spartan force was marching hard to join them, something had to have happened that propelled them to attack prior to its arrival. Some historians have argued that the Athenians had no choice as to when to fight, as the Persians, also aware the Spartans were approaching, attacked first. As this involves throwing out just about everything Herodotus, the only historian who met the combatants personally, has to say on the battle, one must discount such a theory. To accept such a fabrication as true is to say we know nothing of this battle or any of its preliminaries, as we have tossed aside our only contemporary witness.

After much thought and a thorough consideration of what dozens of others have said about this battle, I concluded that only a Persian withdrawal could have prompted the Athenians to risk battle without the powerful addition of the Spartans. The Athenians simply could not allow the Persians to sail off and threaten them at some other point. Besides, the confusion that would inevitably ensue in any boarding operation must have been a great temptation to attack. It was a moment of weakness that Callimachus would have been waiting and hoping for. Of course, I completely reject the notion that the Athenians attacked so they would not have to share the glory of victory with the Spartans. Generals such as Callimachus and Miltiades did not reach their sixth decade by taking foolish and unnecessary risks.

The Shield Signal

Herodotus tells us that after the battle, traitors to the Greek cause used a shield to reflect the sun and send a message to the Persians out at sea. At the time, many Greeks interpreted this act as a signal that Athens was undefended and, if the Persians sailed immediately for Phaleron, the city would be theirs for the taking. At the time, it appears that some Greeks blamed elements of the Alcmaeonidae clan in league with Hippias for this treasonous act. Herodotus, however, is vehement in their defense—a sure indication that one of his interviewees was an Alcmaeonidae.

Although I believe there was a shield signal, I have left this event out of my reconstruction. I did this because there is no way to know who signaled, what the signal meant, or whom it was meant for. Moreover, unless knowledge of the signal encouraged the Athenians to march that much faster to their city's defense, it apparently had no effect on the battle or subsequent military events.[15] The debates over this issue may have influenced Athenian politics in the years after Marathon, but how they did so remains unrecorded.

Who Commanded?

Callimachus commanded. In doing so, he was ably advised and assisted by Miltiades. As Callimachus died in battle, Miltiades returned to Athens as the hero of the hour. That he died in prison just a short time later suggests that Athenians did not judge his contributions at Marathon much superior to those of others. Nevertheless, it should be noted that the Athenians had a nasty habit of punishing even successful generals.

I understand that overturning two eons of glorification of Miltiades is an uphill task, but I believe earlier chapters make a good case for Callimachus's primary role.

Where Was the Persian Camp?

The Persians were a professional army, and as such they would have built a fortified camp almost immediately upon arrival at Marathon. Neglecting to do so invited the Greeks to launch a devastating night attack that might have seen the entire Persian army annihilated. This camp would have played into Callimachus's calculations before the battle, and its location would have determined how he would attack. As there is no evidence, literary or otherwise, on the camp's true location, one can attempt to determine it only by applying sound military judgment.

Therefore, the most likely location is at the base of the Great Marsh, at the entrance to the beach where the Persian ships had beached. Here the camp would have easy access to water, plenty of warning of a Greek attack, and a prime position from which to guard the beached ships. The course of the battle presents further support for this location. If the camp was where I believe, it makes even more sense to stop the flanks, particularly the right flank, before they ran into an easily defended camp. Although it is likely the camp was partially disassembled in preparation for a move, the Greeks would not have known that when they were making their plans. Moreover, even a partially disassembled camp made a natural rallying point for the Persians, where Datis could gather troops for a final stand. I contend that it was this fortified camp that made it possible for Datis to build a new line and hold it fiercely while the bulk of the Persian ships escaped out to sea.

The Move to Phaleron

That the Persians sailed around Cape Surion with the intent of approaching Athens is a certainty. Why they did so, one can only guess. It most certainly was not to capture and hold Athens, as such an act would have been disastrous to the Persian cause. Assuming that entering an undefended Athens would have been relatively easy, what next? The Persians would have found themselves locked up in Athens, where whatever stores the city held were by this point nearly exhausted. Outside, there would have been an Athenian army with blood and vengeance on its mind. Joining them would have been a Spartan force and hoplites from other cities, all looking to get in on the final kill. It is almost impossible to believe that Datis thought his shattered army could withstand a siege. It is therefore doubtful he was planning to rush into Athens only to see his army starved into submission or slaughtered. Another reason must be found.

It is feasible that Datis just hoped to get ashore and move inland to engage the Athenians on ground more suitable to the Persian way of war. However, I do not judge it likely that a disorganized army that had just lost sixty-four hundred men would be in much of a hurry to try its luck again. Hoplite warfare must have been a traumatic experience for the survivors, and Datis would have had some difficulty convincing his men to go another round. And of course that assumes he had some way of talking to them and coordinating a plan while sailing, which was probably impossible. Of course, if the Persians were already withdrawing before the Athenian attack, then the ships may have been following a prearranged plan that Datis was powerless to change. That he would have continued on this course is all the more likely if some of the Persian ships had departed as soon as they were loaded and Datis now had to round them up.[16]

The most likely scenario, though, can be guessed at if one remembers what brought the Persians to Attica in the first place. At the start of the Ionian revolt, the Athenians burned Sardis. The Persians had come to Eretria and Attica to exact revenge. Datis was going to return with the slaves he had collected from a wrecked Eretria.[17] However, that was a job half-done, and Darius was sure to ask of Athens's fate. Datis could have hidden or explained several thousand casualties, as the loss was not great for a mighty empire.[18] But failure in the campaign's key objective could not easily be explained. It is my contention that Datis intended to repay the Athenians in kind for Sardis. His plan was to land and make a lightning march to seize Athens, burn as much of it as possible, and return to his ships. He most assuredly wanted to do this before the Athenian hoplites returned to inflict another terrible beating on his army. Surely the Great King would be satisfied with his Eretrian slaves and the destruction of Athens. With just a bit of luck, Datis might even have been able to round up enough Athenians to make a suitable present to Darius. If this was his plan, seeing the Athenian phalanx arrayed and prepared to throw any landing attempt back into the sea dissuaded him from the attempt.

Conclusion

Despite Sir Edward Creasy's listing of Marathon among his fifteen decisive battles in history, the battle's importance has been obscured by the far larger Persian invasion that fell upon Greece a decade later. For many historians, the Battle of Marathon was little more than a sideshow that inflicted a mere pinprick on the mighty Persian Empire. This general dismissal of the importance of the Battle of Marathon, however, misses a key point. Had the Athenians and their Plataean ally failed at Marathon, Greece would have been doomed. With Athens lost, the Spartans would have retreated into the Peloponnesus to await the final Persian assault. For their part, the Persians would have wintered in Attica and completed their conquest in the next year's campaigning season. Most likely the Persians would have been greatly reinforced during the winter, both by new forces sent from the empire and by Greek cities that would have gone over to the Persian side in the wake of Athens's defeat.

In the spring, the Persians would have faced a radically transformed Greece. Every city north of the isthmus would have Medized, while Sparta would either find itself standing alone or trying to keep wavering allies in line. Moreover, the Messenians, seeing their opportunity for freedom, would likely have risen up in support of Persia. Sparta might have prevailed in such a situation, but the odds were long. In reality, they probably would have fallen in a glorious but futile battle.

Many have also neglected the effect that Athens's victory had on the morale of all Greece. Up until Marathon, the might of Persia caused all of Greece to quake. Although Greeks had fought Persians in Ionia, Marathon was the first time the two had met in pitched battle. The result proved to all Greeks that sturdy, disciplined hoplites were more than a match for the Oriental hordes of the Persian Empire. In no small measure, it was Athens's triumph at Marathon that convinced Greece to stand against the overawing force that marched with Darius's successor, Xerxes, in 480 BC. Unfortunately for the heroes of Marathon, it is this second invasion ten years later that is best remembered today. The story of the three hundred Spartans' last stand at Thermopylae is the stuff of legend, while the massive Battle of Plataea pitted an estimated forty-five thousand Greek hoplites against upward of one hundred thousand Persian soldiers. Furthermore, the Greek naval victory at Salamis definitively ended Persian plans to dominate the Mediterranean.

Of course, a second Persian invasion would not have been necessary if Athens had lost at Marathon, as all of Greece would already have been incorporated into the Persian Empire. Moreover, it is unlikely that the rest of Greece would have found the fortitude to resist a much larger Persian invasion if Athens had been crippled by the smaller initial invasion force a decade before. At Marathon, victory was not enough. A win, just barely eked out, that saw Athens's hoplites roughly handled would have doomed Greece.

In the decades after the battle, no Greek doubted its importance. In Athens itself there was a cult of Marathon, and the men who fought that day were honored until their death. They were the equivalent of Athens's "greatest generation." At the time Herodotus was reading his *Histories* (425 BC), Aristophanes was putting on his great play *The Acharnians*, in which he referred to the "Marathon Men" still alive: "They are veterans of Marathon, tough as oak or maple, of which they are made for rough and ruthless."[1] For those who fought at Marathon, it was the life event they never forgot. The great dramatist Aeschylus, for instance, wrote his own epitaph, in which he did not mention his career as a dramatist. His only desire was to be remembered as a "Marathon Man" despite having also fought at the great naval battle of Salamis. On his tombstone was written:

> Beneath this stone lies Aeschylus, son of Euphorion, the Athenian, who perished in the wheat-bearing land of Gela; of his noble prowess the grove of Marathon can speak, or the long-haired Persians who know it well.

At Marathon, Athens saved itself, Greece, and by extension all of Western civilization. Some have proposed that Marathon made little difference in the creation and development of a unique Western civilization. After all, this argument goes, Pericles, Aristotle, Plato, and Socrates still would have been born. They still would have been brilliant, and their achievements would have been as great. One is hard-pressed, however, to think how these great minds and independent spirits would have soared as slaves to a despotic empire. In truth, Western civilization owes its existence to a thin line of bronze-encased "men as hard as oak" who went bravely forward against overwhelming odds, to victory and never-ending glory.

Acknowledgments

No book ever gets written without the help and encouragement of a number of other people. In my case I first want to thank my agent, Eric Lupfer, who believed in this project from the beginning and was instrumental in steering it to its final conclusion. I also wish to thank my editor, Jessie Waters. Her expert guidance, patient work, and friendly support were greatly appreciated. During the writing of this book, I also received the encouragement and assistance of two of the country's foremost historians, Williamson Murray and Paul Rahe, both of whom provided me with invaluable advice and suggestions. Still, this book deals with an area of history where there remains much for scholars to debate. So where there are interpretations in this book that may trouble others, the responsibility for my claims rests solely with me.

Finally, I wish to thank my wife, Sharon, whose encouragement and support made it possible to write this book. I am fortunate to have found a wife willing to read multiple iterations of the same book and still remain ready to give cheerful advice. Without her, this book would have been much the poorer.

Notes

Introduction

1. For evidence of this, one has to look no further than the depiction of the Persians in the recent hit movie *300*.
2. The Athenians were aided at Marathon by a small force of hoplites (one thousand) from Plataea.
3. Edward Creasy, *The Fifteen Decisive Battles of the World: From Marathon to Waterloo* (Cambridge, UK: 1994).
4. J. A. S. Evans, "Father of History or Father of Lies: The Reputation of Herodotus," *Classical Journal* 64, no. 1 (October 1968): 11–17.
5. A new edition of Herodotus's *Histories* has recently been released and is strongly recommended for anyone looking for a starting point for delving into the original source material on the Greco-Persian wars. See Robert Strassler, *The Landmark Herodotus: The Histories* (New York: Pantheon Books, 2007). All endnotes to Herodotus's works refer to Strassler's book.
6. In this last regard, one needs to make exceptions for Professors Donald Kagan and Victor Davis Hanson.
7. Most historians now agree that while Plutarch caught some minor errors, Herodotus's major problem, as far as Plutarch was concerned, was that he dared to criticize some Greek cities that Plutarch thought had saved Greece from the Persians. As a hyperpatriot, Plutarch could not let these "insults" to Greek national pride go by uncontested.
8. The Behistun inscription was engraved by King Darius at the site of his greatest victory at the end of the Persian civil war that marked the first year of his rule. The engravings were made on a cliff face approximately one hundred yards off the ground. The Babylonian Chronicles, which include the Nabonidus Chronicle, are a collection of clay tablets and cylinders that detail the great events of the Assyrian and Babylonian empires. All of these works are translated online at http://www.livius.org/.
9. A. R. Burn, *Persia and the Greeks: The Defense of the West 546–478 B.C.* (New York: Minerva Press, 1968). This excellent volume begins with an extensive review of the ancient sources of the Greco-Persian wars and is a wonderful starting point for anyone desiring to dig deeper into this aspect of events.
10. Ephorus (400–330 BC) wrote a universal history of Greece in twenty-nine

volumes. Unfortunately, nothing but isolated fragments of his work survives. Cornelius Nepos's work, *The Lives of Eminent Commanders*, includes a short history of Miltiades. A translation of the work can be found at http://www .tertullian.org/.

Chapter 1: AN EMPIRE RISES

1. The Cimmerians were a tribe of nomads who inhabited the Caucasus region. In one of their great raids south in about 652 BC, they destroyed a large part of the Lydian capital, Sardis, which they captured in its entirety a decade later. Between 637 and 626 BC, Alyattes II in a series of campaigns broke the back of Cimmerian power and forced their retreat into the Caucasus.
2. A solar eclipse was visible in the region in late May 585 BC.
3. The following pictures and story are drawn from Crawford H. Greenewalt Jr., "When a Mighty Empire Is Destroyed: The Common Man at the Fall of Sardis, ca. 546 BC," *Proceedings of the American Philosophical Society* 136, no. 2 (June 1992): 247–271.
4. For a thorough discussion of Croesus's fate, see J. A. S. Evans, "What Happened to Croesus?" *Classical Journal* 73, no. 1 (October–November 1978): 34–40.
5. The Median Wall was constructed between the Tigris and Euphrates rivers to the north of Babylon by Nebuchadnezzar II. Its purpose was to stand as a first line of defense against a Median invasion.
6. Ctesias's original has been lost, but a fragment was copied by Nicholas of Damascus (Nicol. Damasc. Frag. 66, Ctes.; Frag. Pers., II, 5). According to Ctesias, Cyrus starts life as a peasant who rises from street sweeper to become Astyages' most trusted adviser. A complete copy can be found at http:// 64.233.169.104/search?q=cache:mTqEQn5tcK4J:www.sacred-texts .com/neu/mbh/mbh10.htm+%2Bctesias+Astyages+harpagos&hl=en&ct=cln k&cd=2&gl=us/.
7. There are three main sources for this conflict: Herodotus, the Babylonian Chronicles, and the Dream Text of Nabonidus. While these three versions often contradict one another, what follows is a synthesis of the three into what is the most likely historical circumstance.

Chapter 2: LOOKING TO THE WEST

1. Herodotus, 1.153, p. 83.
2. The following regions came under Persian control during this period: Parthia, Drangiana, Aria, Chorasmia, Bactria, Sogdiana, Gandhara, Scythia, Sattagydia, Arachosia, and Maka. All of these regions are listed on the Behistun inscriptions as part of the inheritance of Darius and were not under the control of the Medes when Cyrus assumed control of their empire.
3. As we will see, Cambyses attempted to make his name as a great conqueror in Egypt.
4. Herodotus, 1.162.

5. Ibid., 1.169.
6. That the Carians were capable of greater resistance was proven fifty years later during the Ionian revolt, when they massacred a large Persian army.

Chapter 3: EMPIRE AT LAST

1. Herodotus's account of Cyrus's Babylonian campaign is notoriously flimsy and unreliable. It presents the improbable story that Cyrus, unobserved, diverted the Euphrates River, thereby allowing his army an uncontested entry into the city along the unguarded riverbank. By using various other sources (the Nabonidus Chronicle, the Verse Account of Nabonidus, and the Bible), this chapter hopefully presents a fuller and more accurate account of this war.
2. Isaiah 45:1.
3. Many historians have interpreted the Nabonidus Chronicle's comment "The inhabitants of Akkad [Babylonia] revolted, but he massacred the confused inhabitants" as Cyrus conducting the massacre. However, the joyful welcome that greeted his forces all along their route of march makes this interpretation highly unlikely.
4. The similarity to how the Germans flanked the French Maginot Line and broke through at Sedan in 1940 is too alluring a comparison to go unmentioned.
5. Herodotus gives a different version of the fall of Babylon (1.190–1.191). According to him, Cyrus besieged Babylon and finally took the city by lowering the level of the Euphrates River and then sneaking his assault troops in along the lowered river, which was unguarded.
6. Unreliable accounts by Berossus, writing in the early third century BC, state that he was permitted to live and was exiled to Carmania.
7. The Babylonian Chronicles of the seventeenth year of the reign of Nabonidus state: "Till the end of the month, the shield carrying Gutians were staying within Esagila [Marduk's temple], but nobody carried arms in Esagila and its buildings."
8. James Bennett Pritchard, *Ancient Near Eastern Texts Relating to the Old Testament* (Princeton, NJ: Princeton University Press, 1969): 315–16.
9. The cylinder was discovered in 1879 by Hormuzd Rassam and is currently on display in the British Museum. It confirms much of what is found in the Nabonidus Chronicle and the Nabonidus Verse Account (both of which are at odds with Herodotus's account, which states that Babylon fell only after a long siege). The cylinder has been called by many the first "declaration of human rights," and a replica is on display in the United Nations. Unfortunately, this is probably a misinterpretation of the document's meaning and is better looked upon as a masterful act of propaganda not untypical of the kinds of pronouncements many rulers of the period made upon their accession to the throne. A complete translation of the cylinder can be found online at http://www.livius.org/ct-cz/cyrus_I/cyrus_cylinder2.html/.
10. In the *Anabasis:* "For it is a fact that Cyrus came here with the intention of invading India, but found the going so bad and the country so wild and barren that he lost nearly all his men before he could do so."

11. Herodotus, 1.201–1.216.

12. Herodotus comments that there were many versions of Cyrus's death circulating and that he finds this one the most credible. He does not give any indication as to what other stories were known to him.

Chapter 4: THE RISE OF DARIUS

1. A small statue in the Vatican Museums, purported to have the autobiography of an Egyptian admiral, Wedjahor-Resne, presents a different and much more balanced portrait of Cambyses, portraying him as a beneficent ruler who made every attempt to appeal to the Egyptian people. As there is no account of any naval fighting during Cambyses' invasion of Egypt, it might be assumed that Wedjahor-Resne was bribed to desert his pharaoh and then rewarded with the position of adviser to Cambyses.

2. As will be discussed later, there is a strong possibility that Darius and his co-conspirators murdered Cambyses and therefore would have seized on any excuse to justify their actions.

3. This explanation of the death of Smerdis (he is called Bardiya in the Persian sources) is considerably more satisfying than the account given by Herodotus. For a full analysis of the various traditions regarding Smerdis's death, see Mabel L. Lang, "Prexaspes and Usurper Smerdis," *Journal of Near Eastern Studies* 51, no. 3 (July 1992): 201–207.

4. Egypt had joined Lydia in a defensive alliance against Cyrus. Although Lydia collapsed before the Egyptian army could come to its relief, the act must have marked Egypt as the next target on the Persian agenda of conquest.

5. Herodotus, 3.12.

6. Ibid., 3.14.

7. See *Archaeology* 53, no. 5 (September–October 2000): "A Helwan University geological team, prospecting for petroleum in Egypt's Western Desert, has come upon well-preserved fragments of textiles, bits of metal resembling weapons, and human remains they believe to be traces of the lost army of the Persian ruler Cambyses II."

8. As was mentioned above, in the historical records, Smerdis is also referred to as Bardiya. He is often also referred to as Gaumata. All three names are the same person. Herodotus relates that the man pretending to be Cambyses' brother Smerdis was actually named Smerdis himself.

9. The Magi were originally a Median tribe. From this tribe were drawn most, if not all, of the Median priesthood. Over time, the Magi tribe became a religious caste, with considerable power throughout first the Median Empire and then the Persian Empire.

10. This Gobryas does not appear to be any relation to the Gobryas who was of such great assistance to Cyrus in his assault on Babylon. Also, Herodotus gets Aspathines' name wrong, and in this case we refer back to the Behistun inscription on the assumption that Darius had a pretty good handle on who helped him overthrow the established order. Finally, Otanes is the son of Prexaspes, who is credited by all with killing the real Smerdis on Cambyses' orders.

11. Soon after his rise to ultimate power, Darius had Intaphrenes and most of his family killed, claiming they were plotting his overthrow.
12. Also called in some histories Sikayauvatis.

Chapter 5: TRIAL BY FIRE

1. Dadarshish is referred to in some histories as Dadarsi and as such should not be confused with another general in Darius's service of the same name, fighting rebel forces in Armenia concurrent with Dadarshish's campaigns.
2. The chronology of Darius's first year has been a matter of great dispute among historians for over a century. For what I still believe is the single best effort to make sense of this chaotic year, see Arno Poebel, "Chronology of Darius' First Year of Reign," *American Journal of Semitic Languages and Literature* 55, no. 3, (July 1938): 285–314.
3. He also remained in Media to make sure it would remain loyal and peaceful when he marched south.
4. Herodotus states that Darius placed Babylon under siege for almost two years before it was taken by the ruse of sending a supposed traitor into the city who would eventually gain enough trust to position himself in a place where he could give up the city. However, Herodotus appears particularly uninformed about this period, and there is no reason to give his account much credence. In this case, his account should certainly not be given any precedence over Darius's own testimony on the Behistun inscription.
5. The new Smerdis, whose actual name was Vahyazdata, had marched into the province of Arachosia to attack the loyal satrap, Vivana, but was decisively defeated.
6. Fravartish is often referred to as Phraortes.
7. Although he is not referred to by the sources, it is likely that Darius obtained substantial funds within Babylon, which would have bought quite a bit of continued loyalty from his army. He of course would not have been as concerned with Babylonian sensibilities now that they had shown themselves to be rebels. A heavy-handed approach might also account for Babylon's renewed rebellion as soon as Darius departed the city to deal with Media.
8. There is still some historical debate as to which army first marched against Armenia. The Behistun inscription is the only reference, and it starts its description with Vaumisa marching first. However, Darius often tells the story of this revolt in geographic order of events and not in chronological order. In order to validate the timeline the inscription presents for the entire course of events, most historians have placed the march of Vaumisa first. Also, there is general agreement that the fighting in Armenia and Media was concurrent, although they appear to be sequential on the Behistun inscription.
9. Kundar is also referred to as Kundurus in some histories. Ahuramazda, which translates as "wise lord," was the supreme god of the Persians, whose cult was spread by the prophet Zarathustra.
10. Ragae was a Median religious center and Magi stronghold at this time. It is currently a suburb of Tehran.

11. Here, where Darius learned that his forces were successful everywhere and that his empire was finally secure, was to be the location where his descendant Darius III was to lose the empire to Alexander the Great.

12. It is interesting that on the Behistun inscription Darius refers to the rebel leaders as kings and not rebels. Why he did so is a mystery, but perhaps it enhanced his image with the people to be seen as the conqueror of kings like himself, rather than just a ruler who crushed inferior rebels.

13. Herodotus, 3.128. It is just as likely that Darius paid off some of Oroites' guards to murder him and Herodotus is reporting a fable concocted at a later date.

14. The only major exception to this was the short civil war between brothers (Cyrus and Artaxerxes) over the throne in about 401 BC, as detailed by Xenophon in the *Anabasis*.

Chapter 6: THE MIGHT OF PERSIA

1. As this work deals primarily with the military aspects of empire, particularly as they pertain to the momentous first clash between East and West on the Plain of Marathon, topics such as Persian art, architecture, religion, and law are not examined in the detail they deserve. Those interested in delving deeper into these topics are encouraged to start their readings with Richard N. Frye, *The Heritage of Persia* (Cleveland: Mentor Books, 1963); A. T. Olmstead, *History of the Persian Empire* (Chicago: University of Chicago Press, 1959); and Josef Wiesehofer, *Ancient Persia* (London: I. B. Tauris, 2001).

2. Zoroaster himself reportedly had three wives, as did his father.

3. Artystone was a maiden; however, Atossa had earlier married her brother, Cambyses, and was later forced to marry Smerdis (the pretender) when he seized the throne in a coup.

4. The reader may see some parallels with Caesar giving his daughter in marriage to his ally and later great rival (after her death), Pompey.

5. For a similar achievement, we have to turn to the accomplishments of Augustus at the end of the Roman civil war.

6. Herodotus, 3.89.

7. The Behistun inscription lists almost thirty peoples within the Persian Empire, and many historians have held that this is a list of satrapies. This may indeed be the case, and there is evidence that some on this list were added at a later date, probably reflecting new conquests. However, the jury is still out on this interpretation, and Herodotus's detailing of Darius's administrative arrangements remains our best source in this case.

8. Translating ancient currency amounts into something understandable to a modern reader is always difficult, but some effort must be made to present an impression of the awesome wealth at the empire's disposal in the event of war.

9. Readers of Donald Kagan's masterwork on the Peloponnesian War will see different weightings than given here, as his calculations needed to account for the tremendous inflation that war sparked.

10. Donald Kagan, *The Peloponnesian War* (New York: Penguin Books, 2004), p. 61.

11. J. B. Bury, ed., *The Cambridge Ancient History* (Cambridge: Cambridge University Press, 1960), p. 200.
12. Herodotus, 5.52–5.53.
13. Ibid., 8.98.
14. He had linked the Nile to the Red Sea by means of a canal running from modern Zaqaziq in the eastern delta through Wadi Tumelat and the lakes Bohayrat al-Temsâh and Buhayrat al-Morra near modern Suez.

Chapter 7: THE RISE OF ATHENS

1. Later, Athens would have the silver from its Laurion mines to fall back on, but during this period the richest veins had yet to be discovered.
2. Herodotus, 5.78. This was written after Athens had decisively defeated a Theban army and annihilated a Chalcidian army within twenty-four hours of each other.
3. For a fuller example of Herodotus's thoughts about democracy as compared with other systems of government, see Herodotus, 3.80–3.85.
4. Some histories place this event in 612 BC.
5. As quoted in Bury, ed., *Cambridge Ancient History*, vol. 4, *The Persian Empire and the West*, p. 36.
6. Ibid.
7. Plutarch in his *Life of Solon* tells this story and says the poem was one hundred lines long, but only small fragments exist today. Plutarch also states that Solon led the expedition against Megara, but given his age and the fact that other chroniclers make no mention of his participation, this appears unlikely.
8. Solon fragment 1–2; see Ivan M. Linforth, *Solon the Athenian* (Berkeley: University of California Press, 1919), 129–173. For an account of Salamis, see pp. 249–265.
9. *Plutarch's Lives* (New York: Modern Library, 2000).
10. For an excellent account of Pisistratus (with a different spelling of the name), his family, and the basis of the family's power, see A. French, "The Party of Peisistratos," *Greece & Rome*, 2nd ser., 6, no. 1 (March 1959): 46–57.
11. This short sketch of early Athenian political developments, of the reforms of Draco, and of the legal system instituted by Solon fails to do justice to these and many other important developments in Athenian society. This is a fascinating story, but not truly pertinent to the central theme of this work. For anyone interested in pursuing this background, see John Boardman and N. G. L. Hammond, eds., *The Cambridge Ancient History*, vol. 3, part 3, *The Expansion of the Greek World, Eighth to Sixth Centuries B.C.* (Cambridge: Cambridge University Press, 1992); N. G. L. Hammond, *A History of Greece to 322 B.C.* (Oxford: Oxford University Press, 1986); and Bury, ed., *Cambridge Ancient History*, vol. 4, *The Persian Empire and the West*.
12. For an excellent account of this period, see Brian M. Lavelle, *Fame, Money, and Power: The Rise of Peisistratos and "Democratic" Tyranny at Athens* (Ann Arbor: University of Michigan Press, 2005).
13. The exact dates of Pisistratus's seizure of power or, for that matter, any of the

key events of his long career and those of his sons are still matters of dispute. The dates presented here are at best assumptions based on the estimates of numerous scholars in the field. For a thorough academic study of the matter, see P. J. Rhodes, "Pisistratid Chronology Again," *Phoenix* 30, no. 3 (autumn 1976): 219–233.

14. Herodotus, 1.61. According to Herodotus, Thebes gave more money to Pisistratus's cause than any other Greek city.

15. For reference, this is the year before the Spartans and the Argives began the war that led to the Battle of the 300 Champions in about 545 BC.

16. Soon after the Battle of Marathon, a new rich vein was found in these mines, which at the behest of Themistocles was used to construct a fleet of two hundred ships. These ships won the great naval battle at Salamis a decade later and propelled Athens to empire. The silver from this mine would also finance much of the Peloponnesian War, particularly after Athens was cut off from the revenues of the Delian League.

17. The importance of this grain trade became apparent in the Peloponnesian War. Although Athens had suffered many severe setbacks, it was not until their fleet was destroyed at Aegospotami and they were thereby cut off from the Black Sea that they finally surrendered rather than starve.

18. Here I have taken a position that directly contradicts what since Victor Davis Hanson's publication of *The Western Way of War* has become the widely accepted view of the historical community. I will not defend my position here but will come back to it in detail later in this work. See Victor Davis Hanson, *The Western Way of War: Infantry Battle in Classical Greece* (Berkeley: University of California Press, 2000). Also see Victor Davis Hanson, *Warfare and Agriculture in Classical Greece* (Berkeley: University of California Press, 1998).

19. Herodotus recounts a fable in his version of events. He relates that the Dolonci asked the Delphi oracle and were told to walk along the Sacred Way until they met a man who offered them hospitality. They were instructed to offer that man, whoever he may be, the leadership of the Chersonese. After a long journey, Miltiades was the first man to offer them lodging and refreshment, so in accordance with the oracle's orders, they asked him to be their king.

Chapter 8: A STATE CREATED FOR WAR

1. Cynosura, Mesoa, Limnae, Pitana, and Amyclae.

2. As this is mostly a military history of the period, very little time will be spent on the development of the Spartan political system, its unique constitution (the Great Rhetra), or cultural developments. For those interested in pursuing these matters further, I suggest Paul Cartledge, *Sparta and Lakonia: States & Cities of Ancient Greece* (New York: Routledge, 1979); or for some new viewpoints based on recent research, see Stephen Hodkinson and Anton Powell, *Sparta: New Perspective* (London: Classical Press of Wales, 1999). For the

nonspecialist reader, see Paul Cartledge, *The Spartans: The World of the Warrior-Heroes of Ancient Greece* (Woodstock, NY: Overlook Press, 2003).

3. During this period, Sparta was known to have established one colony at Taras (modern Taranto) in 706 BC. For what I consider one of the most interesting perspectives on Spartan society and politics, see Paul A. Rahe, *Republics Ancient & Modern*, vol. 1, *The Ancien Régime in Classical Greece* (Chapel Hill: University of North Carolina Press, 1994), 122–171.

4. Most of the histories of the period quote Pausanias, who lived at least eight hundred years after the events he relates (as far as the Fourth Crusade is from the present day). Moreover, it appears that his account can be traced only as far back as the Cretan poet Rhianus, who lived some five hundred years after the Messenian Wars. In the third volume of the 1925 *Cambridge Ancient History*, H. T. Wade Geary says of the Messenian Wars, particularly the revolt: "Of their course we know almost nothing. After the liberation of Messenia in 369 BC, the early wars of liberation were freely treated as themes for romance . . . conceived in romantic enthusiasm in the pages of Strabo and Pausanias, but almost certainly false history." Historians have found very little since then to challenge this judgment, and the version presented in this book is presented in the full awareness that it is more legend than fact. However, it is upon these legends that Sparta built its warrior society and therefore they are integral to understanding the ethos that propelled the Spartan hoplite into battle.

5. For an excellent in-depth discussion that attempts to separate the history from the legends about this revolt, see L. R. Shero, "Aristomenes the Messenian," *Transactions and Proceedings of the American Philological Association* 69 (1938): 500–531. This article also presents an excellent analysis of each of the sources of the Spartan-Messenian Wars.

6. Historical tradition has it that Sparta requested guidance from the Delphi oracle and was told "to ask Athens for a leader." Athens, fearing to disobey the oracle but not wishing to aid Sparta, supposedly sent a lame schoolteacher named Tyrtaeus to command the Spartan army. More than likely, this version of events is an Athenian insertion placed into the story centuries after the event. What appears certain is that a man named Tyrtaeus did rise to command the Spartan army, but it is likely he was a born Spartan.

7. Thomas Kelly makes the case that there was no traditional enmity between Sparta and Argos and this is a later invention of historians. As his own paper on the topic details three major wars between Sparta and Argos, in one of which a generation of Argive manhood was annihilated, I find his case less than convincing. See Thomas Kelly, "The Traditional Enmity Between Sparta and Argos: The Birth and Development of a Myth," *American Historical Review* 75, no. 4 (April 1970): 971–1003.

8. In similar fashion to how the USSR, before its collapse, controlled the separate votes of its constituent parts in the United Nations.

9. Some historians place the battle's date at 546 BC.

10. Some historians make the case that the humbling of Argos is what brought Corinth, Sicyon, Megara, and Aegina into the Peloponnesian League and that

they had not been members prior to this war. See Terry Buckley, *Aspects of Greek History 750–323 BC: A Source-Based Approach* (New York: Routledge, 1996), 83.

11. For a good general description of the *agoge* system, see W. G. Forrest, *History of Sparta 950 BC–192 BC* (London: Hutchinson, 1968). An argument has been made that what we know about the *agoge* is a result of Hellenistic and Roman myth making and that Sparta's education of its youth was little different from that in any other Greek city. I remain unconvinced by these arguments, but for those who wish to pursue them, see: Nigel M. Kennell, *The Gymnasium of Virtue: Education and Culture in Ancient Sparta* (Chapel Hill: University of North Carolina Press, 1995).

12. Paul Cartledge says a more accurate term is a "similar," as there were levels of society within Sparta and men were not peers, except when they took their place in the battle line.

13. Willis West, *Ancient World: From the Earliest Times to 800 A.D.* (Boston: Allyn & Bacon, 1905), 109.

14. If a hoplite ran away from battle, the first thing he would discard would be his heavy shield. Also, a dead hoplite would be carried home or to his burial place on his shield.

15. Jean-Pierre Vernant, ed., *The Greeks* (Chicago: University of Chicago Press, 1995), 93.

16. Herodotus, 5.39.

17. Ibid., 5.42.

18. Five ephors were elected annually. They could advise and influence the king and summon the assembly and the more powerful *gerousia* (selected only from Sparta's noble families). They also acted as judges and punitive powers and could bring other officials to trial. Sparta was ruled by two kings, who to some degree were overseen by five ephors elected annually. The institution may have arisen as a result of a need for leadership while the kings were leading armies in battle.

19. Sparta had two kings descending from two royal houses, the Agiad and the Eurypontid. Of the two, the Agiad was considered superior.

Chapter 9: SPARTA VS. ATHENS

1. There is some evidence that the Alcmaeonidae exile from Athens was not as clean a break as Herodotus reports, and even that during the rule of Hippias, Cleisthenes himself may have served as an archon. For a discussion of this possibility, see Wesley E. Thompson, "The Archonship of Cleisthenes," *Classical Journal* 55, no. 5 (February 1960): 217–220; and James W. Alexander, "Was Cleisthenes an Athenian Archon?" *Classical Journal* 54, no. 7 (April 1959): 307–314.

2. Herodotus, 6.108.

3. J. A.O. Larsen, "A New Interpretation of the Thessalian Confederacy," *Classical Philology* 55, no. 4 (October 1960): 229–248.

4. Herodotus, 5.62.

5. This is a pretty strong indication that the mass of people in Attica had not yet turned on Hippias, and he might even have still drawn considerable support from the countryside. This would mean that his more murderous tendencies were restricted largely to the noble classes and were of little interest to the mass of farmers, who still felt a lingering loyalty to the Pisistratidae for the rights to their land.

6. A policy they happily put aside during the Peloponnesian War, when they accepted substantial Persian support in order to defeat Athens.

7. Herodotus, 5.69.

8. For an excellent discussion of the political maneuvering leading up to Cleisthenes' assumption of power in Athens, see George Willis Botsford, "The Trial of the Alcmeonidae and the Cleisthenean Constitutional Reforms," *Harvard Studies in Classical Philology* 8 (1897): 1–22.

9. It is unclear if Isagoras was aware of his wife's affair or even if Herodotus was just passing on malicious (but possibly untrue) gossip.

10. The date for these reforms is still a matter of great debate. A straight reading of Herodotus seems to indicate that they were made while Isagoras was still in power. But how they could have been enacted during a time when Cleisthenes held no political power is a mystery. My belief is that the promise of reform was made to the people during Isagoras's rule and later delivered on. For an excellent discussion of this dating problem, see Charles W. Fornara and Loren J. Samons, *Athens from Cleisthenes to Pericles* (Berkeley: University of California Press, 1991), 169–171.

11. For an excellent review of Athenian politics during this period, see C. A. Robinson Jr., "Athenian Politics," *American Journal of Philology* 66, no. 3 (1945): 243–254.

12. For an excellent discussion of these reforms and changing Athenian politics, see A. Andrews, "Kleisthenes' Reform Bill," *Classical Quarterly*, new ser. 27, no. 2 (1977): 241–248.

13. There is some debate as to whether Cleisthenes was the first to enact laws on ostracism, as it may have been done during the time of Pisistratus. As it is not central to the theme of this book, we will not delve into the topic. For those with an interest in this unique legal development, see Antony E. Raubitschek, "The Origin of Ostracism," *American Journal of Archaeology* 55, no. 3 (July 1951): 221–229.

14. Historians have long disputed whether Cleisthenes actually enfranchised aliens and slaves. I have accepted the conclusions of Donald Kagan on the matter. See Donald Kagan, "The Enfranchisement of Aliens by Cleisthenes," *Historia: Zeitschrift für Alte Geschichte* 12, no. 1 (January 1963): 41–46.

15. This is the number of demes in the third century BC (according to Strabo), and the number during Cleisthenes' time was likely the same or very close to it. Others give the number of demes at 139.

16. For an in-depth look at the *trittys* concept, see Donald W. Bradeen, "The Trittyes in Cleisthenes' Reforms," *Transactions and Proceedings of the American Philological Association* 86 (1955): 22–30.

17. For a thorough analysis of these reforms, see James H. Oliver, "Reforms of

Clisthenes," *Historia: Zeitschrift für Alte Geschichte* 9, no. 4 (October 1960): 503–507.

18. Athens had developed a system of three concurrent archons: the archon eponymous, the chief magistrate; the archon basileus, for civic religious arrangements; and the polemarch, who commanded the army.

19. Herodotus, 5.73.

20. For an interesting analysis of the pro-Persian faction in Athens, see C. A. Robinson Jr., "Medizing Athenian Aristocrats," *Classical Weekly* 35, no. 4 (October 27, 1941): 39–40; and James Holladay, "Medism in Athens 508–480 B.C.," *Greece & Rome*, 2nd ser., 25, no. 2 (October 1978): 174–191.

21. It is also likely that if one Spartan king did not wish to attack, there were a large number of Spartan hoplites present who also thought it was inadvisable.

22. Athens was burned by the Persians in the 480 BC invasion, and apparently there was still significant scarring when Herodotus was writing.

23. Colonies, once established, were politically independent entities, while settlers in cleruchies kept their Athenian citizenship, rights, and duties, which included serving as hoplites when needed.

24. Pausanias, *Description of Greece*, 1.29.1, http://www.fordham.edu/halsall/ancient/pausanius-bk.html

25. Elizabeth A. Myer, "Epitaphs and Citizenship in Classical Athens," *Journal of Hellenic Studies* 113 (1993): 106.

26. That Herodotus may have ignored his noble or even heroic death in combat (no mean undertaking for a man of his years) could be just one more example of the historian saying as little positive of the Alcmaeonidae as possible.

Chapter 10: PERSIA'S RETURN TO WAR

1. Herodotus, 4.97.

2. Ibid., 4.142.

3. See George Beardoe Grundy, *The Great Persian War and Its Preliminaries* (London: 1901) for an excellent analysis of how Herodotus came to believe so much of a story that was so obviously incorrect (pp. 55–70).

4. The chronology of Miltiades' adventures is open to argument. Apparently, at some unknown point he was forced to flee the Chersonese because of a Scythian incursion. Some important historians have stated that he was forced to flee not by the Scythians, but by Megabazos, who had learned of his disloyalty at the Danube bridgehead. The truth seems to be that this Scythian invasion took place well before Darius's march through Thrace and that Miltiades soon returned to defeat the Scythians (or wild Thracians). The spoils of this victory were dedicated to Zeus at Olympia, and archaeologists have discovered his helmet there. Miltiades was definitely in the Chersonese when the Ionian revolt broke out in 499 BC, as coins he issued and dated to that period have been discovered. Some historians have argued that the Scythian invasion took place after Darius had returned to Sardis in 512 or 511 BC and that Megabazos, knowing of Miltiades' supposed treachery at the bridge, refused to come to his assistance. There are two major problems with this the-

sis. First, letting a Scythian force large enough to menace walled cities penetrate that deep into Thrace uncontested would have risked everything Darius had gained in his expedition. There is no reason to believe Megabazos was that militarily incompetent. Next, this reasoning fails to explain why the Persians allowed Miltiades to return and remain in power for over a decade. For a defense of this position, see J. A. S. Evans, "Histiaeus and Aristagoras: Notes on the Ionian Revolt," *American Journal of Philology* 84, no. 2 (April 1963): 113–128.

5. Herodotus tells a story that the future Macedonian king Alexandros had Megabazos's Persian envoys murdered because of their rude treatment of Macedonian women. He later covers up this crime by bribing Megabazos and giving his sister in marriage to the Persian envoy sent to discover what happened to his predecessors. This is almost certainly a fabrication that Alexandros sold to the other Greeks after the Persians had finally been defeated. That he had submitted and married off his sister to a Persian could not be denied or hidden. But it could be explained away as necessary after the slaughter of important Persian envoys. That the murders could have taken place and been left unavenged by Persia must be judged as unlikely.

6. That Darius rewarded loyal Greeks was just good policy. It by no means discounts the hypothesis that there was a Persian force at the bridge to make loyalty the easiest option to take.

Chapter 11: IONIA REVOLTS

1. For the story of the tattooed messenger, see Herodotus, 5.35.

2. See Evans, "Histiaeus and Aristagoras," who is in general agreement with this position but goes further by stating that Histiaeus never revolted but ran afoul of Artaphrenes, who had him impaled because he was determined to crush the revolt with force and did not want his plans hindered by prolonged negotiations. (Histiaeus is Histiaios.)

3. Denied plunder, the fleet and army would have been glad to get paid; Aristagoras paid them out of his own pocket.

4. Bury, ed., *Cambridge Ancient History*, vol. 4, *The Persian Empire and the West*, pp. 218.

5. That the Persians reassessed and lowered the tax burden at the cessation of hostilities is a strong indication the taxes were both ruinous and an underlying cause of the conflict. That the Persians were willing to lower the taxes demonstrates they were doing everything possible to avoid a recurrence of hostilities.

6. According to Herodotus, Koes was a Greek who advised Darius not to dismantle the bridge over the Danube before plunging deep into the Scythian hinterland. For this good advice, Darius had granted him Mytilene to rule. If the bridge had been dismantled, there was a strong possibility that Darius and his army would have been lost.

7. The term *anabasis* (a large military expedition) comes from the title of a book by Xenophon describing a Greek military expedition into the heart of the Persian Empire in 401 BC.

8. Herodotus, 5.51.

9. Ibid., 5.96.

10. Plutarch, in a story impossible to evaluate, relates that Eretrian ships had defeated a Phoenician fleet off Cyprus that had been ordered to move against the Ionians.

11. See *The Malice of Herodotus (De Malignitate Herodoti)*, p. 24. This book is considered by many to be the first scathing literary review, and it does catch Herodotus in some errors; but mostly it's a rhetorical exercise conducted by a writer who appears viscerally upset that Herodotus often makes negative comments of the Greek cities Plutarch worshiped.

12. Grundy claims that it must have taken some weeks for the Persians to raise a force of this size. However, it is unlikely the Ionians would have remained in a ruined city where they did not control the citadel, while the Persians mobilized an army to fight them (Grundy, *Great Persian War*, p. 98).

13. Various reasons were given for the Athenian desertion, including the very good one that war had just erupted with their close neighbor Aegina. Also, there was already a substantial peace party in Athens, and it would probably not have taken much to turn volatile public opinion against a war on far-off shores, when there were so many pressing threats nearer home.

14. It seems obvious that Artaphrenes had been mobilizing his army at Sardis. Logistically, a force of any formidable size would have been difficult to maintain in one location. Prudence dictated that this army be dispersed throughout the region, making it easier to draw supplies off the land. After all, the army that defeated the Greeks at Ephesus did not spring up by magic and could not have force marched from Miletus in time to have affected the course of events.

15. Herodotus, 5.105. There is no way to determine the veracity of this passage, but it is unlikely that the Zoroastrian Darius would have prayed to Zeus. (Of course, it's possible Herodotus may have just inserted the name of a god that would be familiar to his Greek audience.)

16. Grundy and others say that the defeat at Ephesus could not have been as terrible as Herodotus relates, or the revolt would not have spread as rapidly as it did in 497 BC (Grundy, *Great Persian War*, p. 101).

17. Herodotus reports that Hymees became ill and died during these operations.

18. Grundy, *Great Persian War*, p. 111.

19. Herodotus, 5.121.

20. Ibid., 6.1.

21. Some historians, such as A. R. Burn, have a radically different take on the story Herodotus presents. They make the case that Histiaios's squadron was actually there to prevent the Persians, who now controlled the southern coast, from interfering with shipments of grain heading for Ionia. (See Burn, *Persia and the Greeks*, p. 208). However, as there is no evidence to support this position, it remains purely speculative.

22. Most historians tend to doubt the number Herodotus presents when he gives the size of Persian fleets, as three hundred and six hundred come up often. However, it is just as likely that the Persians may have considered these num-

bers to be somewhat standard. In any case, there is no doubt that Persia was capable of making a naval effort of this size, and since this fleet had been three years in the making, it must have been substantial. Sir John Myers, on evidence I have not been able to uncover, claims that of the 600 ships, only 353 ships were war vessels. See John Myers, "The Battle of Lade, 494 BC," *Greece & Rome*, 2nd ser., 1, no. 2 (June 1954): 50–55.

23. Assuming an average of 150 men on each ship (crews and marines).

24. The great square sails used by the Greeks were bulky and would have been either stored securely or more likely left ashore so as not to get in the way. That the Lesbians appear to have had their sails at the ready is a strong indication that thoughts of desertion were probably on their minds before the Samians showed them the way.

25. After the fall of Miletus, the dramatist Phrynichus composed a play, *The Taking of Miletus*, that brought his Athenian audience to tears. For reminding Athens of its desertion of the Ionian cause, he was fined one thousand drachmas.

26. Herodotus, 6.32.

27. This was probably not a universal policy, as tyrants are still reported in Samos, Chios, and other cities in 480 BC (and later).

28. Mardonius was a son-in-law of Darius and the son of Gobryas (one of the seven co-conspirators who brought Darius to power). He became famous as the military commander for Xerxes' later invasion of Greece. After Xerxes left Greece, Mardonius was killed and his army destroyed at the great Battle of Plataea.

29. Herodotus, 6.44.

30. Herodotus also says a number of them were devoured by sea monsters . . . possibly sharks?

31. Herodotus, 6.45.

32. Ibid., 7.133. The Athenians threw the envoys into a pit reserved for condemned prisoners. Sparta threw the envoys into a well and told them to gather earth and water from it.

Chapter 12: SPARTA SAVES GREECE

1. The next, of course, was the sacrifice of three hundred Spartans at Thermopylae, followed by the decisive Spartan assault that broke the back of the Persian army at Plataea in 479 BC.

2. We have already noted the most famous of the oracle's ambiguous predictions, when Croesus was told that if he went to war with Persia, a great empire would be destroyed.

3. This date has been a matter of great historical debate, with the preponderance of historians convinced that the 494 date is correct. See Ignace H. M. Hendriks, "The Battle of Sepeia," *Mnemosyne*, 4th ser., 33, nos. 3–4 (1980): 340–346.

4. Herodotus, 6.76.

5. Plutarch, *Moralia* ("Sayings of the Spartans"). This story can be found in Plutarch, *Moralia*, Loeb Classical Library, vol. 3, translated by Frank Cole

Babbitt (New York: Harvard University Press, 1931), p. 336. This is the kind of story that would have been well-known at the time and just what Herodotus, who never has a kind word for Cleomenes, would have seized on. That he failed to do so is strong evidence that the veracity of this story is not all one could hope for.

6. Ibid., p. 341. Plutarch also relates that Cleomenes would have seized Argos, but when he approached he found the walls were manned by women, and he decided an assault would be too costly. This is a late tradition, and if true, it would be strange that Herodotus had not heard about it.

7. For a thorough analysis of what Herodotus has to say about the continuing war with Aegina, see A. J. Podlecki, "Athens and Aegina," *Historia: Zeitschrift für Alte Geschichte* 25, no. 4 (1976): 396–413.

8. This is Burn's interpretation; see Burn, *Persia and the Greeks*, p. 233.

9. Herodotus (6.65) tells us that Leotychidas was preparing to marry Perkalos, but she was kidnapped by Demaratus, who made her his bride.

10. Despite Demaratus's treason, Herodotus treats him very well throughout his narrative. It is probably a safe assumption that a close relative or maybe an aged Demaratus himself was the historian's informer (I am aware of the claims that Dikaios, an Athenian exile who knew Demaratus, may have filled this role; see Herodotus, 8.65). That would also account for how poorly Cleomenes is treated. As we noted at the start of this book, Herodotus, like many journalists today, tended to write favorably of those who spoke with him.

11. For an excellent account of Cleomenes, particularly his final year, see George L. Cawkwell, "Cleomenes," *Mnemosyne*, 4th ser., 46, no. 4 (November 1993): 506–527. In some particulars, such as what Cleomenes was doing in Arcadia in 491 BC, Cawkwell differs from my account, but he makes a compelling case that should be seriously considered.

12. Herodotus, 6.85.

13. As with almost everything in Herodotus, the date of this fighting is in dispute among historians, with some placing it after the Battle of Marathon. I believe there is sufficient evidence, however, to place these events prior to Marathon. For an excellent account of this period and an analysis of competing claims of historians, see L. H. Jeffery, "The Campaign Between Athens and Aegina in the Years Before Salamis," *American Journal of Philology* 83, no. 1 (January 1962): 44–54.

14. Otanes had captured these islands for Persia in the years immediately preceding the Ionian revolt.

15. Details of Miltiades' life and particularly the dates of key events are murky. I accept the work of H. T. Wade-Gery as authoritative on the topic. He gives the following chronology for key events in Miltiades' life:

1. Circa 550 (554?) BC: born.
2. From 528 to circa 516: Hippias treats him well in Athens.
3. 524: Appointed archon for 524/3.

4. Between 528 and 516: First marriage.
5. Circa 516: Death of his brother Stesagoras; Hippias sends Miltiades to take over the principality in Chersonese.
6. 514: Danube episode.
7. Circa 514: Scyths invade Chersonese; Miltiades retires (to Thrace? to Athens?) for a few months, then returns. At the same time, Hippias breaks with him and makes an alliance with his enemies in Lampsacus.
8. Circa 507: Cimon (son of his Thracian wife) born.
9. From 499 to 493: Ionian revolt.
10. 499 or 498: Occupies Lemnos and Imbros.
11. 493: Leaves Chersonese and comes to Athens; acquitted of "tyranny" at his first trial.
12. 492–489: Elected *strategos* (tribal general) in successive years.
13. 490: Paros fiasco; found guilty of "false public statement" at his second trial; dies in prison.

See H. T. Wade-Gery, "Miltiades," *Journal of Hellenic Studies* 71 (1951): 212–221. N. G. L. Hammond has written an excellent summary of the Philaidae in the Chersonese, which analyzes a number of details of Miltiades' rule. His chronology is not in full agreement with that above, but it's worth exploring further. See N. G. L. Hammond, "The Philaids and the Chersonese," *Classical Quarterly*, new ser., 6, nos. 3–4 (July–October 1956): 113–129.

16. For an excellent account of Themistocles' archonship, see Robert J. Lenardon, "The Archonship of Themistokles, 493/2," *Historia: Zeitschrift für Alte Geschichte* 5, no. 4 (November 1956): 401–419.

Chapter 13: GIANT VS. LILLIPUTIAN

1. For purposes of this analysis, I will focus on Athens as it faced the Persian assault at Marathon alone (I will add Plataea's thousand-hoplite contribution). If this analysis were made for Xerxes' invasion ten years later, there would be justification for including a larger number of Greek cities in the estimates.
2. It is notoriously hard to find any convincing figures for Attica's population. I have discounted Arnold Gomme, *The Population of Athens in the Fifth and Fourth Centuries B.C.* (Oxford: Basil Blackwell, 1933), in favor of Peter Garnsey's analysis; see Peter Garnsey, *Cities, Peasants and Food in Classical Antiquity: Essays in Social and Economic History* (Cambridge: Cambridge University Press, 2004). I have extrapolated the numbers Garnsey presents back to 490 BC, using an estimated population growth rate of 3 percent.
3. These calculations are my own, based on various estimates of the size of the Roman military establishment compared with estimated populations over time. These numbers do not hold up during the republic, when Rome was able to mobilize a far larger percentage, as the Greek city-states were, under a period of stress.
4. Again, Rome had an advantage in this regard over other ancient civilizations.

As its Egyptian and North African fields were highly productive and produced a tremendous annual wheat surplus, Roman society could maintain a large military establishment (or a mob) and still feed itself.

5. I reject out of hand that it was possible for the Persians to manage or logistically support any force much larger than this. For some reason, the historical community has come to a consensus that Xerxes marched with 250,000 troops. Consider that the Romans put more than 200,000 men in the field only once, and to do that they had to supply both armies (the Battle of Philippi, during the civil wars). According to Richard Gabriel, Alexander the Great's 65,000 men required 195,000 pounds of grain and 325,000 pounds of water to sustain it for a single day, plus 375,000 pounds of forage per day to sustain its animals. It strains credulity to believe that the Persians were able to supply four times this amount for a sustained period, particularly when they moved away from their established magazines within the empire. Moreover, expert calculations place the column length of a six-legion army at 22 miles. Extrapolating this for a Persian army of 250,000 gives a column length of over 160 miles. Given an average day's march, that means the first troops made contact at Thermopylae while the rear of the army was still two weeks' march from the battlefield (assuming they were all marching along the coast road). Even in multiple columns or in compressed formations, an army this size would be a nightmare to manage and supply.

6. Sailors were relatively easy to mobilize, as the established merchant marine could always be conscripted. Of course, if it was away for any length of time, it would wreck the trading economies of the coastal cities.

7. Herodotus gives the number of male citizens as thirty thousand (5.97).

8. It helps to think of the purchase of a person's own armor and weapons as a form of tax. It is doubtful that any able-bodied man who could afford it would have been able to avoid the obligation. Even if the state did not require it, the social pressure must have been irresistible.

9. Typically, the entire hoplite panoply would cost seventy-five to one hundred drachmas, or about three months' salary for a skilled worker; see Hans van Wees, *Greek Warfare: Myths and Realities* (London: Duckworth Publishers, 2004), p. 52.

10. A. H. M. Jones, "The Economic Basis of the Athenian Democracy," *Past and Present*, no. 1 (February 1952): 13–31. This paper covers the period through the Peloponnesian War but delivers a number of insights for the period covered in this book. The *thetes* class consisted of any Athenian citizen who held wealth of fewer than two thousand drachmas.

11. Rachel L. Sargent, "The Use of Slaves by the Athenians in Warfare," *Classical Philology* 22, no. 2 (April 1927): 201–212. For a good discussion dealing specifically with the use of slaves at the Battle of Marathon, see James A. Notopoulos, "The Slaves at the Battle of Marathon," *American Journal of Philology* 62, no. 3 (1941): 352–354.

12. Sargent, "The Use of Slaves," p. 203.

13. Bury, ed., *Cambridge Ancient History*, p. 248.

Chapter 14: PERSIAN WARFARE

1. The center of Assyrian power was at the upper Tigris, in modern Iraq. At its height, the empire ruled most of Mesopotamia and Egypt.
2. Richard Gabriel, *Empires at War*, vol. 1 (Westport, CT: Greenwood Press, 2005), p. 177.
3. Jackson J. Spielvogel, *Western Civilization* (New York: Wadsworth Publishing, 2005), p. 41.
4. Herodotus, 6.103.
5. The Immortals were so named because whenever they lost a man, he was immediately replaced, so that their number never fell below ten thousand.
6. Herodotus, 7.161.
7. Ibid., 7.83.
8. Of course, the army that Darius commanded during the civil war (and that proved so capable of rapid marches in day or night) was of a completely different nature from those that came after it.
9. Paul A. Rahe, "The Military Situation in Western Asia on the Eve of Cunaxa," *American Journal of Philology* 101, no. 1 (spring 1980): 79–96. I am indebted to this paper for a number of insights on Persian vs. Greek warfare.
10. Ibid., p. 82.
11. John Keegan gives the only known example of cavalry breaking a square. But on that occasion, both rider and horse were killed by musket fire while at full charge. Unfortunately for the infantry in the square, the momentum of the dead horse carried into and through their line. The rest of the cavalry regiment then swept into the gap. See John Keegan, *The Face of Battle* (New York: Penguin Books, 1976), 153–159.
12. Herodotus, 1.136.
13. As the inscription on Darius's tomb states: "My body is strong. As a fighter of battles I am a good fighter of battles. . . . I am skilled both in hands and in feet. As a horseman, I am a good horseman. As a bowman, I am a good bowman, both on foot and on horseback. As a spearman, I am a good spearman, both on foot and on horseback."

Chapter 15: HOPLITE WARFARE

1. A growth rate of 3 percent means Greece's population doubled every generation.
2. The development of colonization policies by many Greek cities helped to deal with this population explosion but never fully alleviated the land shortage.
3. Whereas the literature available on Persian fighting methods is sparse, the sheer volume of material accessible for study on Greek and hoplite warfare may easily intimidate any interested historian. For the most comprehensive and authoritative study, Pritchett's five volumes still set the gold standard; see Kendrick Pritchett, *The Greek State at War*, parts 1 through 5 (Berkeley: University of California Press, 1991). However, for the most informative, readable, and thought-provoking works, see Hanson, *Western Way of War*; Victor

Davis Hanson, ed., *Hoplites: The Classical Greek Battle Experience* (New York: Routledge, 1993); and van Wees, *Greek Warfare*.

4. Also known as the Battle of the Golden Spurs, for the large number of these items removed from the dead French nobility.

5. Quoted from the *Annales Gandenses/Annals of Ghent*, edited and translated by Hilda Johnstone (London: Oxford University Press, 1951). The complete passage can be found at http://www.deremilitari.org/resources/sources/goldenspurs.htm/.

6. In fact, in the following years, continuing even after the start of the gunpowder revolution, Swiss pikemen took the art of phalanx warfare to new heights. It is interesting, therefore, to note that Swiss society was also town based and that the canton is probably the closest political entity to a Greek city-state that has existed since the fall of Rome.

7. The *hoplon* shield is where the name *hoplite* is drawn from.

8. See Pritchett, *Greek State at War*, part 2, for an analysis of Greek military training (pp. 208–231).

9. Sparta, of course, is an exception, as the helots provided the economic underpinning that allowed the Spartans to remain mobilized on a permanent basis. Furthermore, Athens's switch to olives (requiring less attention than grains) and a greater reliance on trade probably allowed it to keep men under arms for a much greater period than the other city-states. Although it could not carry this burden or expense indefinitely, it was a decisive advantage in the two decades of war before the Battle of Marathon.

10. See Peter Krentz, "Fighting by the Rules," *Hesperia* 71, no. 1 (January–March 2002): 23–39.

11. Of course, there were exceptions to these general rules, such as the Spartan conquest of Messina. Moreover, this restraint broke down in later generations, from the Peloponnesian War onward. Greek armies were much more likely to fight a battle of annihilation and persist in their wars for years or decades.

12. Herodotus, 7.9.

13. Only the Spartans were known to advance at a slow walk, kept in step and at an even pace by flute players.

14. Euripides, *Heracles*, http://classics.mit.edu/Euripides/heracles.html

15. The heretical view is a recent development whose main champion is G. L. Cawkwell. See: G. L. Cawkwell, *Philip of Macedon* (London: Faber & Faber, 1978), pp. 150–153; and G. L. Cawkwell, "Orthodoxy and Hoplites," *Classical Quarterly*, new ser., 39, no. 2 (1980): 375–389. Another follower of the heretical view is van Wees, *Greek Warfare*, pp. 184–197. For a concise essay expressing the traditional view, see A. J. Holladay, "Hoplites and Heresies," *Journal of Hellenic Studies* 102 (1982): 94–103; and Robert D. Luginbill, "Othismos: The Importance of the Mass-Shove in Hoplite Warfare," *Phoenix* 48, no. 1 (spring 1994): 51–61. Also see any of the classic works listed in the third endnote for this chapter for the traditional view (which I accept as the accurate one).

16. Athenian hoplites at Marathon had been in a state of almost continuous war for the preceding two decades. It is therefore likely that they possessed individual fighting skills at least on a par with the Spartans.

Chapter 16: THE WESTERN WAY OF WAR

1. Victor Davis Hanson, *Carnage and Culture: Landmark Battles in the Rise of Western Power* (New York: Doubleday, 2001); and John Lynn, *Battle: A History of Combat and Culture* (New York: Basic Books, 2004).

2. Having admitted my conversion, I must also say that I found Lynn's perspective compelling, and some of his statements paralleled my earlier misgivings on the topic, although he put them far more thoughtfully and lucidly than I was capable of at the time.

3. See Lieutenant Colonel Bob Bateman, "Carnage, Culture, and Crapola," posted on the website Altercation, October 22, 2007 (http://mediamatters .org/blog/200710220002/). In this essay, posted on several military history–related websites, Bateman says that Hanson better not take him on, as unlike Yale and University of Wisconsin professors, he is "an academic historian, with 18 years studying the field, and an Army Airborne Ranger." Besides being a breakdown of civility, Bateman's attack is an unusual way to characterize the work of one of the world's foremost historians and an expert on classical Greek warfare. Despite this recent incivility, the debate is important and should not be surrendered to those who claim victory through tossing the most scurrilous invective.

4. Similarly, the aerodynamic laws we worked with for two generations were proven wrong when it was shown that if they were applied to a bumblebee, its flight would be impossible—yet bees do fly. The laws were wrong, of course, but they were good enough to build long-distance aircraft and rockets for space travel. Economists also know that the model they use to explain global trade is wrong, but nothing better has come along yet, and as the model explains most market activity, it remains in use.

5. Hanson, *Carnage and Culture*, p. 5.

6. Lynn, *Battle*, p. 25.

7. Recent studies have revolutionized our understanding of the so-called Dark Ages. It is now clear that far more was transmitted over these centuries than previously believed. See Chris Wickham, *The Inheritance of Rome: Illuminating the Dark Ages, 400–1000* (New York: Penguin, 2009), and Peter Heather, *Empires and Barbarians: The Fall of Rome and the Birth of Europe* (New York: Oxford University Press, 2010).

8. Vegetius, *The Military Institutions of the Romans*, edited by Thomas R. Phillips (London: Kessinger Publishing, 2008).

9. For the best recent work on the Dark Ages, see Wickham, *The Inheritance of Rome*.

10. Lynn, *Battle*, p. 25.

11. See the start of chapter 2 for a discussion.

12. For an excellent discussion of this phenomenon, see James J. Sheehan, *Where Have All the Soldiers Gone?: The Transformation of Modern Europe* (New York: Mariner Books, 2009).

13. Harry G. Summers Jr., *On Strategy: A Critical Analysis of the Vietnam War* (Washington, DC: Presidio Press, 1995).

Chapter 17: THE PERSIANS SAIL

1. Herodotus tells us that the Saka fought at Marathon. It is possible that he picked up this contingent in Ionia, but I find it more probable that they were serving closer to Susa or Ecbatana at the time.

2. Herodotus, 6.95. As noted earlier, historians have long debated Herodotus's ship numbers. In this case, further doubt is cast on the numbers as so many ships were lost at Mount Athos. However, if we accept that the Persians had about six hundred ships at the Battle of Lade, even if over half of them were lost in storms and battle, they could easily have been replaced in the interval before the invasion. Remember, Darius would have been able to level the remaining ships of every Ionian city, along with everything the ports of Ionia and Phoenicia could produce.

3. Herodotus, 6.95.

4. Herodotus tells us (6.95) that the Persian fleet was six hundred "triremes." This is open to dispute, but if it was accepted that the Persian fleet sailed without transports (highly unlikely for an army that took logistical concerns very seriously), then the size of the Persian army would be cut in half, unless space was made by removing sailors from a number of ships.

5. The actual weight of a talent is still in dispute, with most guesses ranging between 75 and 150 pounds. On either end of the range this was a substantial offering, as frankincense was literally worth its weight in gold (or more).

6. Transitioning a horse from fodder to grass too quickly can kill it.

Chapter 18: THE PLAIN OF MARATHON

1. While I believe the Persians fully intended to take a large number of Athenians into slavery, they had only enough transport for several thousand at most. It can therefore be assumed that Hippias would be left in charge of the remainder and that most of those enslaved would be enemies of the Pisistratidae clan. It is unlikely that the Athenians looking at what happened to Eretria were making such finely reasoned calculations. However, given the fact that the Persians had removed most of the tyrants in Ionia, it is hard to fathom why they would place one in Athens, as that was a sure recipe for future problems. In the end, we will never know the true reason Hippias was brought along, but it may have been just to give advice and in the hope that his presence could sow some dissension within Athens.

2. Herodotus states that the prime reason the Persians selected Marathon was that it provided excellent ground for cavalry options. However, this is true of many possible landing sites on the Attic coast. Quite possibly Hippias used Marathon's horse-friendly location as one of the reasons he presented to the Persians for selecting the site.

3. A number of historians have declared that given the Persians' overwhelming numbers, they landed near Eretria at the same time. They suggest Datis's reason for waiting at Marathon was that he was waiting for Artaphrenes, with the

other half of the army, to finish off Eretria and join him for a joint march on Athens. If this is accepted, then the reason the Athenians attacked before the Spartans arrived is that after the fall of Eretria, they had to make their move before the forces joined up. I, however, discount this entire theory, as there is zero evidence for it and its originator never presents an analysis of why it was possible, other than that he wished it that way (see F. Maurice, "The Campaign of Marathon," *Journal of Hellenic Studies* 52, part 1 [1932]:13–24). Besides, it breaks a tenet of warfare that no ancient general would violate without good cause: Never split your army in the presence of the enemy!

4. I learned this as a young officer, when my unit had a chance to attend the Marine Corps Amphibious Warfare School. While we were often able to sort out the confusion, it took time. If we had ever had to attempt it against a waiting enemy force, we would have been slaughtered. My respect for those who did this in World War II, under fire, rose by an order of magnitude after these experiences. Still, a number of classical historians state that such landings were a minor matter. For instance, one of the greatest of them, Arthur Munro, states: "It is scarcely credible that the Persians were afraid of the Athenians, that they doubted their own power to force a landing on the shore of the Sardonic Gulf. There can have been no insufferable difficulty in effecting a disembarkation at some point on so extensive a coast from so numerous a fleet. The advantage of an unopposed landing may have counted for something, but it cannot have been a reason for putting in at Marathon." (See Arthur R. Munro, "Some Observations on the Persian Wars," *Journal of Hellenic Studies* 19 [1899]: 187.) I for one can think of no greater nightmare scenario than to be still unloading his ships as a phalanx bore down on him. As learned as Munro was in classical literature, his unfamiliarity with military affairs leads him to say a number of ridiculous things about Marathon, and I have thereby been forced to discount him as a serious source, although many since him have followed his path.

5. A tactic the Britons tried against Caesar's 54 BC invasion of their lands.

6. Of course, Datis could have viewed this as an advantage, as once he had posted it with good troops, it would be impossible for the Athenians to march down on his landing site.

7. At the very least, the Marathoni (residents of the deme of Marathon) would probably have been in the area, and there were at least several hundred hoplites in this group. This would be one of the groups that Hippias would have expected to come over to him (Munro would find fault with this, as he believes the deme was part of the Aiantis tribe, not known as strong supporters of the Pisistratidae). To find them strongly outposted at the exit of the plain and unalterably opposed to his return accounts for his pessimism on the beachhead better than the reason Herodotus presents (a quaint story of him coughing up a tooth, which he uses to interpret a dream that predicts his failure to return to power).

8. Munro claims that the Persians' failure to send forces to secure the passes proves that they had no intention of marching on Athens. It apparently never

occurred to him that the Athenians may have already been on the passes when the Persians arrived. Besides, the Persians had come a long way and gone to a lot of unnecessary bother if they were not planning to march on Athens.

9. Some historians have stated that Athens could not have mustered its forces in a central location, as it would have been impossible to feed them for any lengthy period of time. Therefore the hoplites must still have been at their homes or at least scattered widely, and it would have taken a considerable amount of time to mass them. This theory, however, neglects some basic facts. By this time, Athens was importing over half of its wheat supply, which was stored in granaries in Piraeus (Athens's port) or Athens, for distribution as required to the rest of Attica. As the harvest was not in yet, Attica was probably subsisting almost entirely on this food supply. In fact, by concentrating the army to the food stores, the distribution of food was probably greatly eased.

10. The Decree of Miltiades; see Plutarch (*Moralia*, 628e) and Aristotle's *Rhetoric* (3.10.7) (http://www.attalus.org/info/moralia.html).

11. One historian has made the case that protecting their land was probably not a factor in the Athenian decision, as "the land near Marathon was not good enough for the Greeks to risk an army for its protection." Apparently, he believes the Persians would be content to lay waste to Marathon and spare the rest of Attica. And he neglects to consider that no matter how poor the soil was, it was all Athens had. They would surely fight for it, as they did many times before and after Marathon. See W. R. Loader, "Questions About Marathon," *Greece & Rome*, 16, no. 46 (January 1947): 17–22. Loader goes on to conclude that the Athenian army was tricked into going to Marathon by those who wanted the Persians to win. They figured the best way to accomplish this was to send the army out to certain destruction.

12. Or if the grain had been harvested, it was stored in easily destroyed granaries throughout Attica.

13. I am aware of Victor Davis Hanson's claims that agricultural destruction was difficult in ancient times. Still, all of the evidence from the period indicates that area devastation was widely practiced and highly effective.

14. I will not enter into the debate on whether Herodotus meant Pheidippides and not Philippides. Athens employed a contingent of professional runners to deliver messages who were famous for their ability to run all day.

15. *Laws* iii, 692d–698e.

16. For an excellent analysis of this position, see W. P. Wallace, "Kleomenes, Marathon, the Helots, and Arkadia," *Journal of Hellenic Studies* 74 (1954): 32–35.

17. It is remarkable how many historians neglect the fact that Athens did have its own small cavalry force (that was not present for the main battle), along with thousands of light troops that were particularly well suited to the job of exterminating foraging parties.

18. Although I had witnessed this myself on several military operations, I tended to block it from my mind when I reflected on events afterward. If I had thought about it, I would have remembered that after fighting and feeding, sanitation (another delicate term for the problem) was the third major con-

cern for any unit. How important a factor it is was brought home to me in an absolutely hysterical essay by First Sergeant Ron Gregg. The article is entitled "SCHITZSQUIE," and a copy can be found in the book *War on Two Fronts* by Chris Hughes (Havertown, PA: Casemate, 2007).

19. N. G. L. Hammond makes the case that the Greeks took this route, but given the military disadvantages such a route would have encumbered them with, I do not find his reasoning convincing. See N. G. L. Hammond, "The Campaign and the Battle of Marathon," *Journal of Hellenic Studies* 88 (1968): 13–57. Norman Doenges agrees with him, but his reasoning is also suspect, as it places the three-mile difference in the route at the center of his argument. However, in this case, a three-mile-shorter route does not equate to less marching time. The longer route, being a much better road over flat ground, would have allowed the Athenians the fastest approach to Marathon. See Norman A. Doenges, "The Campaign and Battle of Marathon," *Historia: Zeitschrift für Alte Geschichte* 47, no. 1 (1998), 1–17.

20. The location of the Grove of Herakles was a matter of great dispute for a number of years but has now been definitively located by Eugene Vanderpool, in the southeast corner of the Plain of Marathon. See Eugene Vanderpool, "The Deme of Marathon and the Herakleion," *American Journal of Archaeology* 70, no. 4 (October 1966): 319–323.

21. Herodotus, 6.109.

22. Ibid.

23. Herodotus, 6.110.

24. Even though this is not certain.

25. And if he had been dead or infirm, they would have turned to someone else who had distinguished himself in these earlier fights.

26. A possible answer to the question of why Miltiades got so much of the credit for victory if Callimachus was the real hero of the day is given in chapter 11.

27. His son Cimon later had a statue erected in honor of his father's "victory" at Marathon, which is notable as the first work of Athens's greatest sculptor, Phidias.

28. Nicholas Sekunda, *Marathon 490 BC: The First Persian Invasion of Greece* (Oxford: Osprey Publishing, 2002), p. 10. For an excellent discussion of the memorial and the breakthrough 1940 discovery that allowed it to be understood, see A. E. Raubitschek, "Two Monuments Erected After the Victory of Marathon," *American Journal of Archaeology* 44, no. 1 (January–March 1940): 53–59.

29. Cornelius Nepos in his brief biography of Miltiades confirms some of this: "The next day, having set themselves in array at the foot of the hills opposite the enemy, they engaged in battle with a novel stratagem, and with the utmost impetuosity. For trees had been strewed in many directions, with this intention, that, while they themselves were covered by the high hills." The trees could only be *abittis*, designed specifically to impede cavalry. One can easily picture the hoplites moving forward while hundreds of light troops or slaves move along the flank, placing *abittis* in depth to stop the Persian cavalry from sweeping into the Greek rear—or, alternatively, making sure that greater Per-

sian numbers could not easily overlap the undefended flank of the phalanx. The reliability of Nepos has come into question, as he was writing five hundred years after the event. However, for a source he probably used Ephorus (who was writing much closer to the Battle of Marathon); and besides, the Greeks had used *abittis* in the past, and it made good sense to use them now. For anyone who wants Nepos's short biography, an English translation may be accessed at: http://www.tertullian.org/fathers/nepos.htm#Miltiades/. For an interesting essay on the reliability of Nepos and his sources, see W. W. How, "Cornelius Nepos on Marathon and Paros," *Journal of Hellenic Studies* 39 (1919): 48–61.

Chapter 19: THE DAY BEFORE

1. There is a weak tradition that states that spies in the Persian camp (possibly Ionians) approached the Greek camp and signaled that the cavalry was away. Unfortunately, the source (*The Suda*, authored by Suidas) is a Byzantine text, written over fifteen hundred years after the event, and it gives no source for this information.

Chapter 20: BATTLE

1. Creasy, *Fifteen Decisive Battles of the World*.
2. Pritchett, *Greek State at War*, presents some colorful examples from lead pellets discovered by archaeologists at various sites.
3. Ancient Greeks rarely ate much for breakfast (a piece of bread dipped in wine or honey). Moreover, nervous soldiers are always disinclined to eat, not least because of an awareness that food in the stomach made belly wounds much worse than they would be otherwise—though such wounds were always a bad thing.
4. Aristides, *Plutarch's Lives*.
5. There are several reconstructions of the order of the Greek line as it formed to meet the Persians. I have accepted that of Raubitschek, as it is listed by Sekunda *(Marathon 490 BC)*.
6. I imagine the pursuit could not have halted on its own and would require a signal. Bugle calls were common in Greek armies, and only a bugle could be heard over the din of battle.
7. Philip Sabin has presented a new look for what a Roman battle must have looked like at the level of the individual soldiers. I have found his reconstruction convincing and believe that the battle in the center probably played out in close approximation to what Sabin lays out. Given the evidence presented by Herodotus, I do not believe his reconstruction of ancient battles applies to what took place on the flanks during the Battle of Marathon. See Philip Sabin, "The Face of Roman Battle," *Journal of Roman Studies* 90 (2000): 1–17.
8. This probably counts only Athenian hoplites and excludes Plataean losses as well as slaves and light troops.

9. Plutarch, *Moralia*, 347C; and Lucian (*Pro Laspu* 3; a translation is available at http://www.sacred-texts.com/cla/luc/wl2/wl204.htm).

10. F. Frost, "The Dubious Origins of the Marathon," *American Journal of Ancient History* 4 (1979): 159–163.

11. It is odd that Herodotus does not make any mention of this fleet (or that of Eretria) in his account of Marathon or its preliminaries. The Athenians may have considered that their seventy ships were not sufficient to make much if any impression upon the overwhelming Persian naval force.

12. Nepos, *Miltiades*, VII.

13. Probably enough to pay for one summer's campaign for the Athenian fleet.

14. Herodotus, 6.133.

Chapter 21: THE GREAT DEBATES

1. For an interesting essay on the difficulty of reconstructing Marathon or any other ancient battle, see N. Whatley, "On the Possibility of Reconstructing Marathon and Other Ancient Battles," *Journal of Hellenic Studies* 84 (1964): 119–139.

2. Herodotus, 6.95 and 6.101.

3. The only ancient literary source stating the cavalry was definitely present is Nepos, *Miltiades*.

4. See Evelyn B. Harrison, "The South Frieze of the Nike Temple and the Marathon Painting in the Painted Stoa American," *Journal of Archaeology* 76, no. 4 (October 1972): 353–378; and Gordon Shrimpton, "The Persian Cavalry at Marathon," *Phoenix* 34, no. 1 (spring 1980): 20–37.

5. I will assume the Persians had no idea how difficult it would be, as they probably had the use of docks in Ionia and Eretria, when they previously loaded the horses aboard ships.

6. See the Battle of Pharsalus for an example of how Caesar took three thousand men from the veteran *triarii* cohorts and used them to rout many times their number of cavalry.

7. Herodotus, 6.112.

8. For a list of scientific papers on the topic by the research scientist who discovered this phenomenon, James L. McGaugh (research professor, neurobiology, University of California–Berkeley), see http://64.233.169.104/search?q =cache:cTT1sGQMxVoJ:www.faculty.uci.edu/profile.cfm%3Ffaculty_id%3 D2140+James+McGaugh,+a+professor+of+neurobiology+at+the+University +of+California&hl=en&ct=clnk&cd=1&gl=us/.

9. These interviews were conducted for my book *Takedown: The 3rd Infantry Division's Twenty-one Day Assault on Baghdad* (Annapolis: Naval Institute Press, 2007). After Baghdad's fall, participants in the heaviest fighting were taken back to the location of those fights and filmed as they described events. This was done in front of their compatriots, which kept the level of exaggeration to a minimum, as others who were present in the fight were on hand to question anything they thought was inaccurate. A copy of all these tapes has been donated to the Military History Institute in Carlisle, Pennsylvania.

10. Charging at the run was not unknown in Greek war, and in fact, despite Herodotus's claim that he knows of no other case (remember that Herodotus was not a soldier and had no personal experience in battle), many examples are known to historians. Pritchett (*Greek State at War,* part 4, p. 73) says, "It was disadvantageous to remain stationary and receive the onset of the enemy," and then presents some examples of when the Athenians had charged at the double. As we have already looked at Pharsalus as an example of how cavalry was no match for unbroken infantry, it is worth noting that Caesar sent his men into the attack (about the same distance that the Athenians had to cover at Marathon) on the run and fully expected Pompey's legion to meet him the same way.

11. Walter Donlan and James Thompson, "The Charge at Marathon: Herodotus 6.112," *Classical Journal* 71, no. 4 (April–May 1976): 339–343.

12. Despite this level of conditioning, which included running ten or more miles day after day, I still recall when the boss brought in an aerobics instructor to conduct physical training one morning. Within half an hour, every paratrooper involved was panting and close to death. As I said, exercise is specific.

13. Pritchett (*Greek State at War,* vol. 2, p. 211) gives examples from Xenophon and Socrates lamenting the sorry state of military training in Athens. However, we cannot assume this was the case during this period, when the threats were many and immediate.

14. N. G. L. Hammond, "The Campaign and the Battle of Marathon," *Journal of Hellenic Studies* 88 (1968): 28. A brilliant, if flawed (in some places), essay. His footnote listing of each of the major historians who have rejected one or more of these events in their entirety, without much (if any) analysis and without presenting any evidence, is particularly valuable.

15. For an excellent essay on this topic, see Harris Gary Hudson, "The Shield Signal at Marathon," *American Historical Review* 42, no. 3 (April 1937): 443–459.

16. For an excellent analysis of the voyage and especially how long it would take to complete, see A. Trevor Hodge, "Marathon: The Persians' Voyage," *Transactions and Proceedings of the American Philological Association* 105 (1975): 155–173.

17. The Persians had collected the Eretrians from an island they had left them on when they landed at Marathon. They were later taken to Darius in Susa, "who did them no further harm and instead settled them in the land of the Kissians . . . about twenty-three miles from Susa" (Herodotus, 6.119).

18. Although the loss of the Persian core of the army might have raised a few eyebrows.

Conclusion

1. Aristophanes, *The Acharnians.* A copy can be viewed online at: http://classics.mit.edu/Aristophanes/acharnians.html/.

Index

About the Author

JIM LACEY was an active-duty military officer for twelve years in the 82nd Airborne Division and the 101st Airborne Division. Lacey is currently a professor of strategy, war, and policy at the Marine War College, and an adjunct professor in the Johns Hopkins National Security Program. He also works as a consultant on a number of projects for the United States military. Lacey has written for several publications, including the *New York Post* and *The New York Sun*, appears regularly in *Military History* magazine, and was an embedded journalist for *Time* magazine during the invasion of Iraq.

About the Type

This book was set in Berling. Designed in 1951 by Karl Erik Fors-berg for the Typefoundry Berlingska Stilgjuteri AB in Lund, Sweden, it was released the same year in foundry type by H. Berthold AG. A classic old-face design, its generous propor-tions and inclined serifs make it highly legible.